·IN STYLE·

· IN STYLE ·

100 YEARS OF CANADIAN WOMEN'S FASHION

C A R O L I N E   R O U T H

First published in 1993 by
Stoddart Publishing Co. Limited
34 Lesmill Road
Toronto, Canada
M3B 2T6
(416) 445-3333

CANADIAN CATALOGUING IN PUBLICATION DATA

Routh, Caroline
In style: 100 years of Canadian women's fashion

Includes index.
ISBN 0-7737-5568-3

1. Fashion – Canada – History.   2. Costume –
Canada – History.   I. Title.

GT620.R68 1993   391'.2'091   C92-095636-X

Design: Gillian Stead
Printed and bound in Canada
Cover illustration from the 1906 Eaton's fall and winter catalogue

Stoddart Publishing gratefully acknowledges the support of the
Canada Council, the Ontario Ministry of Culture, Tourism and
Recreation, Ontario Arts Council, and Ontario Publishing Centre in
the development of writing and publishing in Canada.

To my mother, my sister, and my daughter

◆ C O N T E N T S ◆

◆ F O R E W O R D ◆

WHAT, IF ANYTHING, DISTINGUISHES CANADIAN WOMEN'S DRESS FROM mainstream Western fashion in the twentieth century? Were there specific Canadian factors that determined what Canadian women wore? How pervasive was the influence of American, English, or French fashion? Can Canadian regional differences be determined? Following in the pioneer footsteps of Katharine Brett of the Royal Ontario Museum and Eileen Collard, founder of the Costume Society of Ontario, Caroline Routh has turned her talents as an artist, researcher, and teacher to an important facet of our Canadian heritage. Despite the efforts of her distinguished predecessors, the significance of dress and fashion as part of Canada's cultural past has for the most part been overlooked and neglected. Caroline Routh has addressed this neglect, and, from her examination of surviving garments and extensive research into print and picture sources, has presented us with a lively chronicle of women's dress in the century that saw Canada become a nation.

Routh has assembled an impressive quantity of information; not the least of her achievements has been her skill as an artist which has enabled her to bring to life the garments she has chosen from public and private collections across Canada. She has accomplished the difficult task of presenting a coherent general picture from the particular dress choices made by individuals under widely varying conditions.

The decision to select garments representing high fashion, everyday wear, formal, informal, outdoor, and recreational dress through the decades allows the reader to understand how changes in dress and social conditions interact over the years. The many uses to which this publication will be put by fashion designers, theatre designers, social historians, students, and teachers will undoubtedly increase awareness of the importance of dress in our Canadian heritage and should encourage museums and institutions across the country to redouble their efforts in collecting and preserving what we wore and in helping us to understand why we wore it.

ALAN SUDDON

◆ P R E F A C E ◆

DRESS FOR WOMEN IN THE TWENTIETH CENTURY HAS UNDERGONE A remarkable degree of change. Totally encased in layers of fabric, in boning, stitching, and ruffles, Edwardian women expressed the rules and conventions of a society considerably more formal and often more gracious than that of the present.

In a few successive decades women gained the right to bare their legs and arms in public, reveal the real shape of their bodies through a single layer of fabric, wear men's trousers as well as many other parts of their costume, and generally broaden the range of acceptability of dress for many occasions.

During this time they have also found it necessary to remodel their body shape in favour of the prevailing silhouette, to exaggerate, subdue, or call attention to shoulders, breasts, hips, and waist. Reputations of great designers have been built on the ability to work well with these and other variables.

Changes in technology, mainly in the areas of textile design and construction methods, have contributed greatly to the simplification of dress for women, but the eternal urge to create and embellish will never allow dress to disappear as an art form.

This book provides a survey of the development of Canadian women's dress as it was worn throughout this century. Drawings of actual garments from each decade are shown at the end of the chapter. They include typical examples of daywear, evening-wear, outerwear, sportswear, and miscellaneous. Throughout the text, references to these drawings are indicated in brackets, thus: **[1]**.

Some people whose assistance to me has been invaluable are Eileen Collard, through her books on Canadian women's fashions, and Alan and Mary Suddon, through their collection of costume and archival material. I also gratefully acknowledge assistance from the following: Nancy Legate, two John Rouths, Mary Holford, Ivan Sayers, Jonathon Walford, Isobel Jones, Betty Ann Crosbie, Mary Humphries, and Bella Pomer.

Novi-Modi   Spring 1905

a *The idealized Edwardian woman was more self-assured than her Victorian mother, but still ultra-feminine, with softly upswept hair, delicate gowns, and elaborate hats.*

THE
1900s

THE EDWARDIAN ERA, FITTING FAIRLY NEATLY INTO THE PERIOD FROM the turn of the century almost to the First World War, is named after King Edward VII. He came to the throne in 1901 on the death of his mother Queen Victoria. As the Prince of Wales, Edward had established an active social circle which influenced the dress and lifestyles of the upper classes in England and Canada. His reign brought a new emphasis to fashion that was absent during the long years of Queen Victoria's widowhood.

Canada was a mere thirty-four years of age in 1901. Roads and highways were poor or nonexistent and the railway had just recently connected the west to Ontario, Quebec, and the Maritimes. People were not only regionally divided, but also their lives were kept separate by class distinctions.

Well-to-do Canadian women lived in grand city mansions maintained by servants. Summer brought elegant garden parties, picnics, and outings, as well as travel abroad and excursions to lodges and country houses. The Muskoka area was already established as a summer retreat from the heat and dust of Toronto. Resort hotels like the Royal Muskoka, Beaumaris, Elgin House, Clevelands House, and Windermere drew fashionable summer guests for fine dining, dancing, golf, croquet, and tennis. East to west, from the Pines at Digby to Banff Springs and the Empress in Victoria, the great hotels drew fashionable tourists from Canada, the United States, and Europe. If they chose not to vacation in Europe, the Montreal elite escaped to St. Andrews, or to the Hotel Tadoussac on the Saguenay, or to splendid summer homes along the St. Lawrence.

Canadian society was male dominated. Upper- and middle-class etiquette and mores were restrictive for women; they had few of the morale-boosting freedoms of men. Women did not have the right to vote and many were poorly educated. Nursing and teaching were two careers open to them and, in spite of being poorly paid, some preferred this work to social and financial dependence.

Canadians showed signs of progress in the 1880s when some universities began to admit women as students, but few of these fortunate women pursued careers. Young, unmarried, middle-class women were gradually being accepted in the workplace although the issue of working women was widely debated. People recognized that women needed better education and training, but many still felt that women's suffrage was unnecessary.

The new career women were employed in offices as clerks and typists or as telephone operators at a time when individual calls were handled manually. The supply of good servants for wealthy homes was depleted by the entry of young women into the business world. These social changes brought about different needs in dress and redirected fashion's progress.

b *Edwardian corsets flattened the stomach and subtly adjusted the stance, rigidly shaping the figure for an S-bend silhouette.*

shape to the chest. The skirt, formerly full and cut with straight seams, now curved smoothly over the hips, flaring fuller only below the knee and often ending with a train. Seams, yokes, and gores kept the skirt fitted over the abdomen and hips; sometimes extra fabric in the back helped to produce a protruding derrière.

These features, along with the correct stance and corset, created that counter-balancing act now referred to as the Edwardian S-bend silhouette, fashionable until about 1907. A small waist was a requisite of beauty in spite of the necessary underlayers of dress and belts that commonly drew attention to the waist. Even in warm summer weather, a lady wore an undervest, a boned corset, drawers, corset cover, and petticoat or chemise, and then a dress, often lined and boned [5].

The manners and customs of the social elite were reflected in the dress of both men and women. The Edwardian lady's gown sensuously proclaimed her femininity and stated her status in society. High collars kept a very superior tilt to the head and the rustle of soft petticoats radiated sexual allure [9]. The elegant woman had to be correctly attired for morning activities, luncheon, afternoon calling, walking, motoring, boating, riding, and other sports and gowned in appropriate splendor for dinner, receptions, balls, fêtes and the theatre. Hats were an essential part of being well dressed for any out-of-doors activity and gloves were worn for every formal occasion. Intricate detailing, even in daywear, expressed both the femininity of the period and the extravagant amount of labour needed for dress construction.

The ideal beauty at the turn of the century was a tall, queenly figure with a voluptuous hourglass shape, a long neck, and abundant upswept hair. The American illustrator Charles D. Gibson, whose work was seen in many women's magazines in Canada from the 1890s until about 1910, created the Gibson Girl. She was an image that came to symbolize the spirit and confidence of the new young woman, a creature of fashion with decided opinions on many matters.

Late Victorian dress was generally rigid and rather sombre, but even before the turn of the century the lines started to soften and droop in the languid manner of art nouveau design. The bodice lengthened, often coming to a V at centre-front waist, and by about 1901 delicate dress fabrics were being gathered and pouched at this point, giving the characteristic "pouter-pigeon"

DRESSMAKERS AND SPECIALTY SHOPS

Even with the increasing availability of ready-made clothing, much worn by Canadian women at the turn of the century was still made at home or by a local dressmaker or tailor. In the *Toronto City Directory* of 1901, 150 tailors were listed and as many as 550 dressmakers, all of the latter married or single women. Plain and fancy sewing skills were an important part of women's general education and many women used these skills to earn a living. Dress styles were so intricate that real talent and a great deal of concentrated effort went into the creation of each garment.

Treadle sewing machines sold for about twenty dollars and no home was complete without one. After 1908 the "electrified" machine was available. Knowing about the latest styles and how to achieve them was also an important part of production, both for the home sewer and the professional dressmaker.

In most cities and towns there was a ready supply of textile goods. On Yonge Street in Toronto, for example, numerous department stores and dry goods shops in the Queen and King Street area sold all kinds of fabrics and notions. Certain shops were known for their specialties; R. Walker and Sons, on the site of the present King Edward Hotel, was the place to buy underclothes and linens. Other well-known downtown Toronto names were G.L. Mackay, McLean's, and Bilton Brothers, as well as two Fairweathers, known for furs, at 446 Queen West and on Yonge Street. On King Street were Holt Renfrew, O'Brien's, John Catto and Son, Stitt and Company and W.A. Murray and Company (with a second shop on Colborne Street).[1] G.L. Mackay was at 495 Yonge Street.

Ready-made gowns from Paris, London, and New York were worn by those who could afford them; still, many fashionable women patronized Canadian establishments. The finest dressmakers in Montreal and Toronto produced quality competitive with the world's fashion centres. Two prestigious establishments

W. A. MURRAY & CO., Limited
17 to 27 King St. East and 10 to 16 Colborne St.
The High Class Dry Goods House of Canada

....

DEPARTMENTS

Mantles	Silks	Curtains
Millinery	Dress Goods	Hosiery
Ribbons	Prints	Trimmings
Dressmaking	Laces	Linens
Order-Tailoring	Corsets	Men's Furnishings
Boys' Clothing	Trunks	Carpets
Fine Shoes	Glassware	Stationery

Ordered Tailoring There's a smartness about the tailoring--we do chiefly the result of years devoted to bringing this branch of our business to the highest degree of perfection. No extravagant prices asked, merely a fair price consistent with first-class work—we're equally proficient in the making of suits, overcoats or trousers. Place your next order with us if you wish to get the best there is.

Costume Making Our costume making department is under the supervision of most capable modistes and designers so that there's always a marked degree of the beautiful about gowns made here. We look carefully after every detail and have to our credit the designing of some of the most elaborate costumes ever made in Canada. In addition to dressy costumes we are particularly capable in the making of tailor-made gowns.

W. A. MURRAY & CO.
17 to 27 King St. East, 10 to 16 Colborne St , Toronto   Limited

c *W.A. Murray on King Street in Toronto claimed to be particularly capable in making tailor-mades, but also had to their credit the 'designing of some of the most elaborate costumes ever made in Canada.''*

in Toronto who catered to vice-royalty and ladies in diplomatic circles were O'Brien's Ladie's Tailor[2] and Stitt and Company.

Bilton Brothers had a lady's tailoring department in the English tradition. Their English supervisor married J.A. Boase, chief stockkeeper at O'Brien's and together they established a business in 1905 at 262 College Street. Mrs. Boase's ground-floor showroom carried imported French fashions and other frivolities,

d *A young Ontario bride wears a brown suede, fur-trimmed coat from Creed's, Toronto, about 1910. Her hat is also of suede trimmed with fur, possibly beaver, to match her muff.*

DEPARTMENT STORES

The department store was a phenomenon that changed earlier retailing methods. Toronto's electric streetcars, which began operating in 1892, brought great numbers of shoppers to the downtown area where both Simpson's and Eaton's were providing easy access to a broad range of goods.

Timothy Eaton, early to recognize the market potential of the Canadian woman, catered to all her needs as no one had ever before. Eaton's policies of fixed prices rather than barter, cash only, and goods satisfactory or money refunded, appealed to women shoppers. In the early 1880s, the new Eaton's at Yonge and Queen Streets boasted the first electric lights in any Canadian store and the first store elevator. Complete with doormen and floorwalkers, full-length mirrors, a lounge, and baby-sitting services, it also offered the first café in any Canadian department store. Fashion shows, beauty contests, and lessons by experts on everything from hairdressing to golf took place on the fifth floor.[3]

Competition was keen. In 1896 Robert Simpson rebuilt his large department store on Queen Street after a disastrous fire the year before. His business was to compete with Eaton's for many decades. In 1905 Simpson's bought out the Montreal firm John Murphy Limited and expanded into that city.

Ogilvy's and Holt Renfrew were already established in Montreal before the 1890s, when Henry Morgan and Company (Morgan's) moved uptown into a new three-storied department store in Phillips Square on St. Catherine Street.[4] The area quickly developed into the prime fashion centre of Montreal. Five years later Ogilvy and John Murphy relocated nearby on St. Catherine.

Other major department stores opened across Canada in the 1890s. Woodwards began, on what later became Hastings Street in Vancouver, as a department store aimed at the working class. H.H. Layfield and Company, at 16 Cordova, was a smaller store

and her fitting rooms and workroom employed a good number of craftswomen. It was the Boases who brought Jack Creed to Toronto to head their tailoring department. A few years later Creed opened his own small shop in the front of a house on Bloor Street. With the custom-tailor business on the wane, he eventually established Creed's, at first mainly a high-quality furrier on Yonge Street and later on Bloor Street where it was famous for fashion until 1991.

which carried such luxury items as cashmere shawls, silk and kid gloves, fans, hose, corsets, and yard goods. In 1906 David Spencer opened the first of his department-store chain in Vancouver. His later store, opened in the 1920s on Hastings Street, eventually became an Eaton's.

1905 marked a new era of progress and cultural development for Winnipeg and district when Eaton's opened the then largest retail store in the entire west, with catalogue operations attached. It catered to Winnipeg's South End, particularly Armstrong's Point, which was developing in these years as an area of fine living for the upper-middle classes. However, another company inevitably provided competition in the west. By World War I, the Hudson's Bay Company had major department stores in Victoria, Edmonton, and Calgary. In 1916 the Vancouver store at Granville and Georgia was replaced with the classic-columned emporium known as "the Bay." The department store was by now entrenched in the Canadian lifestyle, each store had its loyal following.

MANUFACTURING

Fashion items in shops and department stores were both imported and made locally. Mass production of some basic items of clothing was established in Canada in the nineteenth century. In 1901 the Canadian census recorded fifty-eight firms making men's and boys' clothing and twenty-six making women's cloaks, skirts, and shirtwaists (a long-sleeved blouse, usually with high choker neckline and buttons at the back). Shirtwaists were one of the first widely sold ready-made items for women.

Most manufacturers were based in Montreal or Toronto, but there were also firms in the Hamilton–London–Kitchener area of southern Ontario. Many of these firms produced work clothes, hoisery, and knitwear. Around 1900 Timothy Eaton began large-scale manufacturing of dresses, cloaks, underwear, shirts, and shirtwaists for his own stores.

Style 1315

Style 1314

e   *In 1906 the Morton-Browne Company of Toronto styled their skirts after those worn by the best dressed women of New York.*

Local manufacture and distribution accelerated with wider trade advertising in print. An illustrated ad by the long-established Montreal and Toronto firm A.E. Rea and Company presented their fall line of 1906 to retailers thus — "We throw down the gauntlet of style and value to the entire trade, having the best showing we ever had of silk waists and suits, silk and sateen underskirts, fancy ruchings and pleatings, collars, belts and Valenciennes lace and Swiss embroideries. We originate styles in Ladies' wear; you can depend on something different here."[5]

Suits and tailored skirts were sometimes offered to the public as "semi-ready," to speed up production, but made-to-order could also be done in a very short time. The Morton-Browne Company of Toronto in 1906 was producing made-to-order taffeta and sateen petticoats and gored, pleated, circular skirts in five different qualities of goods. Fabric samples and a catalogue of illustrated styles were available so that a customer could order by mail and be assured of delivery within ten days.

As ready-made dress styles became more varied, manufacturers competed with the individually made garment. High fashion tried to keep ahead with modes increasingly complicated, fragile, and nonwashable. Skilled home sewers could keep pace very well, and manufacturers of ready-made fashions were ever adapting to provide the middle market with lower-priced versions of the newest look. Although clothes-conscious women might build up a considerable wardrobe, nothing was wasted. Clothing was not discarded when out of fashion or favour, but passed on to "poor cousins" or altered or recut as a different garment.

The ubiquitous ready-made shirtwaist was in great demand for everyday wear. *Toronto Saturday Night* in 1903 published an account of a Dressmaker's Convention in the United States. Dressmakers were fighting a losing battle against an invasion of mass-produced shirtwaists. They were declared common, bourgeois, a menace to the profits of the hard-working dress-maker, and not pretty, anyway. A leading speaker asked her audience to talk them down all they could: "How can we expect to do a successful business when shirtwaists, which are in the mode, can be bought at any of the department stores for from $8. to $12. Can we afford to spend our time making shirtwaists which net only a trivial profit?"[6] They were certainly in trouble; current catalogues advertised shirtwaists at less than half those prices.

CATALOGUE SHOPPING

Catalogue shopping was extremely important in this era before the automobile, when so much of the population was rural. There were many fashion and household retail catalogues circulated, some quite large and others small booklets. The T. Eaton mail-order catalogue service was begun as early as 1884 with the enlarging of the Toronto store. It was Timothy Eaton's aim to bring to rural women and their families the same comforts and luxuries he sold to city customers.

The opening of the west through the Canadian Pacific Railway made the whole Dominion available as clients. Widely circulated across the country, the Eaton's catalogue was referred to as "the wishing book" by struggling families. Prices listed in it did not include shipping costs. You could have your goods delivered quite cheaply by freight to your nearest railroad station, or sent by mail at a cost of about sixteen cents per pound in 1901. Five cents extra guaranteed safe delivery. By 1903 Eaton's catalogue operation had grown so large it was housed in its own building.[7]

Along with every conceivable item needed for home and farm, Eaton's catalogues advertised personal goods for men, women, and children. Ladies' fashions opened the book. In 1901 they were illustrated, carefully drawn in black and white with photographed heads. The female silhouette was shown as a

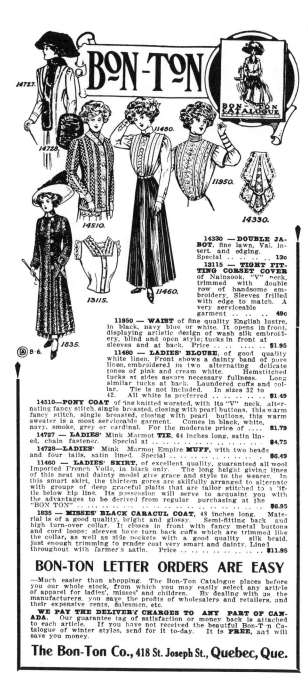

severe S-bend shape. Fairly standard styles were given a little glamour with such references as "navy cheviot serge, Paquin sleeve, has front and sleeves of tucked black taffeta silk . . . "8 One problem about buying fashions from the catalogues: even with a Paquin sleeve everyone knew where you got your dress and how much it cost.

Simpson's mail-order catalogues were published regularly after 1894 and expanded across Canada over the next several decades. Eaton's and Simpson's catalogues were major competitors for many years. In 1953 the mail-order section of Simpson's was transferred to Simpson-Sears Limited; Eaton's catalogue sales ended in 1976.

There were other smaller Canadian competitors for catalogue shopping in the Edwardian era. Murray-Kay Limited, Toronto, as early as 1908 offered a variety of goods by catalogue. The 1917 Murray-Kay book combined colour-tinted photographs of fashion items with black-and-white illustrations.

In 1910 Goodwin's of Montreal, then owners of A.E. Rea and Company, regularly published a catalogue of fashions for women, children, and men, plus some items for the home. An order form stamped with a two-cent stamp and mailed in the preaddressed envelope provided brought your goods to your nearest railway station. In contrast to Eaton's, Goodwin's catalogue prices included the shipping costs.

Smallman and Ingram of London, Ontario, established in 1877, began catalogue operations in 1912 and during the war years were prepaying shipments to any destination in the Dominion. "This free delivery mail order service coupled with the new parcel post service and the rural delivery is the means of placing our out-of-town customers in almost as advantageous a position

f *The Bon-Ton mail order company advertised in the* Canadian Pictorial *magazine (Montreal) in December 1910. The magazine featured black-and-white photos of international scenes, and stories and articles for both men and women.*

6716 K

6706 K

6706 K

6716 K

6619 K

6909 K

Northway GARMENTS

6619K. Ladies' coat of brocaded silk velvet, satin lined throughout, collar and cuffs of silk velour, fastens with handsome silk frog.

6620K. Same style as 6619, but made of silk velour, lined throughout grey satin, collar and cuffs of brocaded velvet and fastens with large silk frog without drops.

6716K. Misses' skirt, wide French front, slashed side closed with buttons, wide tuck down back gathered at band and finished with tabs. Made in grey mixed, green mixed, brown mixed or black and white mixed tweed, also in black, navy or brown serge.

6909K. Stout ladies' skirt, panel front, fancy cut side trimmed with ornaments and buttons, double box pleat back. Made in fine black serge.

6706K. Misses' skirt, slot seam down left side, front trimmed with combination buttons, plain back finished at top with outside darts and belt. Made in tweed in tan mixed, green mixed, brown mixed and grey mixed. Also in two-toned diagonals in grey and white or brown and white.

13

g *The White and May Company promoted their Northway line as neither ultra-conservative nor too extreme.*

as if actually visiting the store . . . Our Aim—A One Day Service."[9] Smallman and Ingram carried a wide selection of women's, children's, men's, and household goods.

Sometimes the descriptive text would be rather picturesque. The White and May Company of St. Marys, Ontario published a ladieswear catalogue in 1913, showing "the two best makers' lines. Northway Garments, and Rogers Garments are known from coast to coast as possessing style, quality and form, to a degree that outclasses all other lines . . . "[10] The catalogue showed skirts, suits, and coats, including a dashing evening number for $32.50 "of Moleskin, satin lined throughout . . . closes with large silk frog."[11] Customers were urged to visit the White and May showrooms, also in Ailsa Craig, Parkhill, and Strathmore, and "try on the Coats, and you will find that they possess a grace and beauty far beyond . . . the plates, for these garments were not got up to look well in a catalog—they were designed to delight the customer when actually in use."[12]

WOMEN'S JOURNALS

Women in Canadian cities and towns kept in touch with developments in housekeeping, etiquette, literature, and fashion through the numerous daily newspapers, books, and magazines of the period. No less than a dozen women's journals were published in Canada between the 1880s and 1905. Although this time period could be looked on as a kind of golden age for the industry, all editors were men. Many Canadian magazines never managed to compete successfully for very long with the bigger and more colourful imported productions, although a few did survive for some decades. The most popular were brought in from the United States, England, and France.

Some women's magazines of the Edwardian era that were published in Canada were *Everywomen's World, The Canadian* (lasted until 1939), *Canadian Home Journal* (1910–58 when it was absorbed by *Chatelaine* begun in 1928), *Canadian Queen,*

The Moon, Women's Century, as well as Canadian editions of the British *Weldon's Ladies' Journal* and *The Young Ladie's Journal*. These and other publications covered a variety of subjects considered of interest to women, including styles in women's attire.

The Canadian fashion trade magazine began as early as 1888 under the name of *The Dry Goods Review*. At that time it dealt mainly with millinery, corsets, cloaks, furs, and even some men's furnishings. Editorial illustrations were limited in number and awkwardly stylized, rather cartoonlike. By the 1940s *The Dry Goods Review* had changed its name several times and then stayed with *Stylewear* until 1946 when it became *Style*.

The *Delineator*, begun in 1885 by the American Butterick Pattern Company, and available in Canada, was an important catalogue of fashion patterns in the early years of the century, but by 1907 the *Delineator* was more a general ladies' magazine with an emphasis on fashion.

The American *Harper's Bazar* (changed to *Bazaar* in 1929) and *Vogue* dominated all fashion journals in North America after World War I. French women's magazines—*Femina, Les Modes, La Gazette du Bon Ton*—also inspired fashions in Canada. The earliest issues had engraved illustrations, but as photographs were used increasingly in the Edwardian era the quality of illustration degenerated even in the French publications.

DESIGN INFLUENCES FROM ABROAD

Turn-of-the-century Paris, the centre of art and design for Europe and North America, was dominated by art nouveau. This graceful belle époque style, with its soft colours and sinuous forms based on nature, had an enormous effect on women's fashions although it was rare to see an obviously art nouveau dress. However, luxurious and delicate fabrics in pastel colours, the refined, linear use of braids, ribbons, and lace, the draping of fabrics around the figure, and swirling, spreading trains, are all typical art nouveau features [2].

Along with French couturiers, many illustrators, jewellery designers, furniture makers, and other craftsmen adopted the characteristics of art nouveau. The Edwardians decorated the interiors of their homes in the new lighter colours and more elegant, graceful forms. Wallpapers and interior fabrics favoured whites and subtle pastels; furniture was smaller, less weighty, rooms less cluttered than in Victorian times.

One of the ways that art nouveau travelled to Canada was through the medium of the graphic arts. Tom Thomson and most of the artists who later formed the Group of Seven, including J.E.H. MacDonald, Varley, Jackson, and Lismer, worked in their early years as commercial illustrators when they were influenced by American and European artists and designers working in the art nouveau style.

The style was also expressed in the collections of the finest French designers. The top names in Paris couture at the turn of the century were the long-established House of Worth, the Callot Soeurs, and Madame Paquin, all famous for beautiful and romantic eveningwear, and Jacques Doucet, highly respected designer of extravagant ball gowns, tea gowns, and elegantly cut tailored suits.

Paris fashion designers were considered the most prestigious, but London was important, too. Two well-known English names of the time were Lucile and Redfern. Lucile, or Lady Duff Gordon, grew up in Ontario as a Saunders and her sister was the well-known actress Elinor Glyn. Lucile designed fanciful tea gowns and oriental-inspired evening gowns. Redfern's reputation was established with early sportswear for yachting and riding and for beautifully tailored suits.

DRESSING FOR DAY AND EVENING

Dress structure was even more complex than it looked. Bodices were cleverly lined and boned for fit, with a softly draped outer shell [8]. Much of the construction was done with hand stitching. Dresses were often in two parts: the bodice and a matching skirt edged at the waist with a minimal waistband; occasionally some dresses had both a day and an evening bodice for the same skirt. Dresses were sometimes constructed in one piece as well.

Solid colour dress fabrics were favoured, these lavishly trimmed with lace, ribbons, braid, or embroidery, and further enriched with fine tucking or pleats [1]. Commonly used winter daytime fabrics were fine woollens, viyella, tweeds, suiting, velvets, brocades, and heavy silks and satins. Summer dresses were made up in lightweight linens, cotton muslins, lawn, cambric, dimity, organdy, gingham, piqué, and cotton or silk voiles. The dainty outer fabrication camouflaged the rigid construction underneath.

As early as the 1890s the tailored suit, comprising jacket and skirt, was established as popular daywear. This suit represented the first visible signs of the masculization of women's wear. Depending on the suit's quality and styling, it was correct for business in town, travelling, and various sporting activities. The jacket, with neatly fitted lines and full sleeves, was worn over a crisp, white, high-collared shirtwaist and often finished with a mannish tie or foulard bow. A simple, long, flared skirt over high-buttoned boots and a severe straw boater hat completed the uniform.

The full leg-o'-mutton suit-jacket sleeve of about 1895 had subsided, at the turn of the century, to a normal fit, and the skirts of the jacket had shortened or were nonexistent [4]. By 1905, the fuller puffed sleeve was beginning to return.

The neat and professional-looking tailored suit was the symbol of the newly emerging working woman, and its popularity

h
Novi-Modi in 1905 illustrated this design with an extreme S-bend silhouette and promoted it as "representing the acme of French modes, a gown for the Horse Show or any very smart affair. Blouse coat with braid 'militaire' . . . Skirt is nine-gore pleated. $32.00."

continued on through the Edwardian era. The full-chested early Edwardian look was often reinforced in dressy afternoon styles with the use of a bolero jacket, popular until about 1907. For a couple of years after that date, the new longer jackets and waists often showed the full leg-o'-mutton sleeve revival [10].

Separates in the form of blouses and skirts for both day and eveningwear were accepted before the turn of the century. Both items were mass-produced and readily available. In the Edwardian period they became the great favourites of the North American woman who had traditionally favoured simple, functional styling. She wore the plain washable cotton or linen shirtwaist, often with detachable linen collar and cuffs, at work or at home. White, or sometimes in colours, shirtwaists might have tucking or lace insertions, nearly always full-length, down the front. But for dressier occasions, the shirtwaist was made in finer fabrics, more imaginatively trimmed with ribbons, lace ruffles, tiny buttons, and pintucks [6].

The T. Eaton catalogues of 1901 advertised summer shirtwaists in white lawn, as well as printed percale, striped madras, sateen, and chambray in assorted colours. The range of prices (seventy cents to two-and-a-half dollars) showed the versatility of the style and also how important it was to know your fabrics. For fall and winter Eaton's offered lined silk waists in beautiful colours, generously tucked and trimmed, in taffeta and Duchese satin, as well as albatross cloth, cashmere, velveteen, and fine French flannel. Popular colours to choose from were black, navy, sky, old rose, cerise, royal, white, pink, and heliotrope. Prices were from two-and-a-half to eight-and-a-half dollars.[13]

The everyday skirt no longer trailed as afternoon dresses did during the first three years of the century, but just cleared the ground for easier movement. A sporty walking skirt was several inches shorter still. Made up in cheviot homespun, serge, tweed, heavy cotton duck, and other serviceable fabrics, as well as silk broadcloths and taffetas, the separate skirt was always trumpet-shaped, flaring near the hem and fitting smoothly over the hips by means of gored shapes or darts.

While daytime fashions expressed a sense of dignity and propriety, dinner and ball gowns were naturally about seduction. High collars were exchanged in the evening for a sometimes extreme décolletage [2 and 3]. Sleeves shrunk to the merest confection at the shoulders, but by about 1908 many evening gowns reflected the leg-o'-mutton revival, these, no doubt, being the puffed sleeves so wished for by the character Anne in *Anne of Green Gables* [11]. Waists were as small as possible, often dropping to a V at centre front. Trailing hemlines were draped in a froth of ruffles and lace over rustling silk petticoats and were sometimes held off the floor for the waltz or two-step. Fragile fabrics were carefully selected: mousselines, chiffons, crepes, satins, peau de soie, pongee, and Japanese silks were combined with nets and laces, most often in cream, pale beige, silvery grey, and other delicate pastels.

CORSETS, TEA GOWNS, AND LINGERIE

Corsets were worn for support and control of the figure for many centuries, mainly by the fashion-conscious upper class. The ideal figure in the last years of the nineteenth century was the curving hourglass—a very small waist with a full bust and rounded hips and abdomen. By 1900 the straight front corset had become an integral part of achieving the newer S-bend silhouette. These corsets tipped the bust forward and flattened the abdomen with a long and straight busk (heavy, central boning). Straightening the front created more fullness at the rear. By 1901 the T. Eaton catalogue stated that "the Erect Form and Straight Front Corsets are in great demand."[14]

Corsets moulded the figure usually up to the nipples, thereby encasing the lower curve of the breasts. A high-bust version had shoulder straps. Corsets varied in length; most covered the hips and abdomen but short-hip styles were available. There were a number of different motives for wearing corsets: to support tired or weak muscles; to slim the figure and control bulges; to create the ideal shape currently in fashion; and to support hose. Four elastic hose-supporters were usually clipped to or permanently attached to the front and sides of a corset. Most corsets were of firmly woven cotton jean or heavy cotton coutil, the silhouette maintained by a series of shaped vertical

A straight front B and C corset advertised in the Eaton's catalogue of 1901 was steel-boned, made of non-stretchable jean, and sold for one dollar.

bones of steel wire. Some French corsets still used whalebone at this time. Corsets were imported from America, France, or England, but one of the largest suppliers was D. & A. Corsets, (later the Dominion Corset Manufacturing Company in Quebec). Their corsets were available in sizes from eighteen inches to thirty inches, and they cost from one to four dollars between 1900 and 1905.

Corsets generally hooked up centre front, and the back was closed by lacing, making the fit adjustable to a degree. How tightly you laced your corset depended on how much you valued fashion and conventional concepts of beauty over comfort and health. D. & A. Corsets made nonrustable, durable corsets that helped to "increase the beauty of the figure without harsh pressures,"[15] and were conveniently front-lacing.

The top edge of the corset at the fullest part of the bust could create an unattractive ridge through dress bodices of light

j
Morton-Browne claimed hundreds of satisfied customers all over Canada for their petticoats in taffeta (guaranteed) or in less expensive English sateen.

fabrics, therefore a corset cover was worn by fastidious ladies of fashion. Corset covers were white, lace-trimmed under-bodices in fine cotton or silk. The chemise was a sleeveless, one-piece, straight-cut undergarment essentially combining the corset cover with the petticoat skirt. White, washable petticoat skirts of cotton or fine cambric, or coloured percale, moreen, or taffeta were hemmed with flounces for volume and edged with frills, cording, ruching, and ribbons.

Tea gowns, Wrappers, and Sacques: An item that bridged the gap between dress and undress was the tea gown. Ladies who had been corseted for afternoon calls and were destined for a corseted evening as well were glad to take an evening meal with the family in a tea gown. These concoctions were as ornate as afternoon dresses, but more comfortable because they were one-piece, often in the cut of a wrapper or coat, and could be worn without a corset. They had a less formal air about them due to their softer lines and were worn only at home [7 and 16]. A sacque was a short version of a tea gown and a wrapper a more casual one.

Underwear: In the Victorian era there was much debate on the practice of wearing wool next to the skin, and it was still considered important by many to keep all parts of the body protected from draughts as well as the public eye. Even the summer catalogues of 1900 offered short- and long-sleeved rib-knit vests, full-length drawers, and combinations (called union suits in the United States) in cotton, wool, Viyella, and silk knit. Drawers in fine cottons, the wide legs tucked and hemmed with ruffles and lace, were also worn and silk drawers were gaining favour.

Two interesting and distinctive underwear accessories from this period, which were worn by certain figure types, were bust-improvers and bustles. Both might be required by the straight and thin woman in order to achieve the admired S-curve shape. The bustles were small horse-hair pads or shapes of tempered wire, merely to give more substance at the back. They were not meant to create a bustle silhouette. The bust-improvers were in the form of a wire distender, mono-breasted like a fencer's shield, or like wire falsies to be sewn into the underlayers of dress. There were also subtler ruffled fabric types.

Hosiery: Thigh-length stockings in silk, cotton lisle, wool, or cashmere, or a blend of cotton and wool were worn in shades of black, grey, cream, beige, tan, or white. Plain, ribbed, or finely striped for day, open lacey knits or with embroidered panels or a simple clock (a decorative motif near the ankle) for evening. Sources were local as well as American and British.

Nightwear: Mother Hubbard styles were common: a square yoke to which was gathered the fullness of the straight-cut long gown, with added short or long sleeves and a frilly collar, usually in white washable fabrics like cotton flannelette, lawn, or nainsook, (fine, soft, plain-weave cottons) and, of course, in silk.

OUTERWEAR AND ACCESSORIES

Perhaps because the Edwardian woman's full-length daytime skirt was made of sturdy fabric and layered over petticoats in winter, short jackets and capes were very popular. The jacket often took the form of the double-breasted reefer with set-in sleeves and hemlines varying from waist to hipline. Black was a favourite colour choice followed by navy, grey, various browns, and even red and dark green, for jackets made up in wool cheviots, covert, cozy napped wool kersey, and napped beaver cloth.

Fingertip capes were available in these same coatings with tailored details for daywear, or in silk brocade, ottoman, silk plushes, and other dressy fabrics, trimmed or lined with fur for winter afternoons and evenings. Full-length, richly decorated opera cloaks were worn on formal evenings. Capes were so much a part of the scene they were even offered in sporty fabrics and fancy plaids for playing golf.

Overcoats, sometimes still called ulsters, were serviceable, full-length coats, often with one or more shoulder-capes attached. Waterproof rain cloaks were available in covert cloth or rubber-lined fabrics in the form of single or double-breasted coats often with shoulder capes.

Winter furs were plentiful and varied. Many kinds of furs were styled into garments for men, women, and even children and sold through fur outlets and salons in the fashionable stores. Two of the twenty-five furriers listed in the 1901 *Toronto City Directory* were Robert Simpson and Holt Renfrew. Holt Renfrew used the line: "Canada's Leading Furriers Since 1837."

This Persian lamb jacket in the Windsor style of 1906 was trimmed with the finest natural Canadian mink and lined with best grade black satin.

l

Large, elaborately trimmed hats accessorized the Printzess spring line sold by J. and D. Ross, London, Ontario.

Short-haired furs such as sealskin and lamb were styled like cloth coats and jackets. Storm coats and jackets were made of Persian and grey lamb, astrachan, Hudson Seal (muskrat), Canadian mink, Hudson Bay Sable (marten), beaver, fox, raccoon, and others.

The mass market was offered, some at fairly reasonable prices, fake and disguised furs such as Hudson Seal and Hudson Bay Sable, as well as weasel treated to resemble mink and rabbit treated and dyed to resemble everything from sealskin (Sealette) to Imperial Mink to Kolinsky Coney. Muskrat was not always disguised under a different name; by the end of the decade, the M. Davidson Company, on Rideau Street in Ottawa, advertised Canadian muskrat automobile coats for fifty-five dollars.[16]

Winter hats, fancy scarves, and caperines, boas, stoles, and muffs were very fashionable in snowy ermine, Alaska sable, fox, lynx, wolf, seal, mink, as well as marten, raccoon, squirrel, and beaver. A Canadian winter had its own kind of elegance in these days, but summer could be stunning, too. Boas and ruffs of ostrich and other feathers were worn for summer evenings, and fancy parasols carried for sun protection and flirting, as were fans of linen, silk, palm, gauze, and feather.

Special coats were designed for protection in the new automobile. Autos were unreliable, clumsy, and difficult to operate and roads were rutted and muddy in spring and fall and dusty in summer. Most early autos were open to the elements and as speed increased, automobile dress became more protective. As early as 1901 women's and children's driving coats and jackets were advertised as automobile coats although they differed very little from regular merchandise. The connotations of prestige associated with motoring dress, speed, and chic, caused the automobile coats to have their own distinct image. In an attempt to demonstrate that the machines were easy to drive, automobile advertising often showed a woman at the wheel; she would be dressed in a roomy, loose-sleeved duster topped off with veiled motoring hat and goggles [12]. As windshields became more common and cars more enclosed, the specialized auto coat faded from the scene.

Hats: Hats were worn for all occasions, perched on top of full upswept hairdos. Made of light fabrics, or natural or coloured straws for summer and felt for winter, most hats were variations on the boater shape, with straight or curved brims. Severe and mannish fedoras could be worn as sportswear. Toques and turbans had more intricately folded shapes and were often trimmed beyond recognition with artificial flowers, ribbon bands and bows, buckles, net, and ostrich and other feathers.

Hats grew bulkier by the decade's end. The new narrower figure was topped by "heavily draped, enormous befeathered crowns . . . combined with either large upturned or down sloping brims."[17] With a final surge of excessive decoration just before the simpler prewar hats, ostrich plumes developed into entire birds.

THE SPORTING LIFE

Canadian Edwardians indulged in outdoor activities and sports of all kinds winter and summer; it was part of their rural heritage. Many women were participating in sports once considered male territory, and naturally they found their regular wardrobes of

m *Menswear styling was adapted for Edwardian women's sportswear.*

fragile fabrics and ornate trim inappropriate. Joining men in outdoor games turned these activities into a socially acceptable means of courting and women continued to be restricted to forms of dress within the conventions of the times. Nevertheless, they began slowly to adapt elements from menswear into their own costumes. Simpler styling and more durable fabrics were used, and women were able to participate quite effectively in spite of neckties, buckled belts, hats, and long skirts.

Fashionable activities of the leisure classes had introduced women to lawn bowling, croquet, tennis, and golf in the summer. Croquet runs were laid out on gracious lawns, tennis courts were built in the gardens of summer homes, and golf was offered through clubs and resorts. In 1901 the Canadian Ladies Golf Union conducted its first Open Championship at the Royal Montreal Golf Course.

Winter brought curling, snowshoeing, and tobogganing; downhill skiing was still an expensive European novelty. Skating had long been enjoyed in Canada, especially in Ottawa on the frozen Rideau River.

Summer cycling was the most popular sporting activity. Cycling was available to all because it was both simple and inexpensive. And no small bonus was the fact that it granted a new freedom to many a young Canadian woman. Hop on a bicycle and you were away from the chaperoned atmosphere of home with only your conscience to guide you. On Sundays thousands of people cycled on the dusty roads. Many ministers of the church criticized the growing numbers who replaced church going with "skylarking on a bicycle."[18]

The most correct costume for women cyclists was the cotton shirtwaist and the wool or linen jacket teamed with a matching slightly shortened skirt over breeches or bloomers. Advice for both safe and socially correct cycling costume was given as follows: skirts must be the length and width that ensured safety from entanglement in the chain and wheel, but no shorter than absolutely necessary. The gaiters should be the same colour as the costume, and so should the hose, and of still more importance (especially for bad riders) was to have the underskirts or knicker-bockers of somewhat the same colour as the outer skirt. No clinging material should be used, and the front part of the skirt should be interlined with a fabric such as chamois, and the whole skirt lined with silk or linen. Further advice was offered in an attempt to minimize "the comical way large sleeves quiver and tremble."[19]

A corseted woman found prolonged sitting difficult. Cycling and other sports influenced the introduction of a shorter corset. Gymnasts needed freedom from conventions of public dress, and wore comfortable, but modest bifurcated garments. Gymnastics were performed mainly through private clubs, schools, and universities. The traditional gymnastic costume (established about 1850) was trousers (or bloomers) plus a shortened frock. The bloomer style that was advocated by the American Amelia Bloomer for everyday wear in 1851 had its origin in this early gymsuit.[20]

Gymnasium activities were usually segregated, and women could wear trousers even without the frock: voluminous, knee-length pants plus a shirtwaist and stockings. More common, however, even at the turn of the century in Canada, was the combination of bloomers with a frock or dress [15].

THE NEW WOMAN EMERGES

Women's fashions changed a great deal in the late Edwardian period. As early as 1906 the extremely pouched bodice was starting to disappear. A fitted ribcage made for a more upright figure as the S-bend straightened out. After 1907 haute couture designers Poiret and Lucile introduced the neoclassic silhouette, raising the waistline and giving women an opportunity to leave off the corset if they wished.

The shape of the corset itself changed. Lower on top, less nipped in at the waist, and longer, its new purpose was to slim the hips and thighs for narrower skirts. Sitting became even more uncomfortable. La Diva corsets, made by the Dominion Corset Company just before the war, varied in price from two-and-a-half dollars to a heady twenty-five dollars and were made in silk-knit,

In March 1907 the Robert Simpson Company advertised washable cotton dress goods: French organdies, voiles, batistes, printed Delainette, and mercerized checks and dots.

tricots, or peau de suede. Dominion's new Tango models in tricot-elastic were said to "mould the figure, enhancing nature's charms without strain or compression."[21] The obviously corseted figure was now considered less attractive, although most women still wore corsets out of habit. As the narrow, clinging dress evolved it was more fashionable to be slim without showing a corsetlike shape.

Corsets began to be designed for a more physically active woman. Lighter, pliable fabrics were used, and softer, button-closing edging tape formed the centre front instead of busks or bones. Removable bones could be replaced if they rusted or left out altogether. The athletic corset, for increasingly active sports, led the way towards greater physical freedom.

The mass-produced shirtwaist was still very common. Inexpensive, unlined, and washable, it had long filled a distinct need for relatively easy-care dressing. In summer the same light and washable fabrics used for shirtwaists were made up in skirts. Matching tops and skirts were combined to form the shirtwaist dress, sometimes called the lingerie dress. Speedy dome fasteners instead of small buttons, appeared about 1910 and became the predominant type of closure system. For fall and winter dressing, the two-piece suit [10 and 14] was a favourite, demonstrating the continuing move towards professional business dress.

A little body exposure in regular daywear evolved in subtle ways—barer throats and forearms and less layers of fabric. The "pneumonia neckline," an open V-neck, was introduced in Paris about 1907, but it was some years before Canadian women gave up their high standing collar for day [13].

Social conditions were forcing great changes: A more affordable automobile was speeding up life; many young women were insisting on a university education and a career. The Edwardian woman wanted a less restricted life and more physical comfort and mobility in her clothes. Participation in the business of life in all its facets was a new goal.

1 DAY DRESS, *about 1903*

A two-piece summer day dress in beige eyelette-embroidered linen. The bodice is pouched above a shirred and pointed front waistband. Three-quarter sleeves have faggoting and écru Irish crochet at the wrists matching the high neckline. Edwardians favoured many details in a gown unified through a monochromatic colour scheme.

The pleats of the unlined skirt are stitched down over the hips lower in front than in back allowing the back to flare and helping to give, together with the overhanging bodice, the fashionable S-bend silhouette. Skirt closure is with dome fasteners along the left front pleat. The centre-back bodice closure uses dome fasteners and hooks. *The Suddon Collection*

2 EVENING GOWN

A two-piece formal gown. Alternating bouquets in persimmon and pale blue are printed on cream silk chiffon. Celadon grosgrain ribbon accents the shoulders and a very small and forward-tipping waistline. The gown would have been worn over a corset shaped to create a small waist, a flattened abdomen, and a pronounced derrière.

The narrow-hipped skirt flares into a full train creating an art nouveau swirl. Design detailing is complex with shirring, drooping lace panels, and lace-edged ruffles, but uniformly softened colours provide harmony. The bodice is boned through the waist and there is a great deal of handstitching. The cream taffeta underskirt produces a sensuous swishing sound with movement.
Designer: Violette, Paris *The Suddon Collection*

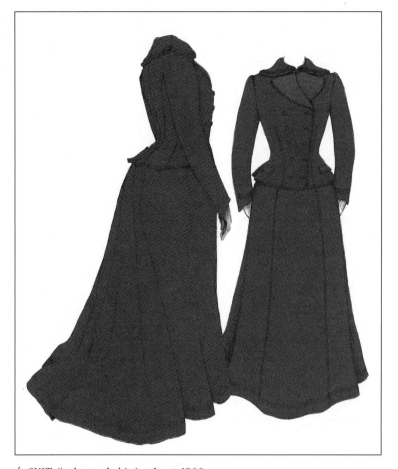

3 RECEPTION GOWN, *about 1905*

A one-piece evening gown in rosy lavender silk brocade trimmed with appliqué medallions of écru lace. The five gores of the skirt are cut to give the very rounded hipline of a sensuous, mature figure. The boned bodice is not pouched but shows the later, more fitted shape and is lined with white cotton. The hook-and-eye closure is along the left side of the centre-front panel. The train is lined with pink taffeta. *Queen's University Collection*

4 SUIT (jacket and skirt), *about 1900*

A tailored two-piece suit for outdoor winter wear in heavy black wool. The double-breasted jacket is moulded to a corseted figure and has black silk-covered lapels, a rolled collar trimmed with black passementerie, and seams generously topstitched.

The three-gored unlined skirt has a narrow silk waistband. The hemline is finished inside with a five-inch band of black silk, and a narrower black velveteen brush braid over it for soil and wear. Sturdy fabric edging would be needed as the skirt would drag in the dirt of winter weather.

The cut of both the jacket and the skirt produces an accented derrière which is reinforced by a small horsehair-stuffed bustle pad of black silk tacked inside the centre-back waist of the skirt.

Label: A.R. Kerr and Co. of Hamilton, Ontario *The Suddon Collection*

5 AFTERNOON GOWN

A two-piece dress in delicate off-white dotted muslin. The bodice and sleeves are worked completely with rows of fine tucks. Even though this is a dress for warm summer weather, it has long sleeves and a standing collar. There is a small gathering of fabric at the throat to act as an anchor for a brooch. The bodice is short-waisted in the back and pouched in front, intricately worked with lace insertions, edging and ruffles.

The skirt has a lace-trimmed panel emphasizing the derrière. Tiers of ruffles create a train also trimmed with tucking and lace; even the cotton underskirt has a ruffled hem.

The Suddon Collection

6 SEPARATES

Typical Edwardian separates for less formal wear. The fine white linen blouse has pintucks and drawn work in two vertical centre-front panels. The standing collar, tucked and lace edged, is supported with yellow plastic collar stays. Closure is with small pearl buttons in the centre-back placket, and there are skirt hooks near the hem to keep the waist securely tucked in at the back. Two cotton ties secure the front and allow the pouched effect.

The unlined, black ribbed-silk skirt has a centre-back hook and eye closure. The hemline panel is a cut circle and drapes with added fullness below the top row of tucks. Skirts and shirtwaists similar to this were standard office wear except that they were usually in more serviceable fabrics and had plain, starched, detachable collars and cuffs.

Queen's University Collection

7 TEA GOWN, *about 1900*

A summer tea gown in fine white cotton. This one-piece gown for at-home wear has a full-length centre-front opening trimmed on each side with rows of pintucking, white embroidery, and a wide lace ruffle. Tied at the throat and around the waist with blue satin ribbon, it has a fresh Gainsborough look. The long sleeves with a relatively small amount of fullness at the shoulders mark the end of the gigot sleeve of the previous five years. The embroidery and tucking down the centre back is derived from eighteenth-century styling.

Royal Ontario Museum

8 WINTER WEDDING GOWN, *1902*

A wedding gown in fine cream wool, pale peach silk brocade, and cream lace. It was worn with a floral headress, long cream veil, and gloves. A two-piece dress, the bodice closes centre back with small pearl buttons and handworked buttonholes. It is lined with cream cotton, boned, and beautifully finished by hand. The standing collar hooks on separately. Sewing skills were very important in the home, although not normally taught in the schools at this time. Many women's sewing skills were equal to that of a couturière, with their exquisite handwork.

Worn by Miss Sarah Maud Moore for her marriage to Hector Peart Mount on 23 December 1902 in St. Stephen's Church, Montreal

Private Collection

9 AFTERNOON GOWN

A one-piece afternoon dress in ivory corded silk trimmed with matching lace and ribbon. A broad-shouldered effect is created with wide vertical panels accented by lace insertions and silk ribbon. The standing lace collar and the sleeves are couched with silk cording and edged with a pale green silk bias-band, the only touch of another colour. Centre-back closure with a buttoned placket on the bodice changes to dome fasteners on the skirt. Every seam is topstitched and the inside of the garment is beautifully finished by hand.

Queen's University Collection

10 WALKING SUIT (jacket and skirt), *about 1909*

A fall / winter outfit for day in aubergine, checked wool flannel. The princess seamed jacket with lapels is cut away in front like a man's morning coat. In spite of the buttons, the jacket closes centre front with hooks and eyes; the self-covered buttons are trim only. Three very long bones are set into the front and side seams to shape the jacket.

Although the pleats of the skirt are released at about the halfway point, fullness is controlled with the pleats being tacked into place to an inside braid near the hemline. There is a three-inch false hem of black cotton plus a brush braid.

The Suddon Collection

11 RECEPTION GOWN, *about 1908*

A one-piece dress in ivory embroidered net over silk, accented with a sash and large roses in ivory taffeta. The Directoire influence is seen both in the fabric design and the raised waistline. The bosom is accented by a double row of taffeta ruffles gathered to the inside neckline. In spite of the empire silhouette a wide Petersham waistband is tacked inside centre front and there are six seven-inch bones in the lining seams through the waist. The skirt is kept narrow at the hips but flares to a train in back.

Queen's University Collection

12 AUTOMOBILE DUSTER, *about 1905*

This summer automobile coat in heavy white linen is a classic of its genre. It features the new and comfortable raglan sleeve cut full and shaped with five large horizontal darts.

The cuffs, rolled-down collar, and central panel are all chain-stitch embroidered in thick, white thread and trimmed with crochet-covered buttons. The coat is fastened with similar buttons and tabs. The large patch pockets were popular details for dusters.

Given by the Warren family, Toronto   *Royal Ontario Museum*

13 AFTERNOON FROCK

A one-piece lingerie-type summer dress in white eyelette-embroidered linen with a slightly raised waistline. The front and back yokes of embroidered net extend up into a transitional Robespierre collar, open in front but still high in back, supported by three wire bones. Yokes and front closure are trimmed with white braid and crocheted buttons. The three-quarter sleeves are of embroidered net with two panels in each of finer gathered net.

Other transitional characteristics in this dress are that the S-bend pouch is quite gone and the waistline is level, but earlier Edwardian features of white-on-white and the skirt straighter in front and full in back are still present. *Label: The A.E. Rea Co., Ottawa, Ont.* *The Suddon Collection*

14 SUIT (jacket and skirt), *about 1910*

A serviceable walking or business suit in creamy yellow wool serge. The long jacket is cut for the straighter, narrow-hipped, top-heavy silhouette of the period. It is unlined and all inner seams are bias-tape bound. The buttons are silk covered, and the buttonholes are machine stitched. The pleated skirt is kept narrow with horizontal bands buttoned into place. This suit is probably a factory-made ready-to-wear. *Queen's University Collection*

15 GYM SUIT, *about 1910*
A sporty two-piece gym suit of jacket-bodice plus bloomers in black cotton sateen trimmed with white. The bodice has a vestee which is worked with tucks and trimmed with white buttons, but closes with hidden dome fasteners. The modest wrapped skirt covers separate black cotton, full-cut bloomers. They have elastic casing in the back half of the waist and at the legs.

Queen's University Collection

16 TEA GOWN or DINNER DRESS, *about 1909*
A high-waisted, one-piece gown in black chiffon and embroidered black satin. Full sleeves of gathered chiffon are held loosely in place by bands of satin embroidered to match the bodice, with black embroidery, couched gold threads, clear seed beads, and opaque and clear aqua beads. The centre-back closure fastens with hook and eye under a double row of embroidered satin-covered buttons. The deeply trained skirt is lined with black cotton with a silk dust ruffle inside the hem. Beaded tassels hang from the chiffon sash. The gown's languid air suggests tea gown. *The Vancouver Museum*

a *In their 1911 catalogue Goodwin's advertised this dress of imported Parisian voile with "the new Citoyenne effect . . . seen to advantage in the short waist. The skirt has novelty semi-tunic effect. Comes in black and navy. $20.00."*

• T H E •
1910s

FROM ABOUT 1909 IN CANADA ELABORATE EDWARDIAN STYLES BEGAN to simplify, and developments during this period led to the emancipated dress of the 1920s. The fashionable shape for women changed from the unnatural S-curve to a nearly straight cylinder; this more upright silhouette, with minor variations, became firmly established for the rest of the century. The beginnings of modern dress can be seen in the simpler lines that appeared in Paris as early as 1907 when couturier Paul Poiret presented a neoclassical look in day and evening gowns with raised waists and long narrow skirts, not in classical white, however, but in richly coloured fabrics. Unlike earlier Edwardian dress these styles looked their best on slim young women.

The metamorphosis of form inspired by the neoclassical revival in Paris began in Canada with the Directoire silhouette —short-waisted dresses with softer, slimmer skirts, which first appeared in the most fashionable evening gowns [11]. In daywear by 1910 the deeply pointed Edwardian waist had given way to a natural waistline, sometimes even slightly higher (especially in the back) as the short-waisted bodice became a more common feature [22]. Soon these dresses with slightly bloused bodices were left unboned, indeed unlined, and had only a wide inner waistband for control. Daytime hemlines merely touched the instep or were even shortened to show the ankle. Circular, gored, dirndl, and flared skirts lost all excess back fullness. Fabrics did not flare away from the legs over crisp petticoats but hung softly and almost straight. Pleated detailing in many daytime skirts gave movement but kept lines narrow.

Not everyone approved of this trend towards lighter, body-revealing dress. A Canadian reader wrote to the *Hamilton Herald* in 1912: "The freakish fashions which shamelessly display the physical rather than the innocent charms of young girls, are a disgrace, and put their mothers in an equally bad light. With large and amazing hats, transparent [shirt]waists, skirts reaching but a few inches below the knee, so tight that the figure is boldly displayed at every step, with stockings of the thinnest silk, our girls present a very improper spectacle. What has come to be a common street sight today would not have been tolerated ten years ago."[1]

By 1912 the predominant silhouette was top-heavy. Long and slim, only gently curvy, often unbelted, dresses were cut on the lines of a high-waisted figure-skimming skirt, topped by a bloused, short-waisted bodice. The waist, therefore, was allowed its natural shape instead of being pulled in. Even with separates, the skirt often rose three or four inches above the normal waistline in a gentle corselet effect [31]. This top-heavy silhouette was often exaggerated by softly draped bodices featuring Magyar, dolman, or kimono sleeves, or a dropped shoulder seam [19]. Further volume on top was provided by those amazing, extremely large, and excessively trimmed hats perched on top of voluminous hair styles.

The ever-narrowing skirt by 1912 had become difficult to move in easily and a year later it developed a pegtop silhouette with fullness through the thighs and a hobble hemline [17]. The illusion of narrowness at the ankles was achieved by clever pleats or slits that allowed a normal step to be taken, however, these skirts were still far from practical. Newspaper fashion editorials expressed women's frustration: "Everyone has long been praying, or at least hoping, for skirts wider at the foot. The agony of trying to step into a trolley car of the present time when wearing a skirt cut on modern lines is familiar to us all."[2]

EXOTICA FROM ABROAD

Sergei Diaghilev launched a new era for theatre in Paris in 1909 when his Ballets Russes presented theatrical spectacles combining avant-garde music and dance with sets and costumes in vibrating patterns of brilliant colours. The decor and costumes for the Ballet Russes production of *Scheherazade*, designed by artists Bakst and Benois, were the source of great change in the decorative arts.

The exciting visual statements in Paris inspired a new form of graphic design. Innovative illustrators such as Erté, Marty, Paul Iribe, Marthe Romme, Georges Lepape, Georges Barbier, and Benito, whose works were linked to the fashion world, were published regularly in these years. Through these artists the decorative arts were uniquely, creatively interpreted in the issues of the *Gazette du Bon Ton* and other French fashion magazines from 1912 to the war years and afterwards. The special quality of the illustrated plates in the magazines offered an elegant and idealized vision which rivalled the more realistically detailed fashion photography of the period. Later, a romanticized and impressionistic photographic style would emerge. North American fashion illustrators were considerably influenced by these artists.

The designs of Paris couturiers Doucet, Lanvin, and especially Poiret reflected their attraction to these revolutionary arts in Paris. Excessive decorative trim highly favoured during the belle époque soon disappeared. Solid coloured fabrics in contrasts of bright hues replaced delicate pastels.

Poiret responded to the mood of the times with dramatic, theatrical fashions using oriental-inspired themes derived from the Ballets Russes, fabricated in beautifully embroidered and beaded textiles and rich brocades. He put women into trousers (harem pants); he produced his early Grecian lines with raised waists and tunics, which allowed women to abandon or at least loosen their corsets; and he helped to do away with that symbol of the Edwardian age, the standing collar. But perhaps he is most remembered for the narrow hobble skirt teamed with the minaret tunic worn by leaders of fashion in 1913/14.

The minaret or lampshade tunic did not appeal to many conservative Canadians, as we see in a 1914 advertisement by the Toronto Pleating Company: "Probably you don't want a 'lampshade' dress, but you do want your clothes to be stylish and charming . . . then consider the use of pleating —a pleated tunic . . . the most inexpensive way to distinction in your dress."[3]

Poiret was the first couturier to give public lectures. As part of his wartime tour of North America in 1916, he gave two lectures sponsored by Eaton's at the Royal Alexandra Theatre in Toronto. Poiret made the point that a couturier does not arbitrarily change fashion, but rather adjusts as he sees his clients changing. He also indicated that he did not find North American women individualistic enough in their dress.

FASHION PROMOTION

Before the war wealthy and well-connected Canadian women spent much of their lives at one social occasion after another: military balls, concerts, theatre, receptions, private parties, and teas. Correct dress was an understood part of these events. Original models from the best houses in Paris or London were the most highly prized, but the great New York department stores were also sources of high quality merchandise. Canadian travellers and vacationers might have garments made for themselves by leading English or French dressmakers or couturiers, or purchase ready-made clothing in American department stores.

Design houses, for example a firm based in London, might move into international markets by opening second branches abroad. Lucile, a talented English dressmaker of international repute, opened a branch house in New York in 1910, and later another in Chicago. She did a profitable business in America until after the war. Leaders of Canadian society wore Lucile's designs and they appeared in some of the earliest and most exclusive mannequin parades in Toronto and Montreal, and were photographed for fashion articles in newspapers and magazines.

Highly skilled Canadian dressmakers and tailors created one-of-a-kind gowns and suits through the tedious process of innumerable fittings. In Montreal Helen Rhind specialized in exquisite wedding gowns for society brides, and Mrs. McKinney, who catered to socialites like Mrs. Wm. Van Horne wife of a Toronto tycoon, was in great demand for her magnificent wraps and evening gowns.

The best retail establishments in Canada carried imported models, both originals and exclusive copies. Specialty shops and large stores, such as Eaton's and Simpson's in Toronto and Ogilvy's and Morgan's in Montreal, all took orders for models from their salons. Some models were strongly influenced by or even copied from leading designers. Piracy of fashion designs was an established and widely practised procedure since the late nineteenth century with the publication of fashion engravings and early photographs in pattern books and magazines.

b *The adjustable dress form allowed dressmakers to create good fits for a variety of shapes and sizes.*

The large department stores advertised in daily city newspapers. Stores that wished to enhance the aura of high fashion associated with their names took great pains with the content of their advertisements. Advertising aimed at women was changing; appeals to sexuality and to identification with the glamorous and wealthy were being used more often. Famous women such as actress Ethel Barrymore, popular dancer Irene Castle, and ballerina Anna Pavlova endorsed fashion products in print and even on film. In 1918 the Dominion Corset Company hired silent screen star Anita Stewart as a spokeswoman and sponsored her movie *The Two Goddesses*. Dominion Corset even made a short film called *Corsets and How They Are Made*.

Special promotional events in Canada began to show greater sophistication. In October of 1913 in the Arena on Mutual Street in Toronto, Lady Gibson opened a special fashion display of the latest modes arranged through a series of elegant rooms. And again, a New York fashion show was shown on film.

International fashion trade was disrupted by the war and prices were unstable. Newspaper articles analysed the situation: "Prices are higher now than they were and are going higher. The European buying situation becomes more difficult daily, and there is no possibility of replacing lines sold out even at double the prices asked today."[4] Murray-Kay Limited stated in their catalogues of these years: "Trade disturbances due to the war, make it impossible for us to guarantee that a supply of the various lines illustrated will be available throughout the season . . . we suggest that you allow us to substitute."

After the war, fashion promotion took on new dimensions. Live mannequin parades became more popular, window dressing and fashion display in shop interiors improved, and imported French and English wax figurines were used as store mannequins.

More print advertising accompanied the syndicated fashion articles that were included in most newspapers across the country. Angelica Scuyler, May Manton, and Helen Cornelius were

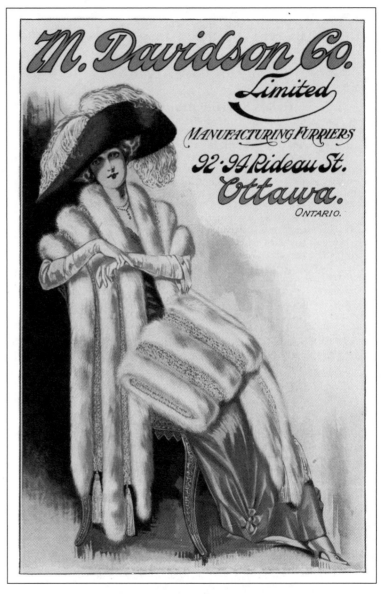

c   *The M. Davidson Company of Ottawa produced an elegantly illustrated catalogue to sell their line of furs for women, men, and children.*

Canadian fashion reporters during the war years. Adele Mendel and Eleda Lednam contributed columns to western newspapers.

Visuals continued to be in the usual form of stylized line drawings, but still giving quite precise information as to design detail. In 1919 the Right House of Hamilton added this note to one of their illustrated ads: "All sketches on this page were made from the merchandise actually on sale—not fanciful pictures drawn from imagination."[5]

In many magazines well-known actresses and society beauties not only were photographed modelling couture gowns, but also lent their names to the promotion of manufacturers' lines. An early example of this was a line of middle-priced dresses and sportswear named after film star Billie Burke and produced in Toronto by the Beauty Lingerie Company at 96 Spadina Avenue.

FACTORIES AND THE UNION

In the last part of the nineteenth century the clothing industry factories in North America had a reputation for being sweatshops. Those workers who lived and sewed in garment districts such as Toronto's Spadina Avenue, endured long hours, poor conditions, and had no union representation. Their situation was typical of all North American garment workers at this time.

In 1907 the Brantford, Ontario Local of the Journeyman Tailors' Union of America reported men's wages were twenty-three cents an hour and women's fifteen. That year the thirty-three women and thirty-two men in the local worked an average fifty-nine hours per week and lost twenty-five days' wages due to seasonal fluctuations.

Clothing manufacturing expanded greatly in Canada during this decade in order to meet a steadily growing market. The industry in Quebec and southern Ontario employed both men and a large proportion of women to work in the factories six days a week running power knitting and sewing machines. The needle trade in Winnipeg was a major component of the city's economy since 1900 and eventually would grow to be the third largest garment industry in Canada, after Montreal and Toronto.

Working conditions were often badly crowded in dark and noisy rooms with poor ventilation. Machinery was primitive and even dangerous. Although some firms were guilty of neglect and exploitation, others like R.M. Ballantyne in Stratford, Ontario boasted of "sanitary and up-to-date conditions with the very latest equipment."[6]

Conservative Canadians considered unions subversive and the workers in the clothing manufacturing industry were slow to organize. In 1911 the New York-based International Ladies' Garment Workers' Union (ILGWU) started a small local in Toronto; union leaders negotiated for improved wages and working conditions until the depression created new problems. A bitter thirteen-week strike in 1929 was followed by a shift of much of the manufacturing industry from Toronto to Montreal, where the laws allowed for lower production costs, mainly at the expense of the workers.

AFTERNOON AND EVENING FANTASIES

In the years before World War I, it was the dressy afternoon frocks, the dinner and ball gowns that best showed Poiret's influence on the Canadian odalisque. The cut of these dresses was actually not very different from daywear: a slim, top-heavy silhouette sometimes with elbow-length sleeves and a fairly modest neckline. Scoop-necked, V-necked, and surplice bodices were often filled with a semisheer, lacy, or embroidered vestee. It was the fabrication and the trim that created evening allure. Rich cloths in murky and mysterious tones and startling combinations of colours—antique gold, nuit d'Orient blue, magenta, mauve, and prune, jade, and almond green—were made up in gowns embellished with fringe and tassels, heavy laces, buttons, and beading. Panniers and overtunics were prominent, drapings of gauzy chiffons, marquisettes, lace, and organdies over long

La Mode Dernier Cri

Dominion Corset Co. Quebec.

d

Clinging satin evening gowns made the most of corseted hips and thighs about 1912. The Dominion Corset Company became Daisyfresh in 1976.

slinky underskirts. Satin was by far the most popular fabric for the underskirts which were usually trained as well as narrow at the ankles [**19** and **20**]. "Long trailing skirts are assured for this winter. They were ultra fashionable last winter, and lovely enough they looked caught up over the wearer's arm by a broad ribbon loop when dancing, or trailing off into serpentine points over the polished floor."[7]

To the pleasures of private dances were added late afternoon public tea dances in restaurants such as McConkey's in Toronto or elegant city-centre hotels like the Ritz-Carleton in Montreal where svelte couples glided to sultry new rhythms. Latin dances were all the rage—the Argentinian tango and the Brazilian maxixe. These physically demanding dances could not have been danced by women laced into heavily boned corsets.

But the most popular dance to replace the waltzes, polkas, and the two-step was the fox-trot. The livelier turkey trot was short-lived but still helped to put an end to the confining hobble skirt. All these dances could be practised to perfection at home to music on the Victrola, before making a public debut.

Important evening accessories included exotic headdresses, draped and jewelled bandeaus worn like oriental tiaras across the forehead, sometimes trimmed with a central feather. Little, intricately embroidered caps in the style worn by dancer Irene Castle were introduced in 1912; these confections worked best over long hair worn twisted and arranged at the nape of the neck.

At the beginning of the war the hobble hemline was quickly abandoned for a shorter, fuller skirt. Bodices, only slightly bloused and with soft deep collars filled in with vestees, fichus, and jabots, were gathered to the natural waist. Flared or tiered skirts were pleated or gathered in and covered by a fairly wide plain or gathered sash [**18**]. Aprons, tunics, and panniers of every variety remained fashionable until about 1917 [**26** and **27**].

Romantic, Paris-influenced evening frocks in 1915/16 had brief, slightly high-waisted bodices and shorter, flaring skirts of diaphanous net, with V or square necklines and shoulders veiled in ethereal arrangements [**28**]. In 1916 Mrs. M. L. Lynch of Granville Street in Vancouver advertised that she was ready to receive orders for fancy gowns for Easter. Her illustrated ad showed the very latest, shorter, full-skirted Paris silhouette.[8]

Early wartime fashions were followed briefly by the barrel silhouette. "In 1917 shortage of materials produced more austerity in clothing designs. This was probably responsible for the introduction of a modified version of the prewar hobble skirt. The widened hipline, first seen in evening clothes in 1918, resulted in the barrel-like contour that was intended to emphasize a youthful appearance. It was not becoming to most women and disappeared from fashionable dress in 1921"[9] [**29**].

In 1911 Novi-Modi offered "High class tailor-made costumes, coats and skirts, in the latest Paris, London, and New York models."

DAYWEAR—PRACTICAL AND DRESSY

Suits continued to be very important. Novi-Modi, a manufacturing firm in Toronto, showed the popular, basic long-jacketed, narrow-skirted suit in black or navy cheviot and grey, brown, or green novelty tweeds for under twenty-five dollars in the fall of 1911. Suits varied from styles with plain long jackets to fancy one-button cutaways or Directoire-styled suits as in **17**. These were sometimes promoted as the Incroyable cut in 1912/13, usually shown with the model wearing a bicorne hat. (An Incroyable was a dandy from the French revolutionary period who wore extreme dress.) Slim skirts often were slit at side or front hem as ankles were liberated, for ease of movement if nothing else.

Women who wanted an air of feminine elegance for day chose a long, slim dress. But even these afternoon dresses had a more tailored appearance than they would have had five years earlier. Contrasting coloured fabrics—worsteds, viyella, serge, duvetyn, cashmeres, cheviots, and velvets—were used and these were brightened up with satin collars, lacy vestees and cuffs, and velvet or soutache braid. About 1912 in Canada the high collar was replaced by the newer "pneumonia" neckline, a short open V-neck or a deep one, filled in with a vestee in light fabric. As the V-neckline became predominant the surplice bodice was frequently seen, and layered styling meant not only the vestee effect, but also jumpers, vests, and overblouses.

Directoire styling was so prevalent that the Robespierre collar was much used. This was a high-standing, turned-down collar widely open at the throat in front, an excellent transitional design for easing into V-necks. Touches, at neck and wrist, of laces such as guipure, Bruges, Battenburg, and Valenciennes continued to be popular in afternoon dressing.

Simple one-piece frocks, buttoning or hooking up at centre back and made up in unlined light muslins, were worn in summer. By now the long Edwardian sleeve was giving way to the alternative choice of forearm or elbow-length, in keeping with the general "body-baring" trend in daywear **[22]**.

The front-buttoning, one-piece shirtwaist dress was gaining in popularity with store clerks, teachers, and office workers because it was practical and neat. "By seaming a bodice and skirt together at the waistline; providing a front opening so that the dress could be stepped into without disarranging the wearer's hair; adding a plain turn down collar and cuffs; and keeping other trimmings to a minimum, a very practical garment resulted that could be made up in a variety of materials."[10]

The war soon made changes to women's lives at home and at work. More practical, less restrictive styles reflected the need for greater mobility and ease of care. Dresses and suits became

444

comfortably fitted through the body, with shorter, easier skirts and often followed the military lines of officers' tunics—neatly tailored, thigh-length jackets with relaxed waists, buttoned and tabbed [32]. Interchangeable separates, skirts and blouses, provided practical wardrobes for work as well as for dressier occasions [31]. Women were encouraged to repair or renovate existing garments rather than purchase new. Coats, dresses, and skirts were unpicked, cleaned, sometimes dyed, and remade. Newspapers and journals supplied directions and diagrams for such procedures.

Parisian designers continued their trade with the United States during the war years and American magazines available in Canada did not reflect the wartime restrictions felt here. American goods continued to be imported into Canada: "Just off the train from Boston, U.S.A. The smartest and latest [footwear] models, all leather" advertised David Spencer Limited in Vancouver, in 1916.[11]

f *Fashionable dress in the years of World War I showed shorter hemlines and a comfortable silhouette.*

The most extreme French-inspired silhouettes were often short-waisted with a full flaring skirt showing a lot of ankle. Elegant leather-trimmed suits for afternoon wear were fashionable in 1916 [30]. During these years many dresses and suits in black fabrics were offered for mourning dress. In 1917 Murray-Kay showed "a design very suitable for mourning wear . . . in black Japanese taffeta silk $20.00 . . . in black crepe de chine . . . $22.50."[12] That same year the flaring silhouette began to be challenged by a new tubular one. It could be barrel-shaped with a little fullness through the thighs or even perfectly straight, with the new lowered waistline foretelling styles to come.

OUTERWEAR

As skirts and petticoats became less bulky early in the decade, coats and capes were more often shown in longer versions such as three-quarter and seven-eighth lengths. Popular full-length coats still included the chesterfield, the polo, and the ulster. Most fashionable coats were cut long with narrow-fitting lines. The looser single-buttoning, straight-cut coat with comfortable raglan sleeves made up in waterproof, densely woven cotton or wool was a basic for travel. Sporty tweeds and mackinaws, in jacket and three-quarter lengths, were popular for everyday wear. Raincoats with similar styling as well as capes were available in rubberized cotton fabrics. Aquascutum and Burberry —two of today's well-known English names in waterproof coats—were also imported into Canada at this time.

As Directoire styling became popular for dresses, it also appeared in coats with large turned-down collars, slightly raised waist seams, and often cutaway "skirts." Coating fabrics used were tweeds, gabardines, serges, poplins, dressier broadcloths, velvets, and fur fabrics, as well as real furs. Where sealskin and lamb had been very popular earlier, long-haired furs—wolf, fox, raccoon—were now favoured, as well as luxury furs such as

g *The large fashion chain, Fairweather, like other early Canadian retailers, began as a furrier.*

sable and mink [21]. By the end of the decade full-length fur coats and capes sold for between $500 and $600. Evening coats and capes of elegant fabric were often trimmed or lined in furs such as hamster, moleskin, and squirrel. Small touches of fur offered luxury at less cost, in stoles, little shoulder capes, or collars in fox, Electric seal (rabbit), wolf, Australian oppossum, muskrat, or squirrel. Fur muffs—bolster or pillow style—matching collars or scarves were also chic accessories. Some well-known Ontario furriers at this time were Creed's, Holt Renfrew, Fairweather's, and Sellers-Gough of Toronto and R.J. Devlin, M. Davidson, and Henry J. Sims of Ottawa.

Through the war years shorter coats with easy bodices and flaring skirts predominated. Fur, or fabrics such as velvet on collars and cuffs, provided contrasting detail. Military styling was fashionable and women adopted versions of the trench coat in khaki gabardine. By the end of the war coats lengthened again

and took on a dressier look. A fall ad for 1917 claimed, "coats are much longer than last season, showing slashed points in several of the models and frequently being ornamented with rows of silk braid."[13]

ACTIVE SPORTSWEAR

A true Canadian heroine at this time was the Sporting Girl. She gloried in outdoor activities both summer and winter, turning her talents to tennis, golf, skiing, curling, and hockey. At the start of the decade tennis dress was the standard ankle-length skirt and shirtwaist, belted, with perhaps the hat omitted in the interest of the game. Laced boots or high shoes in canvas were worn. But within a few years the lighter one-piece dress with an easy-cut bodice, in fact, a sturdier version of the lingerie dress, did very well for tennis [23]. In 1919 Suzanne Lenglen raised eyebrows at Wimbledon when she appeared hatless in a mid-calf, pleated, white skirt and showed quite a bit of leg as she played.

For golf, dressier two-piece outfits were made in comfortable checks or plaids, or in chic solids as in **33**. Skirts were hemmed several inches above the ankles and worn with high-buttoned or laced boots, peaked caps, and gloves. More casual separates such as slim skirts and waists topped with a mannish knit coat-sweater or cardigan were also worn for golf and tennis. One Canadian manufacturer of sporty goods for ladies, gentlemen, and children was R.M. Ballantyne Limited of Stratford, Ontario, whose Beaver Brand knits were distributed through Montreal, Toronto, Winnipeg, Saskatoon, and Regina branches. In 1913 the Ballantyne fall line showed coat-sweaters, aviation caps, tasselled toques, official curling caps, hockey caps, mufflers, mitts, gloves, and hose.

Aviation was already encouraging women to adopt extreme changes in dress. In 1912 Miss Prentice of London, Ontario, put together an aviation costume consisting of a heavy pair of men's

This coat sweater with military collar, made from fine quality Australian wool, was part of the sporty line of sweaters by R.M. Ballantyne, Stratford, Ontario in 1913.

dark-coloured wool with skirts over drawers, short-sleeved or sleeveless, and they did cling to the figure.

Black or navy trimmed with red and white was favoured for bathing costumes in fabrics such as lustre, peau de soie, serge, and sateen, all woven fabrics advertised as not clinging to the figure [24]. These suits, often with sailor collars and other nautical symbols, showed ruffled bloomers below the skirt.

It was about this time that women first began to actually swim and not just stroll on the beach. World-famous Australian swimmer Annette Kellermann who wore knit suits as early as 1910 recommended comfortable dress for swimming, without corsetry or any tight belt because both hindered circulation. Kellermann was quoted as saying that "Most of the costumes I see along the shore are inspired more by vanity than modesty."[15]

UNDERPINNINGS AND ACCESSORIES

Bust-supporting corsets were disappearing from the market by 1910. With the new straight and slim silhouette, corsets were cut lower on top, less nipped in at the waist, and lengthened to go well down over the thighs. The waistline was allowed to be fairly large in proportion to the hips. The new corset was designed to keep the hips narrow for the slim skirts, in fashion until the First World War.

The lower-cut corset now required women to wear a camisole-like bandeau that loosely covered the breasts. Replacing the corset cover and a little shaplier for the fashions of 1915/16, these garments were also called brassieres. By 1918 the soft but flattening bandeaus introduced the bust-subduing bras of the 1920s.

For women who did not adopt the early bra, the knit vest (with separate drawers or as a combination) was worn under the corset. Made of wool, silk, cotton, or a blend, these machine-knit undergarments were produced in Canada and also imported. Over corset, a camisole or a full-length chemise in lace-trimmed light fabric might be worn as a slip under certain gowns.

trousers, a high-necked jacket, scarf, hood, gauntlets, and sturdy, laced shoes: "It could hardly be called a gown," said Miss Prentice, with a shy blush, "but it is dreadfully convenient in a machine."[14]

In the early years of the century bathing dress was derived from fashions for strolling beaches at summer resorts. It was hardly designed for real swimming with collars, sleeves, and skirts over bloomers and sometimes black cotton stockings with laced canvas shoes. As late as 1910 many women still wore corsetry under their bathing costume.

Imagine then, the horror when, about 1915, a few young women wore stockinette knitted suits; they were usually

Homemade nightwear, lingerie, and underwear were often sewn by a maid in upper-class Edwardian homes, or a visiting seamstress might come in for a week of plain sewing and dressmaking for the ladies and children of the house. Fine cottons and, increasingly, silk, were used and trimmed with lace. Shantung silk petticoats were favoured for daywear, and crepe de chine for under delicate evening gowns.

Hats were an important part of the top-heavy silhouette. The very large hats of 1910–12 were followed by styles shaped like a man's bowler, but with interesting brims and trim. Asymmetrical shapes were chic, as were tricornes, turbans, and toques with upswept brims, in beaver, felt, or panne velvet. Wider-brimmed straws were popular for summer. Feathers were still favourite accents (ostrich, pheasant, osprey, marabou) as well as embroidered or jewelled bands or bows or touches of fur in winter. For the winter of 1912 Goodwin's enthusiastic promotion of their millinery led their advertising department to claim that, "every hat is correct in style, so you can't make any mistake in selecting here. And we do not mean mediocre style, but the very newest, best, and most up-to-date."[16] From 1915 on hats were neater, less trimmed, even plain. Crowns deepened and brims often drooped at the sides. Full, floppy berets were favoured for sportswear.

Calf-high laced or buttoned boots with various shaped heels were worn into the war years as everyday wear and even later by some women. Laced Oxfords or shoes with buttoned straps high over the instep were pretty much the only alternatives. They might be of kid, patent leather, suede or, for summer, white buckskin or canvas. In the second half of the decade buttoned spats were a chic way to make a shoe look more like a boot and were worn by both men and women. Dressier pumps and slippers often had high jewelled or buckled tongues, like eighteenth-century shoes. Evening shoes might be made of white, gold, or silver kid; velvet or satin evening slippers were also dyed to match gowns.

WORLD WAR I BRINGS CHANGE

After 1914 as soldiers were called up, women began to replace men at work. As a colourful but anonymous journalist of the period put it, "Johnny Canuck was being replaced by Miss Canada." Three thousand nursing sisters, nicknamed Bluebirds, served during this war in their blue, ankle-length uniforms and white veils. At home, in the cities, and on the farms, women did all sorts of jobs formerly only performed by men. In 1917 there were 35,000 women working in munitions factories in Ontario and Quebec. Women had become a vital part of the work force, but they were paid less than men.

Active participation in war work encouraged simpler, more functional dress. Women needed wardrobes that worked well and expressed feelings of freedom and independence never experienced before. Social pressures helped shorten the long working hours of the middle-class working woman. By 1920 Eaton's had established a five o'clock daily closing time and made Saturday a holiday. The outlook for women was so positive that the publisher of the Canadian magazine *Everywomen's World* in 1918 hired his first female fashion editor, a young New Yorker who dressed in smart suits accessorized with chic turbaned hats and fawn spats.[17]

The first signs of style change took place at the top of the pyramid with the highest fashion. It took some years for simple functionalism to trickle down. Catalogue dresses in 1920 were still complex in structure, as prewar ideas were reworked. Just as complicated were the descriptions: "The bodice gains a dainty air by employing lace-trimmed white organdy for turn-back cuffs, square collar, and . . . vest. [Vest] . . . has two wide tucks and is outlined by box pleats, beneath one of which it buttons. A graceful feature of the full skirt is the pointed tunic with revers caught back by white crochet buttons."[18] All for only $9.50. It would be a few years before the ordinary working girl and the society woman would be wearing nearly identical simple dress styles.

17 SUIT (jacket and skirt), *about 1913*

A fall/winter suit with appliqué designs in heavy, brown, pinstriped wool. The short-waisted jacket has sleeves with a dropped shoulder seam, very fashionable at this time, and a poet's collar. The skirts of the jacket are cut in a style reminiscent of a man's evening coat. The tail is weighted with lead weights inside the hem.

The long, narrow hobble skirt with stylish peg-top silhouette is high-waisted and has only an inner waistband. Like the jacket, the draped skirt is decorated with an art nouveau motif in self-fabric and accented with large buttons. The asymmetrically wrapped and curved hemline allows the foot to be easily seen.

The Suddon Collection

18 GARDEN PARTY FROCK, *about 1913–15*

A one-piece dress for summer in semi-sheer ivory-coloured piña cloth. The straight cut bodice is gathered at the natural waist and has a deep V-neck trimmed with three rows of ruffles and filled in with an embroidered vestee dome-fastened down to the waist. A wide band of twenty pintucks crosses the lower bodice front and back, and the gathered self-fabric sash is trimmed with a rosette. The billowy skirt of ruffled tiers shows a new and shorter hemline for day.

Fabric purchased in Manila and made up in Ontario

Royal Ontario Museum

19 FORMAL GOWN, *about 1912*

A one-piece reception gown in rich gold-coloured satin, bronze silk organdy, lace, and beaded embroidery. The dress shows the slightly raised waistline of the narrow Directoire silhouette. It closes centre back with domes and hooks, which continue through the waist area under the hanging écru lace panel. The bodice, with fashionable kimono sleeves, is tucked at the shoulders. Bronze organdy covers the lower bodice and also falls in two panniers gathered low at centre back to a medallion detail. The satin underskirt ends in an exotic fishtail-, tassel-like train, weighted with lead weights. The asymmetrical embroidered sash is evocative of the passion for Middle Eastern exotica that was generated by the Ballets Russes and Paul Poiret.
Label: The Robinson Co. Ltd., Napanee, Ont.   *The Suddon Collection*

20 FORMAL GOWN, *about 1914*

An embroidered evening dress in pale grey green satin and near matching chiffon. The skirt is cut for a peg-top silhouette and the hobble hemline is relieved by a side vent exposing an underskirt of embroidered beige satin. The heavy embroidery is in satin threads of green, gold, red, and black, with touches of blue and red beadwork. The chiffon bodice is lined with net and the fabric is doubled over the bosom. The stylish features are finished off with bronze metallic tassels.
Purchased in Edmonton   *J. Walford Collection*

21 COAT, *about 1912*

A full-length winter coat in brown civet fur with collar, cuffs, and large button in dark brown, long-haired, sablelike fur. This stylish coat is lined in smoky purple raw silk and has several inside pockets of the gathered patch type in self-fabric.

Made for an Englishwoman who emigrated to Canada in 1913

The Vancouver Museum

22 LINGERIE DRESS, *about 1912*

A day dress in eyelette-embroidered cotton muslin, a simple and popular summer style of the time. Bodice and dirndl skirt are both gathered to a two-inch-wide waistband. The undarted bodice is collarless and slightly bloused in front but is short-waisted in back where it closes with buttons under a central placket. The elbow-length kimono sleeves are edged with a band of the eyelette and white cotton lace.

The skirt is hemmed just above the ankle and its length is the width of the fabric seamed at centre back only. The worked border of the yardage forms the decorative band at the hem and is reinforced with a two-inch false hem of white muslin. The skirt is not very full in order to help create the favoured top-heavy silhouette of this period. *The Seneca College Collection*

23 TENNIS DRESS, *about 1914*

A one-piece summer dress for tennis in white embroidered Indian cotton. The simple cut of the dress makes it loose and comfortable for active sportswear and also easy to wash and iron. The collar is soft and flat; the sleeves are three-quarter length with a turned-back cuff. Closure is centre back with a buttoned placket. The skirt has a serviceable amount of fullness and is shortened for a ladylike run. The belt is missing but the dress probably would have been worn with a simple white leather one.

I. Sayers Collection

24 BATHING COSTUME, *about 1911*

A one-piece bathing dress with attached bloomers in black cotton sateen. The collar and sleeves are trimmed with cream machine-embroidered black braid. The front central panel buttons under the collar on each side.
Label: ''Swim Easy'' Pat'd Approved 1911.
Made by Myers—G. Co. Inc., Los Angeles, Cal., Poughkeepsie, NY.

Queen's University Collection

25 PERFORMANCE COSTUME, *about 1910–13*

A recital costume in natural creamy buckskin and red cotton with ermine and Indian trade silver decoration. The silhouette of this dress follows the fashionable lines of the top-heavy figure of these years, but the materials, detailing, and colours are traditional North American Indian.

The front bodice of buckskin is cut to show the red cotton around armholes and neckline. The sleeves do not match, one is of ermine skin, the other of two embroidered buckskin panels (similar to belt) and long fringe matching the peplum. The scalloped buckskin hemline stands out over the red cotton and is short enough to show some stockinged leg above the high slippers. Waist ornaments are of human hair, buckskin, ermine skin, and trade beads. The necklace is of bear claws and glass trade beads. Over the shoulder trails a red wool blanket.

Worn by the poet Pauline Johnson   *The Vancouver Museum*

26 AFTERNOON OR DINNER FROCK, *about 1916*
This one-piece dress evokes an impression of Harlequin with its silk chiffon printed windowpane checks, combined with crisp black taffeta and pleated collar. The chiffon bodice lies open centre front and is layered over a sleeveless underbodice of white china silk which buttons up centre front in a narrow placket. An ivory organza collar repeats details at the wrists. The bloused bodice is gathered to the waist with a wide and pointed cummerbund plus a full peplum giving a pannier effect. The skirt is finished with a thick corded hem.

The Suddon Collection

27 AFTERNOON FROCK, *about 1918*
A one-piece afternoon dress in chestnut brown silk satin with an apron-tunic of the same fabric. The long-sleeved bodice shows a fashionable basque made of the satin trimmed with dark brown handworked embroidery and self-fabric covered buttons. The basque continues around to the back waist as a loose apron sash. A short-waisted, slightly loose bodice was often teamed with a barrel-like skirt shape in the years before World War I.

Joseph Brant Museum

28 EVENING FROCK

A short-waisted evening dress with the fashionable full and shorter skirt of 1915–17, in three layers of sheer silk nets over gold tissue. The outer black net is over smoky aqua net over suntan beige. Black net is gathered horizontally through the bodice and edged with black sequins and beads. Delicate net drapings over the shoulders and arms are caught up with tiny rosebuds and hemmed with gold thread.   *The Suddon Collection*

29 DINNER DRESS, *about 1918*

A dinner dress in emerald green façonné velvet with a bodice generally skin-toned and covered over by four triangular panels in moss green net. The interesting colour clash reflects the continued appeal of Middle Eastern themes. The dramatic butterfly bow at the waist is of verdigris shot lamé. The skirt's stylized floral motif shows the beginnings of the abstract, geometric designs of art deco. The cream satin bodice is layered with a delicate net worked with sparkling round and bugle beads and larger brilliants, some faintly green.

Worn by Mrs. Charles Band   *The Suddon Collection*

30 SUIT (jacket and skirt), *about 1916*

A two-piece wool gabardine suit with Middle Eastern influences in the trim and showing the new full skirt so fashionable in 1915/16. From the hip yoke the skirt hangs with knife-pleated panniers at the sides. The hem is cut in an arc on each side to expose panels of cream gabardine and give the impression of a shortening hemline. The designer felt quite undecided about the jacket length, too. The collar is lined with cream corded silk; the trim, all in cream, is of soutache braid, embroidery, and ball-fringe. The buttoned straps on the sides are of cream leather.

The Suddon Collection

31 SEPARATES, *about 1915*

A summer skirt in natural linen teamed up with a white cotton blouse. The unlined skirt has long but comfortable lines with a gathered central panel over a slightly raised hip yoke. There is an inner Petersham waistband. Closure is along the back right seam with hooks and eyes.

The blouse of light cotton voile is V-necked with a wide collar. The long sleeves, collar, and bib are all trimmed with scalloped bands of crochet lace.

Joseph Brant Museum

32 SUIT (jacket and skirt), *about 1915*

A neatly tailored two-piece suit with a military air in popular navy blue wool, trimmed with darker blue velvet. The tunic-length, single-breasted jacket is pleated and softly pulled in to the waist with self-belting finished with matching plastic buttons. Wide collar and cuffs are faced with dark navy velvet. The jacket is lined in red satin.

The unlined skirt has no waistband only an inner Petersham band. It hooks and snaps on the left seam and has a double box pleat centre back for added fullness. Two curved slash pockets, hidden by the jacket, are set in at hip level on the skirt front.

The Suddon Collection

33 GOLFING SUIT (jacket and skirt), *about 1919*

This suit in cream wool gabardine has an easy jacket lined with sateen and finished with a second set of revers as a false collar so that no blouse need be worn. The white flannel collar is embroidered with black and white silk threads. The buttons are of ivory bone. Interesting tailored self-belting is typical of its time. The slim skirt hangs from a hip yoke with extra fullness in the back for a seductive swing.

Royal Ontario Museum

T H E

1920s

WHEN THE TROOPS RETURNED HOME IN 1919, ALL OVER CANADA WOMEN were released from their breadwinning wartime jobs and restored to their former positions as housewives. Prewar dress styles were reinstated, too.

The Canadian economy was depressed in the early twenties. Trade was so bad in 1920 and 1921 that the government removed its luxury tax and as a result sales went up. Within a couple of years the recovering economy improved even further when new trade deals allowed American dollars to cross the border.

Canadian women were finally granted the vote at the end of the war. Spurred on by the new confidence that their wartime experiences had given them and bombarded by an influx of American culture through magazines, radio broadcasts, and movies, Canadian women endeavoured to take a more active role in a changing world. An inflating economy further helped to promote a 1920s version of women's lib.

Fewer young women chose to go into domestic service [51]; instead they worked in white-collar jobs in the growing numbers of large offices and retail companies. Canadian clothing manufacturers for the middle market prospered as they responded to demands for a broader range of ready-to-wear dress for working women who no longer had time for tedious dressmaker fittings.

The Edwardian style was an expression of life at the top; the much more democratic twenties style reflected the prosperity of a growing middle class, advances in technology, and exciting innovations in art and design. Mass-produced items now more often had their own standards of quality, rather than imitating prestigious works from the past.

A faster pace of life meant that soon women would no longer relate to the languid, exotic airs of the prewar period. Some of Poiret's vamp image would linger for a few years, but by about mid-decade women would go streamlined. Cutting off their long hair symbolized women's entry into the new era, as did abandoning restricting undergarments and high-buttoned boots for everyday wear. Dress became simpler and briefer; figures appeared more youthful in the straight-cut chemise and feminine curves were considered old-fashioned.

Improved automobiles made travel more accessible to the general public. Young women were going about, farther and faster than their mothers ever did. The spirit of the times was reflected in the lively lifestyle of Canada's "bright young things."

THE TWENTIES SILHOUETTE

Dress styles in 1919 were similar to what was fashionable at the beginning of the war. The short-lived barrel silhouette was an echo of the pegtop styles of 1912/13; note the similarity in silhouette between **17** and **29**. Frock bodices were girlish, cut quite straight with little or no shaping, and waistlines somewhat raised. Skirts were long and often showed fullness through the hipline, again by means of aprons, tunics, side draperies, and panels like earlier pegtops. Wide, loose-fitting belts and the vestee front were still much in evidence. Tucking and tassels, buttons, braid, and embroidery were all decorative details that continued the traditional dainty styling from the earlier period.

By 1921 dress construction in the leading fashions had simplified to a fairly long, childlike, scoop-necked chemise made of a nearly straight-cut front and back. Sleeves were frequently the most primitive form of Magyar or kimono type.

Manufacturers capitalized on the trend towards simpler styling and construction and the use of less fabric in a single garment. The simplicity of design also helped home sewers and small-town dressmakers, who might charge as little as one dollar and fifty cents for making up a chemise. Dress construction was easy to understand by the amateur, especially when the standard flat, block pattern system was devised. Patterns were straight-forward and construction information easier to follow. The Canadian journal *Everywoman's World* made available to its readers Le Costume Royal patterns "plainly and unmistakably marked . . . though the designs be elaborate the actual construction is simple." These patterns were said to be "sister fashions to *Vogue* and *Vanity Fair*."[1]

Decorative trim, mainly in the form of beading and embroidery, continued to be important. Trim for daywear was usually applied in borders of classical design and geometric arrangements. As the middle market caught up, the main difference between mass-produced dress and high fashion was in the quality of fabrication and trim. *Women's Wear* described the fashionable suit of 1921: "Take a really good piece of tricotine; grey, beige, tan, navy or black, fashion into a box coat, tailor

22.50
Lustrous Duchess Satin and
Beaded Georgette Crepe

a
Early 1920s dresses often combined slightly bloused bodices with hipline emphasis and low hemlines for an elongated silhouette.

it straight and well, then submerge it with jet bugles, silk floss and tinsel embroidery."[2]

Styles were now often seamed or sashed through the hip. Long blouson shapes topped slim, nearly ankle-length skirts. In 1922 hemlines were on the rise, but in 1923 they dropped again. By 1924 severely straight lines coupled with mid-calf hems and short haircuts produced the first boyish flapper look. By 1926 the flapper was truly in, and hemlines peaked near the knees where they remained until about 1929.

b

The flapper wore straight easy lines and showed lots of leg. Pullan Garments of Toronto in the fall of 1926 offered this coat cut in "the new straight line . . . trimmed with rows of silk twist stiching and buttons . . . Made in good quality Teddy Bear." $14.50 wholesale.

THE FLAPPER

The flapper was the young extremist of the twenties who wore the shortest bobs, painted her face, rolled her stockings, and adopted the debutante slouch; the aim was to look smart rather than feminine. Where the preceding generation had considered wearing makeup as not quite respectable, the flapper's stylized face had darkened eyes and rosebud lips. She made an issue

c

of smoking and drinking in public; unthinkable a decade before when such things were only done at home, if at all.

The erogenous statement of the later twenties was centred on the legs. Women had never before bared so much of their legs in public. Through the early part of the decade, stockings were lighter in weight and colour. Silk stockings, although they had the best reputation, ranged from beautiful and expensive to cheap and ugly. Cotton stockings were produced in a variety of weights and types. Plain and fancy weaves, and full-fashioned, were of a serviceable weight for everyday. Dress sheers of very lightweight cotton called chiffon were as lovely as the best silk, but almost as expensive. Rayon stockings, flesh-coloured and rather too shiny, were a reasonably priced substitute for silk.

Women who left off their corsets wore pantywaists or garters, plain or fancy, to keep up their stockings. Garters were more romantic than functional.

Well-dressed women wearing frocks and suits in the light, clingy fabrics of this period were very aware of their figures.

Corsetry in some form was still relied on by many curvaceous young women to help create the desirable boyish shape. Hip- and tummy-controlling boned corsets in firm coutil, worn with bandeau brassieres, were standard early in the decade, however, new, rubber elastic yarns allowed underwear manufacturers to do away with boning and stiffening. Soon the girdle was lighter and pliable, made of satin, brocade, or silk, with rubber elastic panel inserts. Eaton's carried the Madam X line of all-rubber, reducing girdles as well as other girdles with panels of elastic webbing. One version of the new girdle that had no closure system was called a step-in. Step-ins were ideal for not showing nasty ridges through light fabrics and were often worn with camisole-shaped brassieres in dobby, tussah, rayons, or cottons whose main aim was to flatten. The twenties woman was determined to be sleek, young, and thoroughly modern.

ART DECO

Art deco, the innovative, modern design of the 1920s and 1930s, is a name that developed indirectly out of the 1925 Exposition Internationale des Arts Décoratifs et Industriels Modernes in Paris. Preferences for simple, pared-down geometric shapes were, in part, derived from the works of earlier artists and painters. Cubism and the postcubist artists were especially influential.

Fine art painters such as Mondrian, Léger, and the Delaunays led the way in the fragmentation of form and severe stylization. The war interrupted this trend in North America, but cubist influences were later seen in the works of Canadian artists and painters—Lawren Harris and other Group of Seven members, as well as Bertram Brooker, Charles Comfort, and Thoreau MacDonald. Art deco-styled graphics and illustrations appeared in many books and magazines in Canada. Illustration of the fashion figure was rigidly stylized, forms were simplified

and almost doll-like abstract shapes were executed in a controlled, linear and two-dimensional manner.

Cubist forms moved into sculpture, jewellery, furniture, and architecture. Art deco interiors and architectural styling was used in Canadian public buildings and department stores. Eaton's College Street in Toronto and Eaton's in Montreal are good examples. By 1931, art deco style was even more visible in such buildings as the Marine Building in Vancouver, the Université de Montréal by the Canadian architect Ernest Cormier, and the Cormier house. By the thirties art deco was the signature architecture for numerous Odeon movie theatres across the country.

Ancient Egypt helped create art deco as well as cubism. The discovery of Tutankhamen's tomb in 1922 was a stimulus for all kinds of Egyptology in designs for interiors, textiles, jewellery, and dress.[3]

Mexico's and Central America's Indian cultures also had much to contribute to design in the 1920s. But by the 1930s, the dominating influence was technology and the machine. The design principle of "less is more," which originated in the German school of design, the Bauhaus, soon became the doctrine of the best thirties product designers and architects.

Art deco characteristics perfectly describe the flapper from 1925 to 1930, however, minimalist principles were not much of a guiding light for thirties fashions.

PARIS AND LONDON INFLUENCES

Coco (Gabrielle) Chanel was the strongest influence on North American fashion through the 1920s. Her revolutionary designs included sailor pants, simple cardigans, attractive workingmen's sweaters, skirts with practical details, and tweed suits. She liked to use comfortable jersey knits in fashionable garments and crisp, white collars on fine, black fabrics accented with pearls and diamonds. Chanel's use of costume jewellery caused it to be widely accepted. Her ideas were always very adaptable to mass production and to the wardrobes of working women.

Chanel's important contemporaries were Poiret (nearing the end of his career), Jeanne Lanvin, Jean Patou, Jenny, Molyneux, and Vionnet. Their original designs and copies of them were available to Canadian women.

What was being worn in New York was also important. *Harper's Bazar, Vogue, Women's Wear, McCalls, Vanity Fair,* and other magazines all brought American and European fashion news to Canada. In the early twenties *Vogue* took on a new sophistication because publisher Condé Nast had connections with the *Gazette du Bon Ton* and hired French illustrators who worked for American *Vogue.*

In 1927 in Toronto Colonel Maclean (one of the founders of Maclean Hunter) launched *Mayfair,* a new fashion glossie aimed at Canada's social elite. For the next thirty years, *Mayfair* published society gossip and fashion news and advertised quality goods. Readers often had strong ties to Britain, so there was news on court functions and English dress styles.

Eaton's began publishing the *News Weekly* in 1923. Styles aimed at the upper-class fashion customer were featured and elegantly illustrated pages of ads were interspersed with fanciful promotional news. A September 1924 issue describes display props from Paris: "waxen ladies, one with the loveliest orchid-hued hair of finely-spun silk," another "vamp with plum-coloured locks and lowered eyelids." These bust forms were to be used in the arcade windows to display scarves, jewellery, and hats. The article concluded with a description of Madame Charlotte of the Parisian house Premet: she "actually dyes her shingled white hair to just such lovely tints — one day mauve, another day green or blue. Ma foi!"[4]

Along with British and American labels, many better stores carried French imports, both originals and copies. Top name fashions from Paris were bought by retail stores along with

d *Martha used rose-blush net, roses and violets for this bouffant gown worn by Mrs. A.B. Harris in 1927.*

permission to copy for their customers. Couture originals were sometimes copied by sketchers who attended fashion shows and put down enough details immediately after the finale in order to produce rough copies for lower-priced manufacturers' lines.

Many of the best-fitting garments of quality were created by local dressmakers and couturiers. Some dressmakers in the fashionable circles of Montreal, Toronto, and Vancouver even achieved a certain degree of fame. Montreal had a lively and fashionable society in the 1920s. Well-dressed Montrealers paraded down St. Catherine Street on Saturday afternoons, pausing for refreshment at the Edinburgh Café or the Castle Blend Tea Shoppe. In the evenings theatregoing was immensely popular and very formal and was often followed by night-club hopping.

Ida Desmarais, who had an elegant salon in Montreal, the match of any in Paris, was considered the grande dame of local couture. Wealthy clients paid high prices for her skills through the twenties and thirties. Desmarais continued the tradition of fastidious attention to detail using numerous fittings. Many items with the Desmarais label that were part of the 1930 trousseau of Mrs. Saul Silverman of Toronto are in the collection of the Royal Ontario Museum.

Clara Faulkner, Katherine MacInnes, Mrs. Eva Harrison, Madame Senior, and Martha were Toronto names of note in this decade. Martha, who in the mid-twenties was designing for wholesale manufacturers in Toronto, was a talented Canadian couturière well known for her charming afternoon and evening gowns. By 1927 she had her own business at 60 Bay Street. Martha gowns were featured in the earliest issues of *Mayfair*.

Many of the important names in ladies' tailoring from the early years of the century continued to prosper: Bilton Brothers, Boase Limited, O'Brien's, George A. Stitt, Posluns Son and Company, The Regent Ladies' Tailors, Stollery Limited, D'Allaird, and John Northway, among them.

DAY AND EVENING DRESS

Postwar dress was increasingly simplified. The short-waisted bodice first gave way to straighter vertical lines only slightly sashed in at the natural waist [34] or even with a dropped waistline. Early bodices were sometimes made up in two layers, the long-sleeved underbodice, topped by a sleeveless plastron or basque as in 27.

As the structure of dresses became more elementary and classical, there was practically no difference between day and evening silhouette and construction. By 1923 the chemise was used day and night, the main differences were in fabrication and trim. Favoured daytime fabrics were finely textured, softly draping, and sometimes shiny (to give the chemise some sex appeal) — silk or wool jerseys and crepes, fine serges, pongee, duvetyn, crepe de chine and Japanese silks, silk shantung, and crepe-backed satins, as well as washable cotton voiles, ginghams, percales, and rayons for summer. Evening fabrics were light organdies, silk charmeuse, satins, and soft silk velvets. Especially popular were chiffons and georgettes used as delicate bases for masses of sparkling beadwork.

Rayon, known as artificial silk or art silk, was used in knits and weaves, alone or in blends. "Plain weave rayon fabrics of rather uninteresting appearance, were used to make mass-produced summer dresses and blouses. These poor quality materials ravelled at the seams and disintegrated if very much heat was applied when pressed. Colours used to dye the cloth bled and streaked."[5] By the end of the decade, better quality rayon and rayon blends were used by prestigious designers.

The interest in the early twenties in simple ethnic styling, the basic, ancient tunic shape of the chemise, and peasant embroidery was in keeping with a classical approach to design. Tidy, geometric motifs in borders of plain fabrics or controlled geometric repeats in prints were preferred. Even

A—*The tunic of her georgette frock sways with the weight of its glistening crystal beads. One of many lovely designs in French frocks of beaded georgette, in all the new browns, green, blue, rose and coral shades. Sizes 36 to 42, $35.00.*

B—*Of coral crepe-de-Chine, striped with rows of tiny coral beads, over which star-like flowers of crystal beads are scattered. It is French, one of many similar frocks of beaded crepe-de-Chine, in sizes from 36 to 42, at $45.00.*

$35.00

$45.00

$65.00

e   *In 1924 narrow evening gowns still might have covered much of the leg but by 1925 evening dress was shorter and "when beading [was] used this season, patterns [were] as exquisite as a piece of jewellery."*

floral motifs were stylized and cubistic, and classical paisley designs were popular.

The Egyptian craze affected all aspects of the fabric arts—textile motifs, colours, and dress styles. Long pleated dresses, perhaps girdled in gold, with motifs of scarabs, sphinxes, or sacred cats were worn [35]. Bright Egyptian blue, jade and emerald green, gold, yellow, apricot and "tango" orange, black and white, silver, beige, and tan were popular colours.

Hemlines for both day and evening varied between lower calf and ankle until about 1924. Collarless, scooped, and bateau necklines were common, and when there was a collar, it was flat and wide, an innocent Peter Pan. Many chemise dresses were slipped on over the head without any closure system [43].

Sleeves were at times only an extension of the body of the dress and were often elbow-length. The long, set-in sleeve, when it was used, was plain and slim with merely a neat finish at the wrist. Except for sleevelessness for daytime, starting in about 1923, there were no innovations in sleeves.

The simple elongated bodices were often loose enough not to require bust darts; indeed the bust was something not recognized by the flapper. Still, the new lines did require changes in cutting methods. "The wrinkles that formed under the armpit due to the straight shapeless cut were unbecoming and sloppy in appearance. When a short horizontal underarm dart was introduced in the 1920s part of the excess material could be removed resulting in an improved line to the garment."[6]

All apron effects and draping side panels had disappeared by 1924 and neater, tailored styles were favoured. Suits for day showed long straight-cut jackets. Machine and hand-knitted cardigan jackets and suits in fine twill, serge, and tricotine were popular.

Separates often took the form of a cylindrical skirt supported by an attached camisole with little or no shaping, covered by a long overblouse, a middy, or a V-necked sweater. Or sometimes the overblouse was shaped like a man's waistcoat at the hem. A mannish shirt worn with cardigan and tie gave a masculine look to the young and daring.

Eveningwear was only slightly more bare than summer daywear. In the early decade the most chic models had a wide, square neckline, a long and straight sleeveless silhouette, and perhaps a scalloped hemline or trailing side panel, but no real train anymore. Exotic styling might still recall the oriental slavery theme [37].

The simple chemise silhouette [45] didn't change much over the years as the hemline rose. Straight-cut, sleeveless silk georgette dresses, often scoop-necked lower in back than in front, were worked with sparkling beads or sequins or finished with silk fringe. The short, beaded, flapper evening dress was the ultimate in sophistication and a true expression of art deco. By mid-decade art deco, with the clean, straight lines of a sure thing, was influencing fashions from Paris couture to Canadian catalogues. The silhouette and design motifs were more geometric than ever [39].

Promotional copy in an Eaton's 1925 *News Weekly* read, "When beading is used this season, patterns are as exquisite as a piece of jewellery. This Paris dinner gown of rose-hued flat crepe uses embroidery of crystal and silver beads. $65. Other beaded dresses $35. up."[7] Large feathered fans, especially of curled or uncurled ostrich plumes, were an exotic accessory for these gowns.

OUTERWEAR AND ACCESSORIES

Coats at the opening of the decade were still full and often had high-waisted lines with loose self-fabric belts. Soon the cut was narrower and longer with the new dropped waist often featured. Hip-level front or side fastenings used a single large button or buckle. Long shawl collars or long revers and kimono sleeves were often part of this look. The 1924 full-length coats for day

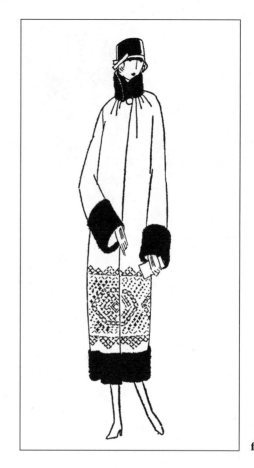

f

showed bands of fur around lowered hemlines, and on collars and cuffs, as well as featuring heavily embroidered panels, yokes, or inserts [38]. Fur-trimmed capes and wraps for evening also indulged in rich embroidery. Fur muffs, tail-fringed shoulder capes, and fur scarves with heads and paws continued to be worn.

Three-quarter length coats, jackets, and various length capes were also worn for day in meltons, wool velours, polo cloth, and tweeds, often trimmed with a bolster style fur collar. The clutch coat, without any fastening, was wrapped tightly around the hips [47].

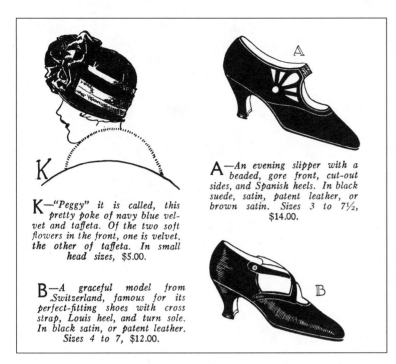

K—"Peggy" it is called, this pretty poke of navy blue velvet and taffeta. Of the two soft flowers in the front, one is velvet, the other of taffeta. In small head sizes, $5.00.

A—An evening slipper with a beaded, gore front, cut-out sides, and Spanish heels. In black suede, satin, patent leather, or brown satin. Sizes 3 to 7½, $14.00.

B—A graceful model from Switzerland, famous for its perfect-fitting shoes with cross strap, Louis heel, and turn sole. In black satin, or patent leather. Sizes 4 to 7, $12.00.

g This cloche-shaped hat of navy blue velvet and taffeta is trimmed with two velvet and taffeta flowers.
Evening shoes of 1924 in black suede, satin, or patent leather, the bottom shoe was also offered in brown satin. All at Eaton's.

As the silhouette shortened and became more geometric, hemline fur trim was used less often, but long-haired fur collars in fox, opposum, wolf, raccoon, and skunk continued to provide a softening accent to the small, neat cloche-covered head.

The demand for fox and other furs was so great that the Canadian fur industry expanded rapidly in the twenties. Farming was the main source of expensive fox pelts since they were rare in the wild, but muskrat, which thrived throughout the country, became the biggest commercial fur in Canada. Muskrat was used to simulate other more luxurious furs, but also as itself in full-length coats. Eaton's had muskrat coats at the end of the decade for $175 and Hudson Seal (dyed muskrat) coats were $350.

Shoe styles showed typical art deco simplicity. Dress shoes often had moderate Louis heels and buttoned or buckled straps. Cut steel or jewelled buckles livened up pumps for evening. Suedes were used, but shiny satin or patent leather were most popular for dress.

As legs emerged early in the decade, high, laced boots were no longer worn for everyday outdoor wear and sportswear. Women wore serviceable oxfords, some with fringed tongues, or, for the stylish, English sports shoes called swagger brogues. Winter overshoes in various heights were buckled or laced at front; some had fur or fur fabric trimming.

Hats in the early part of the decade were still inventive and were often decorated with feathers, flowers, or bows, but began to shrink in size, especially the brims. By 1925 the simple bowler-shaped cloche, sometimes practically brimless, was very commonly worn pulled well down over bobbed hair. The cloche look lasted until early thirties romanticism reintroduced brims and trims.

THE SPORTING GIRL

Serious participation in active sports in the twenties made women think about dress in a new way. This era of liberation put women into pants [41] for a number of activities indoors and out.

Pants often had a flap opening at the waist which buttoned on each side. Sporty knicker outfits [40] were fashionable for camping, hiking, and canoeing. Made of khaki cotton jean (drill) for summer activities and wools and wool tweeds for skiing, snowshoeing, and tobogganing, knickers were often teamed with the Norfolk jacket or the mannish mackinaw in red and black or blue and black checked wool with knit collars and cuffs [42]. More formal approaches offered three-piece tweed suits with the choice of a pleated skirt or knickers for golf or a softball game. Skating costumes often incorporated bloomers and skirts, and skiing brought long ski pants as well as knickers. Riding habits seldom paired the prewar skirt with riding coats, but instead showed breeches or knickers teamed with coats and hacking jackets.

Of course, pants had been worn by women for garden and farm work for some time. With the emphasis on practicality, even coveralls initiated new trends. In 1928 the Kitchen Overall and Shirt Company Limited in Brantford, Ontario, offered coveralls with a front zip fastener: "The genuine Jiffy combination with a hookless fastener—rustproof, dustproof, guaranteed. On and off in a jiffy."[8]

In this decade women wanted freedom for swimming as opposed to wading. As the twenties began, Canadian swimsuits in fine wool or cotton jersey had knee-length drawers topped by a sleeveless, scoop-necked tunic. It wasn't just modesty that kept women covered up, there was also a vague idea that they couldn't take the cold water.

By 1926 suits were becoming briefer and more functional. Eaton's carried a practical Annette Kellerman suit with a back pleat for extra fullness and a Jantzen [49] in various colours.[9] Twenties knitted swimsuits clung to the figure, especially when wet, and the newer suits cut lower in back and sometimes skirtless were considered daring and even offensive by some. By the late twenties knit suits had self-fabric built-in brassieres or bandeaus for shaping and modesty.

Jersey knits in active sportswear took on smarter styling, too, but were not without some problems. Former American golf champion Glenna Collett told this story about playing with Canadian champ Ada Mackenzie in 1925: "Miss Mackenzie wore a knitted suit for the occasion. When we started the day was fine. A cloudburst blew up but we played on, and after one hole in the rain, Miss Mackenzie's knitted frock was touching the ground."[10] Cardigan jackets or men's sporting sweaters were adopted by women for an androgynous look. Some standbys for summer

D—*No fear of catching cold when one wears such a well made bathing suit of pure wool. It is hand-finished, and was knit in Vancouver, and comes in navy, emerald, black or Copen., with narrow bands of contrasting color at the brief skirt hem. Sizes 36 to 42, $3.95.*

$3.95

h

were nautical-styled middy tops, worn by young women since Edwardian times, and neat white sleeveless dresses, often based on tennis dress [48]. At the end of the decade beach pajama outfits with wide legs [57] were all the rage.

MOVIES, JAZZ, AND THE SHIMMY

The twenties are often referred to as the jazz age, that decade when jazz moved north to Chicago. In fact, jazz was played everywhere, from the American speakeasy to the Parisian nightclub. In a 1923 Broadway review called *Runnin' Wild*, the Charleston was born. Bouncy and spirited, it had the flapper kicking her legs and flicking her knees to create the archetypical symbol of the era.

A North American pronounciation of the French word *chemise* came out as *shimmy*. The shimmy was a dance fad from the twenties that was named directly from fashion. "At one performance, singer Gilda Gray, who restlessly twisted and slithered while she performed, was asked what she was doing. She glibly shot back, 'Shaking my shimmy!' She wore a French chemise with fringe and tassels; everything appeared to be going in every direction at the same time."[11] Soon everyone was dancing the shimmy. Young couples at Toronto's Palais Royale were all trying to "Shimmy like my Sister Kate."

Another favourite form of entertainment among the social elite during this lively decade was the grand masquerade ball. Costumed or fancy dress dances brought forth pirates, eighteenth-century courtesans, Spanish gypsies, and clowns. Harlequin, Columbine, and Pierrot [50], characters of early theatre, were particularly popular.

The jazzy novelty dances were not the only ones around. The waltz, the tango, and other Latin rhythms were still popular in the United States and Canada. Not only were all the latest tunes available on sheet music for the piano, ukelele, and banjo, but also many people enjoyed music at home on the gramophone and the radio. Life in Canada was generally quieter than south of the border, but Canadians had a new window on American culture through the radio. In 1921 when commercial broadcasting began in Canada, only six wavelengths were free, American broadcasters had already expropriated dozens of others.

By 1920 the silent movies were replacing vaudeville, and movie houses were quickly opening up in cities and towns across the country. Movie stars had considerable influence on young women's image of the ideal. They sighed over heartthrobs Douglas Fairbanks and Rudolph Valentino. Valentino, in particular, epitomized the romantic Latin lover and tango dancer in films that kept fashion focused on the exotic.

Other fashion roles for Canadian women included the girlish innocence of Canadian-born Mary Pickford as America's sweetheart, the oriental vamp Theda Bara, and as the twenties progressed, the madcap young flapper personified by stars Clara Bow and Joan Crawford.

THE PARTY ENDS

In many ways the twenties woman stretched the lines of acceptability a great distance in a very short time. Especially significant was the wearing of pants. About 1926 that Parisian arbiter of fashion, Paul Poiret, made a thirty-year prophecy on the subject, "Will Skirts Disappear?" He claimed that "trousers for women will not be a mere short-lived fad; they will become as inevitable as bobbed hair, which is here to stay . . . trousers will be found to be more practical, more hygenic, and as a consequence this innovation will keep gaining ground . . . "[12] Was he merely predicting the popularity of lounging and beach trousers around 1930?

By the late twenties, woman as an art deco design, as simple a form as a dressed figure can be, was a product of new, streamlined, man-made technology. But as early as 1927 designer collections showed a weakening of crisply tailored geometric lines and a retreat to femininity. The stock market crash of 1929 forced the issue.

The popularity of pants for daywear receded and skirts and dresses changed form. Softer, fuller skirts, still snug through the hips, showed asymmetrical shaping, hemlines dipped in the back, and there were draped side poufs, and even bustle and train effects. Hanging points of triangular or diamond-shaped godets created irregular handkerchief hemlines, transition stages for the lower hemlines [46]. By 1929 designers were showing North American women longer hemlines for daywear. The economy might be bad, but fashion would have its way in spite of a style change requiring more cloth. The inflated economy of the twenties was gone and with it the sense of easy living and good times.

34 AFTERNOON FROCK, *about 1922*

An elegant afternoon dress in midnight blue silk crepe with aqua green accents. Both bodice and skirt are slashed in vertical strips exposing a lining of green chiffon. Small blue fabric-covered buttons line the edges and are also grouped at the hemline. Fresh white collar and cuffs are of lace embroidered with white threads. There is an underbodice of white silk to which the sleeves are attached and the outer bodice snaps up the left side and shoulder. The skirt is suspended from an inner Petersham waistband.

The Vancouver Museum

35 AFTERNOON FROCK, *about 1923*

An unlined, pull-on chemise in dark jade cotton jacquard. The structure of this elegant dress is simplicity itself: made from a single piece of fabric folded in half vertically, seamed up one side and across the shoulders. Small horizontal darts slightly curve the lines over the hips. The fabric in decorative stripes joined with faggoting suggests columns of ancient Egyptian hieroglyphics.
Label: The R.J. Devlin Co. Ltd., Ottawa *J. Walford Collection*

36 CORSET, *1922*

A pink silk rib-knit, boned corset. It is adjustable to a slight degree, but fastened approximately for a twenty-three inch waist and thirty-two-and-one-half inch hips. It is trimmed with pink satin ribbon and the satin-covered central busks fasten with six, flat metal hooks in front. The central back busks have eighteen pairs of eyelettes laced with pink rib-knit laces.

Label: Langton and Wellington of England. Bought in Toronto by Nellie Bryan for her trousseau   *Private Collection*

37 DINNER GOWN, *about 1923*

A square-necked sleeveless chemise in black net over black crepe de chine. The crepe underchemise is edged at the neck with lingerie lace. The slim outer chemise has a very deep V-neck and long panels scalloped at the hem, all edged with bands of beads framing large floral designs worked in black beads and sequins. A side vent at the hem is filled with a gathered spray of soft black net. Not strictly sleeveless, this dress has two narrow beaded and lace bands falling from back shoulders to hemline and tacked to the chemise down to the hips. The lower ends snap over forming loops to be worn around the wrists.   *The Suddon Collection*

38 COAT, *about 1923*

This seven-eighths length, brown wool coat, embroidered with taupe and turquoise wool chainstitch, is trimmed with a dark brown mouton bolster collar and cuffs. Exotic Middle Eastern tastes linger here in the extended V-shaped sleeves and the tassels. The coat and the sleeves are lined with a bright floral-printed silk in chartreuse, purple, and turquoise—a very timely art-deco-styled print.

The Suddon Collection

39 FROCK, *about 1925*

A light and simple chemise in pale jade green cotton voile embroidered in brown and white. The geometric, art-deco-influenced motifs are made with tobacco brown chain-stitch embroidery and white seed beads. Kimono sleeves are in keeping with the desire for structural simplicity.

Made in France and worn in Manitoba

I. Sayers Collection

40 CANOEING AND HIKING OUTFIT, *about 1923*
A typical example of summer sportswear for this date: a two-piece khaki cotton outfit of shirt and knickers. Breeches and knickers by this time had become not only acceptable but also fashionable sportswear. They often had the traditional naval waistline button closure on each side. The knickers are of cotton twill or jean. The shirt of heavy cotton tabby has grey composition buttons.
Worn by Mrs. Jean MacMahon on her honeymoon at Limberlost, Ontario, in 1923   *Royal Ontario Museum*

41. RIDING SUIT (jacket and breeches), *about 1923*
A two-piece summer suit in cotton twill. The unlined jacket is loose fitting with no waist seam and a somewhat low self-belt. The low lapels and long skirts also give the jacket its 1920s cut. The breeches have a buttoned fly opening at each side waist and eight buttons from knee to calf.
Label: [T. Eaton Co.] E. Vanity Fair, Our Own Make, Toronto and Winnipeg
The Suddon Collection

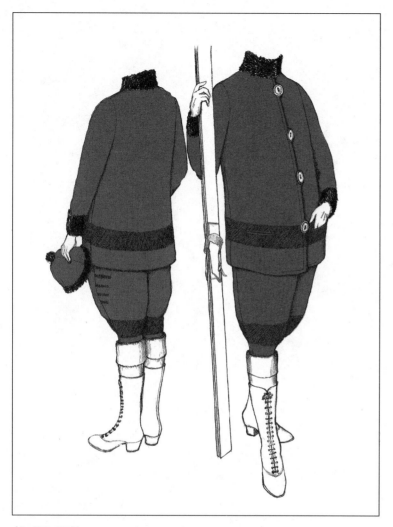

42 SKI SUIT

A scarlet and black winter suit with matching hat, made from a Hudson's Bay blanket and trimmed with black fur collar and cuffs. The jacket is lined with beige wool flannel, fastened with four large mother-of-pearl buttons, and has two double-welt pockets set into the broad black stripe at hip level. The knickers show the four black linear "points" of the Hudson's Bay system for weight and value of a blanket. They fasten at left waist with hook and eye plus domes and have four eyelettes below knees (laces missing).

J. Walford Collection

43 SUMMER FROCK

A simple afternoon dress in embroidered cream chiffon trimmed with blue. This pull-on chemise has a lowered waistline and short set-in sleeves. The scooped neckline is edged with sky blue chiffon ties to do up in a soft bow. The skirt is gathered at hip level by four rows of shirring and seamed with cream chiffon piping. This youthful style is made more sophisticated by the use of delicate chiffon and by the large, colourful, embroidered flowers in blue, coral, soft pink, yellow, and white.

The Suddon Collection

44 ENSEMBLE (jacket and dress), *about 1927*

A dress and jacket for daywear in aqua and cream silk crepe de chine. The unlined, boxy, hip-length jacket in aqua has long slim sleeves and cream-coloured, full-length lapels. The collar takes the form of a simple band in aqua tacked at neck back only. Two patch pockets give an accent at hip level.

The V-necked chemise has front and back yokes in cream crepe that form simple cap sleeves. The dress is very slightly shaped in at the waist, but there is no closure system and it pulls over the head. Although it is belted at the normal waist, strong hip-line emphasis is created by stitched-down pleats at the hip yoke. The permanently pleated skirt is short and straight. The geometric styling of this outfit in two colours of smooth and shiny fabric make it an excellent example of art deco design. *The Suddon Collection*

45 CHEMISE, *about 1926*

A short evening dress in dusty Copenhagen blue silk georgette with blue and silver sequins and beads. Here is the essence of the flapper style. The sleeveless chemise is made of two straight-cut panels stitched up with no closure. The floral and geometric motifs are worked with machine beading using irridescent blue sequins, silver-lined blue seed beads, blue bugle beads and ribbed, metallic silver beads. *The Vancouver Museum*

46 DRESS, *about 1928*

A pull-on sleeveless chemise in gold-embroidered black chiffon over black crepe. This dress is practically identical front and back. There are twenty rows of topstitching through the hip area. A softly fluttering handkerchief hemline is created by means of eight chiffon squares stitched into the bottom of the side and central seams, along one side of square, and left to drape. These irregular hemlines were harbingers of the longer evening dress to come.

The Suddon Collection

47 CLUTCH COAT

A dressy afternoon or evening coat of black satin embroidered in silk threads creating large yellow green flowers and finished with a collar and cuffs of green-tinted mole. The waistless, slightly flared coat has no closure system and was simply clutched and wrapped snuggly about the hips for a narrow silhouette. The lining is of muted grey green silk crepe with an inside pocket of shirred self-fabric.

Label: By appointment, Furriers to H.M. King, George V. Holt Renfrew and Co. Ltd., Quebec, Toronto, Montreal, Winnipeg   *The Suddon Collection*

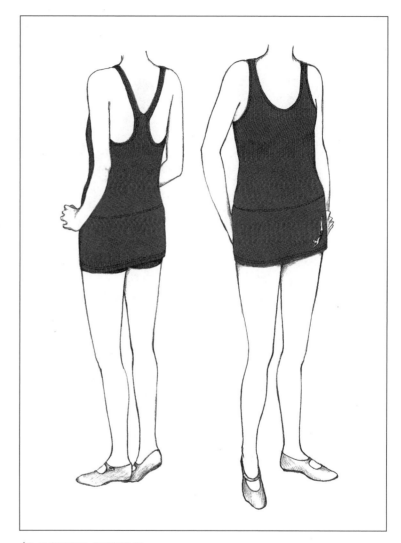

48 FROCK, *about 1928*

A sporty, sleeveless, pull-on chemise in lightweight silk broadcloth for playing or watching tennis. Tennis dress through the twenties created a vogue for summer fashions that were simple, crisply tailored, and often pleated and sleeveless. The flapper was baring both her arms and legs in public.

Private Collection

49 BATHING COSTUME

A one-piece bathing costume in knit black wool. By the twenties women wanted simpler and neater bathing suits like men's for real swimming, and now there was very little difference in styling between them. Merely short panels, the remnants of a skirt, stitched at hip level almost covers the boxy pants.

Label: Jantzen

J. Walford Collection

50 MASQUERADE COSTUME
A Harlequin-influenced masquerade or theatrical costume in black and white.
The dress is black cotton broadcloth with the irregular hemline worked in
white satin appliqué and trimmed with white wool pompons. The neckline
is very low-cut, the hemline short and swingy. The design recalls the costumes
of such characters as Harlequin, Columbine, and even Pierrot, from the
Commedia dell'Arte productions of past centuries.   *I. Sayers Collection*

51 MAID'S UNIFORM
A uniform in fine mauve/purple cotton trimmed with crisp, white dotted
swiss. The loosely cut one-size-fits-all one-piece dress buttons centre front
in a placket closure to below the waist and has two full-length side pleats
in front as well as a large patch pocket. The collar and cuffs are stitched on
loosely by hand for easy removal for washing. The matching separate apron
threads through large belt loops to tie in back.
Worn in a home in Rosedale, Toronto   *J. Walford Collection*

1930s

THE COLLAPSE OF THE STOCK MARKET IN 1929 MARKED THE BEGINNING of a period of depressed economy in North America. By 1933 nearly a third of the Canadian labour force was unemployed, and wages dropped throughout the decade. Not everyone's standard of living fell; those who were well employed, property owners, and the wealthier class of society may have actually benefited by the falling prices. But the majority felt the hard times. More Canadian women entered the white-collar work force than ever before, often as lower-paid replacements for men.[1]

Installment buying increased and credit was extended in nearly every area of consumer spending. The "buy now, pay later" philosophy blossomed in this period, and expectations ran high in a time when real spending money for most Canadians was shrinking. Women's wardrobes had to be serviceable and versatile, qualities found in conventional, classic styling.

In times of insecurity most people revert to familiar, long-standing roles and values, and these are expressed in dress that is traditional in form. The poor economy created traditionalism, but at the same time the attraction of status dressing was very strong. Women's magazines stressed ladylike values and featured socialite news. Advertising of the period took advantage of women's desires to conform to the ideal, playing on their insecurities and the horror of offending in any way.[2]

As prices fell, increased mass production of ready-mades met the demand for reasonably priced fashionable dress. Many manufacturers went out of business, while others attempted to keep prices down through lower wages, more piecework, assembly-line production, and new machinery which allowed faster manufacture. The workshops of the large department stores, including Eaton's with its reputation for on-the-job philanthropy,[3] also employed cost-saving measures. In 1932 when Spadina garment workers went on strike for higher wages and better conditions, many manufacturers relocated in Montreal where there was an abundance of cheaper, nonunion labour. By mid-decade the International Ladies' Garment Workers Union managed to organize a large part of the industry in Canada.[4]

INFLUENCES FROM PARIS

Many Canadian society women still wore exclusive and expensive clothing, more likely than in the twenties to be from local sources. The wealthiest occasionally supplemented their wardrobes with gowns from Paris, but French haute couture lost much of its North American market because of the depression. Fewer originals were imported; the large stores carried more of the less expensive copies. The Robert Simpson Company advertised in 1932, "copies of Paris Originals, after Vionnet."

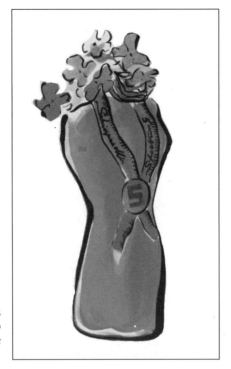

a
Schiaparelli's aim was to create a stir; her famous perfume was called Shocking.

Fashion-conscious women were still interested in the news, however, and Parisian power continued to be considerable.

French houses that made the greatest impact during the thirties were Vionnet, Chanel, Piguet, Patou, Lanvin, Lelong, the American in Paris, Mainbocher, and the Italian in Paris, Schiaparelli. The press played up a rivalry between Chanel and the new star, Elsa Schiaparelli.

Schiaparelli began her career in 1927 with handknit sweaters and sportswear strongly influenced by the current Parisian art world. Her dramatic statements became important for more formal wear, and startling, amusing invention was her trademark. Brilliant colour combinations, her famous shocking pink, unusual fabrication, innovative buttons, jewellery, and amusing hats were some of her specialties [55].

After **Vionnet**

After **Chanel**

Vionnet's collarless coat with tucking, seaming, stitching and a swagger Ascot scarf. New knubby rough crepe.
$35.00

Chanel's dressmaker suit that uses tucking to broaden the shoulders. The wide sleeves disclose a white silk crepe lining. Wool crepe.
$29.50

b *Chanel and Vionnet were two of the most influential designers in the 1930s. Simpson's copies of French designers' fashions meant that these elegant styles were more widely worn in Canada.*

Schiaparelli understood the value of promotion, and the public was entertained by the many fashion articles in magazines and newspapers about the surrealistic quality of her designs. Avant-garde artists such as Dali, Cocteau, and Berard designed some of her unusual fabrics. By the late thirties she had put her seal of approval on culottes, separates, aggressive shoulders, zippers, and synthetics. In the autumn of 1940 she toured North America and spoke to audiences in a number of cities, including Vancouver, Montreal, and New York.[5]

The Parisian couturière Madeleine Vionnet was a designer whose approach to creating dresses resembled that of sculpting. Her training followed the usual route of apprenticeship in various dressmaking houses, a short time in London, and then Paris where in 1912 she opened her own house. Throughout the twenties and thirties Vionnet established a reputation for exquisite feminine fashions. She perfected the technique of cutting fabric on the bias (diagonal grain) so that an unlined dress clung to the figure. Cowl necklines, handkerchief hemlines, the use of crepe de chine as a luxury fabric, and faggoting as a refined dressmaker detail were made fashionable by Vionnet.

CANADIAN COUTURE AND DRESSMAKING

Many fashionable women continued to have their clothes custom-made, particularly dress clothes and fashions for special occasions. Dressmakers were still abundant in Canadian cities. A dressmaker simply sewed to the suggestions of her client, but a couturière produced designs that bore her creative stamp.

Gaby Bernier was a well-known couturière in Montreal in the thirties. Almost self-taught as a dressmaker, Bernier made gowns

c *Home sewers could purchase patterns for Paris-inspired fashions from* The Chatelaine *in 1931. With lowered hems and interesting cuts, most dresses took about four metres of fabric.*

and furs for many of the fashionable elite of Montreal's "Square Mile" for over twenty-five years. Her great skill at creating excellent fit was combined with invention and daring.

In 1927 she was the first couturière to locate on Sherbrooke Street, at that time still largely residential. About 1935 she moved to 1524 Drummond and a year later added to her premises Canada's first boutique, Etcetera reg'd, which was run by Margot Wait. The boutique carried chic leather bags, stylish costume jewellery, and other accessories from New York City's leading suppliers. Bernier's concept of a boutique was more limited than the 1960s version.

In 1938 Bernier presented her first collection for a showing at the Ritz-Carleton Hotel. Although the fashion show was a great success, she never did another. Four years later Bernier returned to the Sherbrooke Street area to an elegant establishment at No. 1669 which housed her business until her retirement in 1958. Some of her famous clients were Dorothy Killam, Margaret Rawlings, Barbara Ann Scott, Mrs. Woodward, and Marjorie Caverhill.[6]

Another important Montreal couturière at this time was Marie-Paule Nolin, who started as a vendeuse for Raoul-Jean Fouré. Nolin set up her own couture house at University and Sherbrooke in the mid-thirties. Here she catered to wealthy and well-dressed clients for several decades.

Bloor Street in Toronto was gaining a reputation for having the finest dressmakers. One of the best-known dressmakers, Martha, created charming frocks for those clients of the Robert Simpson Company who purchased fabrics from that store. Ads in *Mayfair* magazine, promoted Martha as "Designer and Importer of exclusive gowns and accessories at 16 Bloor Street West."[7] Nearby, Polly Ferguson made smart dresses, suits, and coats.

Mayfair wasn't the only Canadian English-language magazine that brought the latest fashion news to its readers. In 1928 Colonel Maclean launched *The Chatelaine* (later known as *Chatelaine*) which competed very successfully over the years with the big American glossies. Its fashion pages adapted Parisian styling for the average woman and for home sewers.

SHOPS IN TORONTO

Fashionable shopping in Toronto was in the department stores or specialty shops in the downtown area, stretching along Yonge Street, along Bloor, and extending into areas such as the west end and along Mount Pleasant and Eglinton Avenue.

Some well-known retail ready-to-wear names on Yonge Street were Ira Berg, D'Allairds, Evangeline, Holt Renfrew (also in the Royal York Hotel), Lourden and Taylor, Julius Simon, and Virginia Dare. John Northway and Son, on Yonge Street, was one of the largest chains selling exclusive ladies' wear with branches in Hamilton, Brantford, Chatham, Stratford, and Orillia. On Bloor Street in Toronto, were Creeds, Joseph and Milton, Ada Mackenzie, Joy Frocks, Sophronia Gowns, and the Madame Worth French Shoppe.

Millinery shops were in abundance; there were over 200 retail hat shops scattered throughout the city, not to mention millinery suppliers.

THE 1930s WOMAN TAKES SHAPE

Fashions of the early thirties expressed a traditional ladylike appearance. As the economy worsened, the ideal look quickly changed from flapper to the conventional "little woman." She regrew her hair into sculptured waves and trimmed her intriguingly shaped hats. Her waistline returned to the normal place and her hemline dropped to hide most of her legs. The cover-up, as much psychological as physical, was necessary even when, for reasons of economy, the times seemed to be calling for dress made of less cloth.

The sombre mood of the times, reflecting the damaged economy, caused customers to choose dark, sensible colours and practical daytime fabrics such as printed cottons, wool tweeds, and jerseys. Fine, drapy evening fabrics were essential

d *The cover for January 1934* Mayfair *illustrates the form-fitting lines through waist and hip on an idealized figure.*

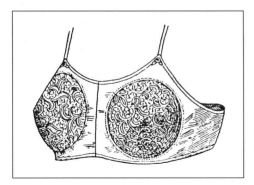

e

Bandeau brassieres of the late twenties had changed by the early thirties to acknowledge the breasts of a slightly more mature figure.

to the fashionable silhouette that skimmed the torso and flared at the hem. The bias cutting of fabric in so many of the early thirties dresses was one way to achieve this kind of fit in woven fabrics. The structure of these garments became quite complex as designers experimented with new kinds of patternmaking [52]. Bodices were softly draped but rather skimpy and bias cutting led to some very chic asymmetrical styling, as seen in the day dress [53]. As if trying to create femininity with a minimal amount of fabric, skirts were invariably close-fitting over the hips without pleats or gathers to the waist seam.

Fashion illustrations of any period always represent the figure in a manner that best symbolizes the ideal, the way women want to be seen. The 1930s elegant woman in illustration was invariably narrow hipped, an ideal most compatible with the popular dress styles; indeed, it is impossible to tell which comes first, the styling or the idealized figure. In any case, James Laver's theory concerning the relationship between the width of the hips and the fertility of women is substantiated by the declining birthrate in Canada during the depression years. *Harper's Bazaar* in 1934 stated: "modern dresses are designed to follow the figure form, and a loosely fitted waist to hip in a dress is not appreciated by the average woman."[8]

A slender hipline meant women wanted figure-controlling underwear, but they wanted it softer and more comfortable. Step-ins, lightweight stretching girdles, and bandeau-shaped brassieres were popular. Soon shaplier brassieres were favoured. Lastex yarns were woven into satin, lace, and other materials that were used in corselettes, combinations, and brassieres. Towards the end of the decade, the ideal figure became more shapely and fashion decreed a raised and pronounced bustline that further influenced the design of brassieres. The audacious sexuality of thirties film star Mae West, with her late Victorian image, helped to promote this curvy feminine figure.

TRADITION IN DAYWEAR

The ubiquitous bias-seamed dress of the early thirties can be directly attributed to the influence of designs by Vionnet. Early in this period, styling often showed V-shaped, softly draped necklines, along with fitted natural shoulders. An interest in inventive shapes included detailing in sleeves and produced a wide variety of sleeve styles, but the raglan fit at the shoulder was particularly popular. Pleated inserts, lantern shapes, medieval flares, angel wings, full puff, bishop sleeves, and many other shapes were used.

In the early part of the decade, fullness and accents were usually centred on the lower arm, with the exception of some styles about 1933 that accented shoulders. Gradually, the emphasized part of the sleeve moved up the arm as the seasons passed, and in the second half of the decade, a broad-shouldered silhouette was often created by sleeves with fullness at the head as well as shoulder padding. Waistlines were usually marked with a narrow self-fabric belt, but were not greatly accented until the end of the decade.

Daywear fashion categories broadened as women's lives became increasingly varied. A complete daytime wardrobe contained everything from skirts and sweaters [67], jumpers, and other items of casual sportswear to cocktail dresses. There were suits, dressy ensembles, and afternoon frocks for every season. The coordinated look of ensemble dressing in two or three parts, such as seen in [60], was considered especially chic. Suits were important. Jackets had long, gently fitting lines, and shoulders were at least somewhat padded. Skirts were long through the early and mid-decade, usually narrow with a central panel or a centre seam finished with kick pleats. Many elegant suits were trimmed with touches of fur. By now, knits, even homeknitted outfits, were often made up as ensembles [58].

Fabric designs in the thirties became more traditional; small florals, polka dots, and fine stripes were favoured. Colours

f
This daytime ensemble, summer 1931, was offered in challenge blue, black, guardsman blue, and chukker green. All with a blouse of alabaster, sizes 13 to 19, by Rosemere.

considered in good taste were generally subdued—darker shades of greens, muted pinks and browns, burgundy, and navy. And, of course, the little black dress was a continuing favourite. Schiaparelli's shocking pink was a way to separate high fashion from the mainstream.

Popular daytime fabrics ranged from sporty wool flannels and tweeds to softer fabrics for afternoon dress: silk or rayon crepes, cotton dimity, georgettes, and voiles, wool crepe and jerseys, even angora in sweaters and accessories. Rayon was an important fabric by the thirties and gave the essential soft, fluid quality at a reasonable price. Rayon was used alone and in blends and, at times, was deliberately confused with silk. Deception was

g
Traditional feminine floral-printed fabrics were a popular choice for dresses in 1934.

not unusual. The National Research Council reported "that many goods labelled wool and cotton blends contained very little wool, others identified as silk and wool contained only synthetic silk, and that many products labelled 'pure silk' had none of this expensive material whatsoever."[9]

Celanese acetate was introduced into Canada in 1927 when Canadian Celanese Limited opened production in Drummondville, Quebec. A low cost fabric used in shirts, sportswear, and linings, Canadian Celanese began to compete for the market in evening fabrics and in 1931 and 1933 the company launched a large promotional campaign, which included fashion shows of designer collections using Celanese satins, crepes, and Celasilk. Cotton was also promoted as a fashionable yet reasonable alternative to silk for afternoon and evening. About 1936 Wabasso in Quebec asked Gaby Bernier to design an entire collection in cotton—day dresses, sportswear, and eveningwear for promotional fashion shows across Canada.

GLAMOUR FOR EVENING

Eveningwear went through a distinctly transitional phase in the last years of the 1920s. Hemlines dropped dramatically making a greater distinction between day and evening styling. The long evening gowns of the thirties were newly romantic and helped to re-establish the traditional relationship between men and women. The flapper was gone and seduction was now more dignified. Over-all-beaded and sequined gowns disappeared, although by the late thirties sequins and beadwork were again used as appliqué accents on solid fabrics. Crisply delineated art-deco-styled evening dress gave way to soft gathers of fabric and ruffles, dresses that moved gracefully when dancing the slow fox-trot.

Evening hemlines varied from ankle-length for dinner and dancing to floor-length for more formal occasions. Although the bodice in front was usually modest, the backs were often cut very low, creating a new kind of erogenous message [54]. In 1931 a revolutionary backless corset, a great boon to the new fashion, was introduced by the Dominion Corset Manufacturing Company of Quebec.

The most desirable fibre for evening was still silk in fabrics such as satins, velvets, nets (or tulle), white or coloured lace [62], printed or plain chiffons, georgettes, lamé, and crepes. But "art" silks (artificial silks) of rayon fibres in different fabrics were used more frequently.

Furs were important for both day and evening. Particularly popular was fur trim on gowns and on evening coats and wraps [69]. Full-length evening coats with fur collars were an essential part of formal dress.

Escapist romanticism, particularly evident in evening wear, expressed itself through the entire decade in a series of references to the past and to ethnic cultures. For example, a Spanish influence was almost inevitable with the silhouette so similar to that of the costume of the traditional flamenco dancer. In the mid to late thirties there were also versions of classical draped effects, of Byzantium and medieval styling often showing up in the sleeves, as well as Victorian influences. Some gowns had train effects, usually created by having godets (a triangular piece of fabric) set into the seams at the back of the skirt and little shoulder capes in fragile evening fabrics, both features recalling dress from just before and after the turn of the century.

Truly experimental were such designer gowns as the McCord Museum's 1934 evening dress, designed by Vionnet and worn by Mrs. G.F. Haden Wallis of Montreal. This fashionable figure-clinging gown has cowl-draped panels of ivory satin in the bodice, which continue as long, floating panels over a flaring skirt.

DEPRESSION ESCAPISM

Canadian author and fashion historian Eileen Collard points out that "although the economic conditions of the 1930s often made buying fashionable clothes difficult, women of all ages expressed their desire to forget everyday problems by dressing up whenever the opportunity arose . . . including a floor-length evening dress in the most modest wardrobe [was] a must, and accounts for the large number of contemporary examples which still exist. These artifacts range from inexpensive ready-mades to exclusive couture models."[10]

The desire to escape the sad realities of life is a need that fashion has always served well and, no doubt, will continue to do so. A little escapism was also at hand in the music, the radio programs, and the movies of the era. By the end of the 1930s there were more than 1.5 million radios in Canadian homes, or for twenty-five cents you could forget your troubles and step right into another life for a few hours at the movies.

Hollywood influenced styles all over North America as movie houses sprang up in every city and town. Films were usually in black and white; successful Technicolor started in about 1935. Hollywood designers chose sensational fabrics and created fabulous outfits for the many style-conscious films of the 1930s. Garments had to photograph well in black and white and be styled to slim the figure since the camera tended to create the illusion of added pounds. Designers used fabrics that were sensuous and rich with highlights and textures or created interesting, memorable details and motifs. Films done in contemporary dress often displayed exaggerated, dramatic, and glamorous styling for leading ladies that at the same time had to be rather classical because a film might be released a full year after the costumes had been designed and then run for several more years.[11]

Some of the best-known film designers of this period were Adrian, Travis Banton, and Orry-Kelly who created fabulous gowns and ensembles for Hollywood stars Claudette Colbert, Loretta Young, Joan Crawford, Greta Garbo, and Marlene Dietrich. Joan Crawford, in particular, was known for wearing an extremely wide-shouldered silhouette and Marlene Dietrich for slacks. Greta Garbo in *Ninotchka* played a Russian Communist visitor to Paris who is tempted by the appeal of the charming dresses and eccentric hats of the thirties.

Some fashions available in the United States and Canada were not only inspired by or copied from Hollywood productions, but also were promoted by the manufacturers with movie stars' endorsements [67]. Magazine ads and editorials in the American publications on Canadian stands and in the *Montrealer* and *Mayfair*, for example, played up more than ever before the connection between the glamorous images of movie queens and manufacturers' lines. *Stylewear* showed a number of Hollywood fashions photographed on movie stars and ran articles such as "Will Hollywood Replace New York as a Fashion Centre?"[12]

Escapism took other forms as well. Fanciful hats replaced the no-nonsense, streamlined cloche. One of the earliest indications of mounting romanticism was seen in the new headgear; it was impossible to be chic in a thirties ensemble without just the right hat. Brims got wider and shapes more varied; asymmetrical lines were considered the most chic. Soon hats were trimmed with flowers, feathers, bows, and veils. As early as 1930 designer Adrian's creation of the Empress Eugenie hat for Greta Garbo's role in *Romance* began a vogue for little velvet hats, trimmed with ostrich plumes, worn tilted over one eye. The Beverley Hat Shop at 150 Yonge Street in Toronto named in an ad some of their 1938 collection: "Saucy Pill Boxes, Pert Poke Bonnets, Clever Bumpers, Young Boleros, New Bretons and Swanky Sailors." Berets, turbans, feminine fedora styles, Robin Hood hats, wide-brimmed picture hats, flat pancakes, cone-shapes; women in the thirties tried them all.

OUTERWEAR

A long slim silhouette in coats opened the decade. The popular wrapped-front cloth coat, belted or unbelted at the waist, was made up in dressier coating fabrics and often trimmed with a fur collar. Sporty styles and travel coats were popular in tweeds, sometimes trimmed in leather. In most cases plain, fitted sleeve-heads produced natural shoulders in the early years. Fashionable coatings were boucles, tweeds, plaids, and smooth-faced solids in blacks and browns, tan, navy blue, dark green, and burgundy. Silk crepes and satins lined the finer quality coats, while less expensive ones used satins, twills, and crepes of rayon. Chamois interlining, to act as a windbreak, was inserted into the backs of better quality winter coats and jackets.

h *Coats, by 1930, were already showing more fullness at the hemline and slightly stronger emphasis at the waist.*

JOSEPH and MILTON
L I M I T E D

FURS ∗ WRAPS ∗ GOWNS ∗ MILLINERY

i *Joseph and Milton at 95 Bloor Street West in Toronto in the late thirties claimed furs were "on the crest of an upward trend in popularity," and showed Persian lamb, caracul, mink, and the "new opossum sports coat for swagger grace with generous warmth."*

Fur coats began taking on dressmaker details as designs became more complex. Because of the complexity of the cuts and in keeping with art deco, silky, short-haired furs and shaved furs were prevalent: caracul, sheared and Persian lamb, muskrat, and beaver. Fur collars showed greater variety, from luxurious fox, Manchurian wolf, and raccoon to dog and rabbit. The separate fur piece complete with head and paws was popular, and even the fur muff had a revival.

By 1933, just as with dress styles, coats had imaginative sleeves—elbow-puff styles or interesting cuffs and dolman and raglan sleeves were used more often. As the thirties progressed, coats were cut with greater ease and more generous fit. "Swagger" was very evident by mid-decade in everything from coats and jackets to dresses. Swagger implied fullness and a jaunty swing to the garment, a defiant note against the depression. A gala fashion presentation at the National Motor Show in 1936 promoted day and evening coats, and furs . . . "princess lines, semifitted, or sportingly swagger, full-length or seven-eighths . . . some in silken-skinned mink, gleaming caracul, or youthful grey lamb."[13]

Later in the decade shoulders began to broaden on coats, through greater padding, cape effects [63] with widened shoulder lines, or epaulettes and military revers. By 1938 the new coat look was V-necked and collarless, or a simple shawl collar, or long tuxedo collar as in 60. Full sleeves and padded shoulders with short lengths produced a boxy silhouette.

A distinctive Canadian coat style is the Hudson's Bay Company's blanket coat, valued for its warmth in the 1930s. English wool blankets were made into coats throughout most of two centuries for stylish and protective, if heavy, winter wear. Hudson's Bay blankets were first introduced in Canada at the end of the eighteenth century and were traded for beaver pelts.[14] Single-striped versions [56] were later made more colourful with the familiar four differently coloured stripes. These blankets were used by Canadian designers in the 1970s and 80s to create updated interpretations of the coats.

Another coat exclusive to Canada was the Red River coat, mainly for young girls. Goodwin's of Montreal showed a version of it in their catalogue of 1911: "only in navy blue Canadian blanket cloth, full hood, trimmed with red piping, lined in warm red flannel and has sash to match. $6.94."[15] Variations of this style were available at least until the 1980s [56].

SPORTSWEAR AND ACTIVE SPORTSWEAR

The new look for leisure was "smart and active," even for spectators of sporting events. Functionally designed clothes for specific sports began to have an impact on fashion and this decade marks the beginning of that category of dress called sportswear, as opposed to active sportswear. Neat, tailored styles derived from tennis and golf were increasingly important for casual daywear, especially crisp linen, cotton, or silk outfits for summer, and sweaters for winter [64].

The simple cotton or wool-knit bathing costume of the twenties was gradually replaced by more inventive swimsuits, in a variety of fabrics in white and brighter colours, and which revealed the shape of the figure in a new way.

Ontario knitting mills, such as P.K. Mills in Listowel, made a name for their high-grade knitted sportswear. Ballantyne in Stratford was also very competitive. In 1933 they showed a smart black, wool-knit suit cut away almost to two pieces and trimmed with a white belt and V-necked collar. Bigger brandname swimwear manufacturers were Monarch and B.V.D., the latter made in Montreal by the Knit-to-Fit Manufacturing Company.

Early in the decade beach pyjamas with very wide flaring legs [57] were a stylish look for resort wear and at-home lounging. As the fit figure became the new ideal, beach pyjamas were replaced by the one-piece white or coloured maillot [66], usually low cut in back, sometimes skirtless, either of knit or woven cloth. Suntanning was becoming very popular. Public taste and local laws were still rather prudish, and beach wraps in the form of robes, jackets, and skirts were a stylish way to cover up when necessary.

A 1933 *Mayfair* fashion editorial reported that "beach ensembles supersede the now frowned-upon gaudy beach pyjama,"[16] and offered instead a wrapped skirt in white duck over a white wool knit swimsuit with coral accents from the Eaton's Toronto College Street store. The 1930s swimsuit often had a built-in bra structure and elasticized fabrics were used.

At the beginning of the decade skirts were still the norm for many sports such as skating, tennis, and golf, and hemlines were still below the knee [59]. In 1930 Livingston and Scott of Toronto advertised a velveteen skating dress in a variety of dark colours with a front-closing lightening fastener. A nearly mid-calf hemline over knickers was worn even for figure-skating competitions.[17] Although used on galoshes in the 1920s, lightening fasteners or sliders (zippers) were not used very often in women's apparel until about the mid-1930s.

Culottes [68] were worn for tennis and golf and paved the way for shorts as casual summer wear. Ada Mackenzie of Toronto, a Canadian golf champion in the twenties and thirties, found a great need for more comfortable dress for women on the links, and in 1930 she started Ada Mackenzie Limited, a sportswear shop at 26 Bloor Street West, that carried imports as well as Mackenzie's own designs.[18]

Increasing numbers of sportswomen dressing in slacks for sporting activities helped to gain wider acceptance of trousers for women. Still, nowhere in formal city scenes were slacks correct. A 1936 *Vogue* decreed that slacks were for golf, fishing, boating, gardening; shorts for beach, tennis, but not golf; culottes were for the country only.

Opposition to trousers for women continued for many years in conservative, male-dominated situations. Marlene Dietrich created a great deal of controversy by wearing mannish pantsuits both in films and in her personal life. Gaby Bernier made perhaps the earliest pantsuit for a Canadian woman, a fashion-conscious client in Montreal in the early thirties, but American ready-to-wear was already onto the look—the 1933 Sears catalogue featured a slacksuit. Slacks of any variety, as the word implies, were considered casual wear, often too casual by many people.

THE DECADE DRAWS TO A CLOSE

As early as 1933, no sooner had dress lines softened and drooped, than the look began to change again, not drastically, but gradually throughout the decade. As fashion focused on nostalgic revival, the silhouette was more extravagantly defined. Fuller shoulders, at first used to narrow the hips, later in the decade symbolized a more assertive woman [65]. Her silhouette echoed the broad-shouldered lines of men's suits and uniforms.

By 1938 the hemline was nearing the knee and the long, slim thigh was no longer so important. A nicely stockinged leg was the sign of good grooming. The full-fashioned, and therefore seamed, silk stocking gave the best fit but had a rather unreliable lifespan. Dupont's nylon fibre promised to create a greatly improved product, especially for durability and fit in a seamless stocking. As well as sexy legs, tiny waists and an uplifted bust were essential.

Paris fashions were moving towards a tightly fitted waistline even requiring the return of extreme corsetry. The Parisian emphasis on the small waist and broad shoulders is shown in the dress by Piguet [61]. Princess lines, the corselet waistline on dresses, waist-to-hip yokes, peplums, and set-in belts, all called attention to the waist. A paddy green day dress by Molyneux, worn by Mrs. Cleveland Morgan of Montreal in 1939 and now in the McCord Museum shows corselet seaming at the waist. The dirndl skirt, with its emphasis on rounder hips, was part of this curvier silhouette of the late decade. There was even an attempt to revive the Victorian bustle in 1939.

The puffed sleeve was winning out over any other, but the fully bloused bishop sleeve was a second variation, as an alternative to narrow, short, or long. Pleats or darts at the sleeve head, along with shoulder pads of some kind, were by now universal.

The commonly worn and sensible knee-length skirt, nearly always flared for comfort and ease of movement, continued into the next decade. In fact, many details seen in the prewar years were locked in for approximately the next eight years: shirtwaist dresses, boleros, sweetheart necklines, slightly draped bodices, shoulders, yokes, and knife pleats, sensible shoes, and rather mad hats.

These features sometimes merged with an exotic, somewhat Spanish feeling. The Latin American influence was becoming quite pronounced through increased contact with Mexico, Cuba, and South America. Favourite tourist spots were Rio de Janeiro and Havana, and for those Canadians who couldn't travel, Latin music, dance, and costume were featured in many Hollywood films. The stage was already set for the styles of the war years.

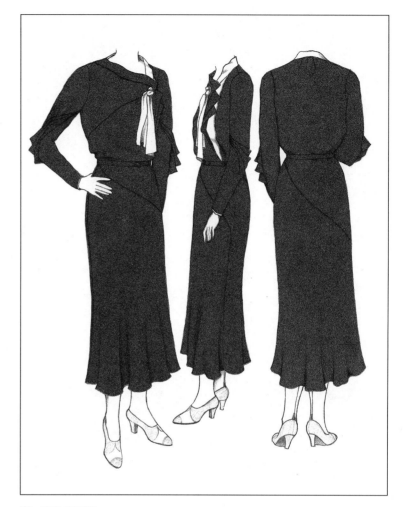

52 AFTERNOON DRESS, *about 1931*

An afternoon dress for summer in a rayon sheer printed with soft multi-florals on a royal blue ground. All the silhouette features for 1931 are here: the collarless V-neckline and long slim sleeves, the shirring, the tucked and moulded hipline, and the fuller flaring hem. By the next season the waistline becomes even more fitted. *Museum of Civilization*

53 DAY DRESS

A form-clinging day dress in black and cream silk crepe with distinctive art deco styling. Three stepped, finlike inserts project from the elbows of the long slim sleeves and along the asymmetrical neckline opening. The simple, bold use of black and cream in a shiny fabric is characteristic of art deco. The bias cut of the skirt allows it to curve over the hips and flare at the hem. Closure through the waist is on the left, with six snaps—two above the waist and four following the diagonal seam in back. *The Suddon Collection*

54 PARTY FROCK, *about 1933*

Green-and-white striped seersucker fabric is used to full effect through the bias cutting in this design. Tiered and ruffled sleeves cleverly slim the hips by emphasizing the shoulders and continue smoothly into a collar in the back, which dips almost to the waist. Here is a dress designed to play up a suntanned back. Shaping at the bust, bias seaming through the waist, and the self-fabric belt all help to introduce new curves to the figure. Edges are bound in white organdy.

The Suddon Collection

55 EVENING DRESS WITH BOLERO, *1933*

An evening dress in sky blue satin with a coordinated, shirred, corded silk bolero. The slinky, narrow lines of the gown are topped with textured plaid in blues, gold, rust, and cream. Raglan sleeves complement the lines and shapes of the jacket as the fabric wraps and is drawn up into a gathered collar. The sleeveless gown shows Schiaparelli's interest in nontraditional closures —the unusual meant-to-be-seen hooks and eyes set in through the left waist seam.

Designer: Schiaparelli
Worn by Mrs. John David Eaton

The Royal Ontario Museum

56 HUDSON'S BAY COAT
A sporty unlined coat made of an off-white, two-and-one-half point heavy wool Hudson's Bay blanket with a wide black band that is also used on the collar and cuffs. It has a black wool tabby belt and large patch pockets.
Label: Hudson's Bay Co. Ltd., Made in England
Purchased in Winnipeg, worn in New Brunswick
Museum of Civilization

THE RED RIVER COAT
Mary Peate in *Girl in a Red River Coat* writes of this classic Canadian girl's coat: they "were the winter costume of Quebec children. They were made of navy blue melton with red flannel lining, red trimmed epaulets, a narrow red stripe down the side seams and a navy blue Capuchin hood, lined with red. With the coat, we wore red woolen leggings, red mitts, and a red sash and toque which lent the costume a dashing habitant air." Many Ontario women also remember them from their youth, including the fact that the leggings tinted the snow pink when the wearer made snow angels.

57 BEACH PYJAMA OUTFIT, *about 1930*

This sunshine-bright beach or lounging outfit is in three parts, one-piece pyjama, jacket, and sash. The "overall" in gold crepe de chine has extremely wide legs and a fairly low V-neckline in back. A wide bias-cut chevron panel is inset through the waist both front and back. The left side seam closes from armhole to hip with eight snaps. The collarless jacket in emerald green has orange crepe lining with gold and orange bands trimming the sleeves and the two patch pockets. The seven-foot-long sash is made of a five-inch-wide bias panel in each of the three colours.

Label: Bonwit Teller, Paris, London, Philadelphia, New York

The Suddon Collection

58 ENSEMBLE (jacket, pullover sweater, skirt), *about 1931*

A three-piece knit ensemble in viscose bouclé yarns of rich purple with light yellow, salmon, pale apricot, beiges, and mauves. The unusual multicoloured motif on the pullover may have been influenced by designs in knitwear by Chanel of about this time. The main body of the pullover in pale apricot has a V-neck and very narrow capped sleeves. The simple purple hip-length jacket is reminiscent of Chanel's straight-cut, nonbuttoning cardigans. It matches the longer flaring skirt, and the whole outfit provides the kind of style and comfort that she helped to promote in the 1920s and 1930s.

The Suddon Collection

59 COORDINATES

A versatile suit with two interchangeable skirts in cotton wide-wale corduroy. Depression-era ingenuity produced an outfit for every daytime need: The jacket teamed with the long, slim skirt made the correct fashion statement for town; with the shorter and fuller skirt, one was ready for walking, cycling, or skating. The asymmetrical design of the unlined jacket is accented by large mother-of-pearl buttons. The long cuffed sleeves have a dropped shoulder seam giving the illusion of added width. *The Suddon Collection*

60 ENSEMBLE (jacket and dress), *about 1936*

A simple sheath dress plus matching swagger jacket in rusty red, lightweight wool tweed. The dress front is cut in one piece and brought in at the waist by two darts on each side under the self belt. The long narrow sleeves are fitted into the armhole with inverted darts and the front bodice is subtly detailed with a chevron of gradated darts. The slim skirt has a centre-front pleat and left side zip-fastener opening. The long-sleeved, hip-length jacket is lined in silk and trimmed with a tuxedo-style collar of soft, grey persian lamb.
Label: Polly Ferguson, 30 Avenue Rd., Toronto   *Royal Ontario Museum*

61 AFTERNOON DRESS, *about 1937*

This romantic afternoon dress in silk crepe has long, fuchsia-coloured sleeves, puffed and gauged at the armhole to create a dramatic broad-shouldered silhouette. A redingote look is created with the black crepe wrapping over gathered fuchsia panels. The bodice, of two draped panels, forms a V-neckline and is gathered to an area of shirring hidden behind the redingote waist. The cummerbund effect with seven buttons is an expression of the ethnic or peasant influence that was developing just before the war.

Designer: Robert Piguet, Paris
Worn by a Torontonian

Royal Ontario Museum

62 EVENING GOWN, *about 1937*

This full-length evening gown is of metallic-embroidered net over ivory silk crepe. A large, black, moiré bow trims the bodice and continues across under the arms, dipping to centre-back waist where it loops around the narrow self-belt and then falls in two, long, graceful panels. The bodice has wide, draped straps that overlap slightly at centre front spreading over the shoulders to exaggerate their width and forming a low V in back.

The skirt is intricately made of handworked shapes fitted diagonally through the hipline, but falling and widening quickly to produce fullness that starts higher on the skirt than was previously fashionable. The underdress of crepe has conventional slip straps and falls with a slight flare to a scalloped hemline edged with lace.

Designer: Chanel, Paris

The Suddon Collection

63 COAT, *about 1937*
A winter coat fitted with princess seaming sports a double-breasted closing with six brass buttons. The notched collar covers the handstitched fastening of an added cape/collar with a wide self-fabric border. Romanticism in the 1930s favoured capes and caped coats. The straight but ample sleeves have three seams and a six-inch vent at the wrists.
Label: Made in France
Worn in Toronto   *Royal Ontario Museum*

64 DAY DRESS
The daffodil yellow silk has the texture of handkerchief linen, light and crisp. The styling is smart, with a sporty air provided by the extended safari pockets and large mother-of-pearl buttons on the false centre-front opening. Belt and lapels are completely top-stitched. Broader shoulders, bustline a little more accented, and a shortening hemline are all new features. The safari pockets emphasize the bust and that short tailored sleeve with puffed shoulders will become standard for some time.
                                             The Suddon Collection

65 SUIT (jacket and skirt), *about 1937*
A casual spring suit in blue-and-cream, tweedy, cotton plaid, worn without a blouse. Tweeds, checks, and plaids were popular, serviceable fabrics for suits and day dresses. This suit has a military look with its three double-buttoned tabs and matching, dark red plastic buckle with bold art deco styling. Fullness of the sleeve head is pleated into the armhole to create fashionable shoulder width further accented with shoulder pads. The shorter, slightly flared skirt shows the trend towards fuller silhouettes in the second half of the decade.
The Suddon Collection

66 BATHING SUIT, *about 1937*
A one-piece bathing suit in Lastex yarn with a textured surface. The bodice bandeau is softly gathered centre front for shaping and fashion interest. Rayon cord straps join in back with red plastic fasteners locking into couplers. The low cut and the narrow straps are designed to show off a beautiful tanned back.
Label: Jantzen
Purchased: Burdines Store, Florida
Museum of Civilization

67 SEPARATES (sweater blouse and skirt),
        about 1935
A sweater blouse in printed, brown wool jersey paired with a tailored, brown wool skirt. The knit top has a front-buttoning bodice down to the wide wool rib-knit waistband matching the treatment of the long full sleeves. The neckline is a softly draped tie fastened at back. The long, slim, unlined skirt fastens with dome fasteners on the left seam through a fairly wide waistband. The front panel of knife pleats is stitched down through the hip area. In another year or so the hemline will shorten to mid-calf.
Label: Sportswear by Billie Burke
The Suddon Collection

68 PLAYSUIT

A one-piece playsuit in peach silk crepe de chine, probably made in France. A self-fabric built-in belt joins the top to neatly disguised shorts with a low-cut crotch. Front fullness is controlled by partially stitched-down pleats; the back shows a simpler fit. The top teams flap pockets, a Peter Pan collar, and short sleeves with a bit of shoulder emphasis. *Museum of Civilization*

69 EVENING COAT, *1939*

A full-length evening coat in royal blue velvet with a collar of white rabbit fur. Fitted to the torso with princess seaming front and back, it closes dramatically at the waistline with an enormous self-covered button and with a hidden dome fastener at the neck. The lining is of cream satin. Elegant coats such as this were an important part of evening dressing in the thirties. *Worn by Laura McQuillan* *The Seneca College Collection*

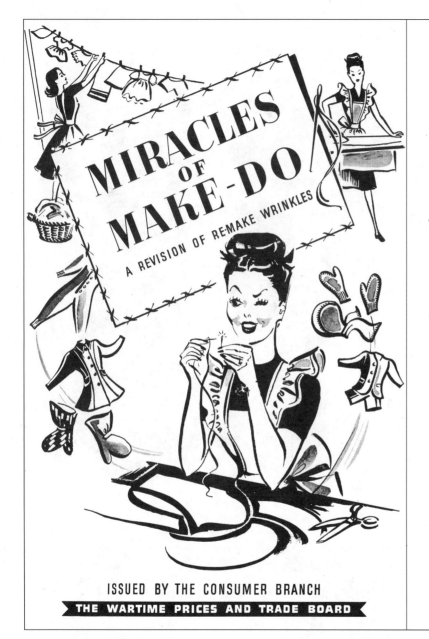

MIRACLES OF MAKE-DO
A REVISION OF REMAKE WRINKLES

ISSUED BY THE CONSUMER BRANCH

THE WARTIME PRICES AND TRADE BOARD

What You Can Make from a Woman's Discarded Coat

WORN BUTTONHOLES—Use twist made especially for working buttonholes on men's suits. If you can't get this buttonhole twist, use double ordinary thread. Wax it for strength and easy handling.

Pick out all worn and ragged stitches of the buttonhole. Be careful not to pull the hole out of shape as you rip out the old stitching. Join new stitching with old carefully so that it won't show where the repair is made.

If the entire buttonhole has to be reworked, work over gimp or several strands of thread twisted together and waxed.

PULLED-OUT BUTTONS—If a button has pulled off and taken a bit of cloth with it—darn it or patch it—depending upon the size of the torn place.

If the hole is smaller than the button, darn with matching yarns over a small piece of reinforcing material slipped under the hole. Then sew the button on again.

If the suiting is torn beyond the button so that a darn wouldn't be strong enough to hold the button, set in a carefully matched block patch as you would for repairing a worn elbow.

To prevent strain that may cause the button to pull a hole in the suiting again, sew the button with a shank.

1. Make the shank by laying a pin or two across the top of the button. Sew several times over the pins and through the button and material.

2. Pull out the pins, lift the button, wind the thread beneath the button, and fasten off. Length of shank depends on thickness of the suiting.

3. For even greater protection, sew a tiny stay button directly under the top button but on the inside of the suit. Sew through both buttons at the same time and make a shank inside the top button long enough to allow the buttonhole to fit underneath without strain on the cloth.

Page 26

a *Canadians at home were encouraged to recycle clothing during these years in order to free up production for the war effort.*

THE
1940s

CANADIANS ON THE HOME FRONT, INFINITELY MORE FORTUNATE THAN those in countries ravaged by war, nevertheless, did suffer privations. By 1942 food rationing was a well-established way of coping with shortages. Gasoline rationing had already changed transportation habits and clothing production was controlled. Imports from Europe were cut off, as well as the flow of design ideas from French couture. Many designers left Paris. Mainbocher and Schiaparelli went to New York. Chanel gave what she thought was her last show in 1940.

New York took on a new importance during this time as did the Canadian industry and local dressmakers and couturiers in cities like Montreal, Vancouver, and Toronto. By the war's end, the industry in Quebec had developed so much that the Montreal Fashion Institute was formed to counteract people's perception of the inferiority of Canadian goods. The institute presented semiannual fashion shows for ready-to-wear buyers and the press and also published a magazine.

The Wartime Price and Trade Board through what were called its A61 regulations curtailed luxury goods and made changes in the manufacture of goods for the home. The board's publication *Miracles of Make-do* gave directions and diagrams for the home sewer on how to "Make a Lady's Suit from a Man's Suit" and how to make children's wear out of an old shirt.[1]

A major task of *Stylewear* magazine during World War II was to keep the fashion industry informed about changing A61 regulations. Fabric colours and patterns in printed rayons, for example, were limited in manufacture, and yardage allowances and other elements regulated for individual garments. By 1942, day dresses could not have zippers longer than nine inches. Less material was alloted per garment than had been in 1941, and the number of garments a manufacturer could produce for the home market was to be cut by one-third. Hems could not exceed two inches in a straight-cut dress, nor one inch in a bias-cut dress. It was forbidden to create dresses with any type of cloth-over-cloth design, to create a hemline sweep over eighty inches for size 16, to create any voluminous or exaggerated sleeves, or a belt over two inches wide. Evening dresses, suits, and coats had their own equally stringent limitations. Manufacturers were hampered in production methods and equipment, too. Factories had to make do with existing machinery.

In the late 1930s, hemlines had risen almost to the knees and legs were more visible. Seamed stockings of nylon, an important synthetic substitute for silk, appeared during the first year of the war only to disappear again until the end of 1945. All nylon was geared toward parachute production. Less glamorous cotton or rayon stockings substituted in winter, and, in summer, leg makeup was a not very successful solution. Sometimes frustrated, determined fashion enthusiasts drew seams with eyebrow pencil

b   *Delicate silk hosiery for chic legwear came in chiffon or service weight in 1940. Seams drew attention to the legs as hemlines rose to the knee.*

up the backs of their legs to give the illusion of the unobtainable stocking. Shoe design often reflected shortages of leather. Ankle-strapped, platform-soled high heels became a characteristic wartime style. In spite of all the limitations, the forties look had a personality of its own and the legs were an important part of it.

FASHIONS FOR DAY

By the late 1930s the fashionable shape was a moulded fit through the torso with an uplifted bust and snug waistline. Paris, reflecting the difficult times, showed confusion of silhouette with a variety of skirts, from hoop-flared or bustle-backed to long and slinky, but the one common feature was the tiny waist. That and the pronounced bustline continued throughout the forties.

Suits were very popular in durable, practical tweeds and gabardines, with styles similar to the army uniform [71]. In the early years the daytime hemline was quite standard at seventeen inches from the floor, just covering the knee. The dirndl or knife-pleated skirt was cut slimmer and had less detail as wartime restrictions were felt. In jackets, the military mood of the time was expressed with pronounced masculine shoulders and traditional lapels.

The classic front-buttoned, belted shirtwaist dress with its tailored, slightly formal air was a great favourite. A sleeveless overdress, called a jumper, worn with a shirt or pullover sweater, was a more casual style, and separates of skirt and blouse were commonly worn.

A sleeve style seen over and over again was the perky elbow-length one that puffed stiffly at the head and was pleated into a tailored narrow edge [74]. Requiring little fabric, this sleeve style still gave emphasis to the shoulder. Other popular details were set-in, self-fabric belts, shoulder yokes, small patch pockets, and bolero jackets [70]. Often, skirts avoided pleats or tried to create a richly pleated effect by other means [77]. The gored skirt gave ease of movement with a minimal use of fabric.

c
*Suits and jumpers were
neatly tailored and often
broad-shouldered.*

More glamorous styles for dressy afternoons were made up in softer printed rayons and sheers, using draping and shirring techniques to create textural richness with relatively little fabric. There was a tendency to choose darker colours as they were more serviceable and more appropriate. The traditional ladylike small floral print predominated. Important forties fabrics for summer were chambray, seersucker, rayon broadcloth, linenlike rayon, printed rayons, piqué, shantung, and for winter, wool plaids (said to be an influence from Hartnell, then couturier for the British royal family), tweeds, velveteen, and men's suiting fabrics.

Glamour and luxury in the war years often took the form of fur: a jacket or coat or even just a collar, choker, or muff [73]. Toronto was still an important centre for the industry, with wholesalers such as the Yukon Fur Company, I.J. Levitt Furs, West Canadian Fur Company, and the Lake Fur Company. The most popular furs were the short-haired types—lamb, mouton, caracul, rabbit, muskrat, and mink.

Hats were varied in size and shape and were still an important part of being well dressed. They perched straight on top, slipped to the back, or even tilted forward, with a mysterious little veil. The influence of factory workwear was seen in the snood (a hairnet) and various turban shapes. The mannish fedora was adapted for women, but the pretty decorated hat was important as a relatively easy and inexpensive way to express femininity in a time when much dress was functional and masculine. Gloves were still an important daytime accessory.

WOMEN'S WORK

Comfort and function were emphasized in daytime clothing in the war years. With servicemen overseas, many previously male-only occupations were filled by women. Women often wore slacks or overalls as they manned assembly lines in munition factories, tested and packed parachutes, or worked as welders and riveters on aircraft production. Turbans were required to prevent long "Veronica Lake" hair from getting tangled in machinery, and they became a fashion statement as a result.

By the war's end, over 45,000 Canadian women had served in uniform, either with the Canadian Women's Army Corps or in the Women's Division of the air force or the navy [76]. Despite considerable criticism at first, women were trained as noncombatant clerks or as technicians for radio, telephone, and auto vehicle operations. In addition, 4,480 nurses served with the Royal Canadian Army Corps or in the medical services of the navy or air force. In 1946 the women's services were disbanded leaving only a small number of nurses in uniform; however, by the early fifties the reserves reinstated limited recruitment for women.

Women's work, both in service and in civilian life, affected dress. Suits and tailored styles were popular for day; practical and serviceable overcoats were highly valued. Men's World War I belted trench coats in densely woven, water-repellent cotton twill were often adopted by women. Reversible coats were a new idea for getting value from fewer resources, and both the lumber jacket and the neat, leather battle jacket were worn by young women.

LATIN EVENINGS AND THE PINUP

Sex appeal in the 1940s was less subtle than in the 1930s. The bosom replaced the back as the erogenous zone and became the winning feature of Hollywood stars like Rita Hayworth and her following of "sweater girls." Legs ran a close second. Betty Grable was the favourite live pinup girl, but for pure fantasy there were the calendar pinups by illustrators Petty and Varga.

Latin culture was at a peak of influence in North America in the forties through movies, music, and dance. Carmen Miranda, the Brazilian bombshell, had a very high profile through her exotically costumed musical films. Illustrations of tropical themes and graphic motifs in print and on textiles trickled northward from Mexico, California, South and Central America, and Cuba: sombreros, cacti, castinettes; also sombrero-shaped dress hats, ruffled peasant and off-the-shoulder blouses and bodices, and tiered and ruffled skirts.

Fashionable eveningwear styles accented the shoulders through crisp sleeves, shoulder pads, boleros, and halter necklines. The sweetheart neckline was very important, also draped and shirred bosoms. Waistlines were kept fitted. Hips were featured, with drapings or peplums jutting out over narrow skirts, both long for formal and short for less formal occasions. Asymmetrical sarongs were fashionable and sometimes the bare midriff was seen in eveningwear.

d

The effect of gathered sheers, often of rayon, over an under-fabric in a similar solid colour was a winning textile treatment for dressy skirts and bodices [80]. Printed sheers, satin, silk faille, velvet, taffeta, and lace in fairly dark colours were all used for evening gowns and afternoon numbers.

In the period immediately after the war, evening dress geared up to include a wider variety of styles for several degrees of formality: short party dresses were worn for tea dances, informal dinners, and the theatre: longer gowns for formal dinners, dances, and opening nights. Not only were exaggerated shoulders starting to disappear for evening, but also they were being bared in off-the-shoulder styles. For the young and daring there were strapless gowns.

Black was still popular, but also wine, fuchsia, and deep rich blues and greens in velvets, crepes, faille, and satin, sometimes with overskirts in nets and sheers or lace. Sequin and beaded embroidery trim was very important [72]. Skirts began to show increased fullness at the hemline, especially the frothy debutante-styled gown in tulle and other sheers.

ACTIVE SPORTSWEAR

War work put many women into pants for day, and they continued to gain acceptance as sportswear. Slacks or culottes were now well established as fashionable dress for cycling, golfing, and boating. The typical winter ski suit paired full-cut heavy wool pants with sporty jackets of the same or contrasting fabric, buttoned or zipped and finished with rib-knit cuffs.

The thirties one-piece playsuit was changed little throughout the forties, especially on the tennis courts where short dresses or separate shorts and tops were also worn [68]. Tennis dress was fairly covered up but soon to become more varied and style conscious. In 1949 "Gorgeous Gussie" Moran caused a furor at Wimbledon with her feminine touches: ruffles and bows and fuller skirts that revealed polka-dotted or lace-edged panties.

Another exhibition sport caught the Canadian interest because of figure-skater Barbara Ann Scott—Canadian champion through the forties, European and the world champion in 1947, and Olympic champion in 1948. The pretty blonde athlete in dainty, short-skirted costumes (which now appear very conservative) inspired many Canadian girls and glamourized skating competition dress for the future. Scott also inspired new hat styles, particularly perky little caps, as well as more sophisticated looks. "Thousands of Canadian girls sported replicas of the odd little hat with the bright red poppy six inches from the crown that Scott had worn home to Ottawa."[2]

A summer suntan was thought very appealing by many

e *Barbara Ann Scott's graceful beauty on ice was an inspiration to young women in the late forties.*

Canadians as beachwear became lighter and briefer. The traditional one-piece, bare-backed maillot, in woven rayon, Lastex, and cotton, or elasticated jersey, was the standard body-clinging swim suit [84], but variations included one-piece skirted suits called the dressmaker style and two-piece suits with pants or a tight, skirt-like front panel, completely hip covering, and a top, bra-shaped without being very brief. In the late forties built-in bras in most swimsuits were stiffened or padded for a busty look, which continued into the fifties.

SLOPPY JOES AND CASUAL DRESS

Chatelaine magazine portrayed the Canadian woman as a neat, domestic creature, mainly wanting to be informed on housekeeping and marital matters. *Chatelaine* in the forties carried occasional articles on fashion and beauty, a good deal of romantic escapist fiction, but the bulk of the magazine was taken up with ads for products—personal hygiene to household—that played on women's insecurities as wives, mothers, and daughters.

In 1947, Canadian young women—in what are now known as the teen years—looked very mature as shown in *Chatelaine*'s suggested checked wool suit with flared skirt or the favourite "shirtmaker dress" with three-quarter-length bishop sleeves and pleated skirt. "Wear pearls or silk ties with it . . . "[3] was the final touch that turned the young woman into a replica of her mother. Teens as a whole independent market had not yet been established; at some point one simply moved from child to adult.

More sophisticated American fashion magazines aimed at the college girl, such as *Mademoiselle*, started in 1935, and *Glamour*, in 1939, helped to create a slightly more daring version of a casual campus look that was still nowhere as casual as it was to become. Knee-covering pleated or flared skirts, usually plaid, check, or tweed, teamed with shirt-styled blouses and topped with cardigans are still the basics for the uniforms of many private girls' schools. Even more casual versions were worn by high school students and as leisure styles for university students and young career girls.

Mary Peate wrote of her teenaged years in Montreal during the war and described her "uniform" thus: "a Sloppy Joe sweater (bought several sizes too large, and worn with the sleeves pushed up); a skirt, generally plaid, or matching the sweater, often pleated, coming to mid-knee or slightly above; pearls, or a detachable white Peter Pan collar; white socks, and brown and white scuffed saddle shoes, or polished loafers."[4] Peate also mentions her passion for bangles and other unbusiness-like accessories that she had to shed for her first job. Her mother took her downtown, "and bought [her] a Glen plaid suit, a beige Helen Harper pullover sweater to go with it, a couple of Tooke shirts, a beret, gloves, a purse, stockings . . . and sensible shoes"[5] to outfit her for the job interview.

As a result of the war, slacks for young women, straight cut and with a left side closure, gained in favour for casual dress [75]. They offered comfort and function at a time when good-looking stockings were not available, although most people still considered slacks appropriate only for strictly informal occasions. Eventually, cycling in a gasoline-rationed society helped to initiate cropped pedal pushers and turned-up jeans.

For summer, shorts and skirts went with blouses in peasant styles often called Mexican. Casual summer dress with feminine styling might include bodices or shirts of bright printed cotton knotted up to expose a tanned midriff paired with shorts, full skirt, or a sarong à la Dorothy Lamour. Hawaiian, Polynesian, and Mexican prints in bright colours were all the rage [83].

THE WAR ENDS

When the war ended in 1945, everyone wanted to return to a normal life as quickly as possible. Although adjustments were seldom smooth, people gradually dealt with new domestic problems at home. The problems were not only about material things, but also about role playing and lifestyles.

A 1946 survey conducted by the fashion editor of *New World* magazine (Canada's short-lived answer to *Life*) asked one hundred returning Canadian soldiers, sailors, and airmen how they wanted to see the girls back home dressed. They were equally divided on the wearing of hats; they definitely favoured

WOOL DINNER SUIT

WITH A SKIRT THAT

GOES INTO A SPIN

OVER A DISPLAY OF ANKLE

typical of the "after five"

collection at **EATON'S**

f *This wool dinner suit of 1947 has the newly dropped hemline, but still shows the broad shoulders of the war-time silhouette.*

sensible Oxfords or high heels over loafers and open sandals; they liked romantic full skirts for evening much more than slinky, narrow ones; fifty-eight percent voted for bare-shouldered tops and forty-two percent for a covered-up look. The men favoured strings of pearls over chunky costume jewellery or the current armful-of-bangles fad, and they liked pale shades for daytime and black for evening. The results of the survey presented a conservative and conforming picture of young Canadian women in 1946.[6]

Many women who had held full-time jobs during wartime returned to full-time homemaking when the men returned. The new job was the old job of pleasing husband and family. All the former values of a patriarchal society carried Canadians into the 1950s.

DIOR'S NEW LOOK

The fashions for 1946 still featured the same basic silhouette of the past seven or eight years—broad shoulders, the bolero, soft drapery effects for afternoon and evening, and the bare midriff. In a manner similar to the way fashions at the end of World War I picked up 1914 styles, the designs of 1946 echoed those of 1939.

The collection presented in Paris by Christian Dior in the spring of 1947 has come to symbolize the beginning of an era. Instantly labelled as the New Look, it spoke to women's desire to return to a stable and prosperous society as it had existed before the war. Dior was an extremely skilled tailor and he presented beautifully sculpted bodices and jackets with an hour-glass shape, doing away with the aggressive wartime shoulders. He showed luxuriously full and lengthened skirts. Sophisticated black was an important component, as were hats and veils, dramatic makeup, gloves, and high-heeled shoes [79].

Other designers in Europe and North America joined forces with Dior over the next years to present a design message that was consistently glamorous and mature [82]. The year after Dior's sensational debut, fashions suggested a further return to the past with hints even at small-waisted bustle styles [78]. The fitted bodices needed corsetry for a perfect fit; evening gowns might require the strapless, wired bra; full skirts spread wide over layers of petticoats [81].

The promotion of the New Look raised a great cry of protest in many countries where there were continued shortages of materials; money was needed for essentials such as housing and education. With the new silhouette, almost a complete wardrobe replacement was required to be truly chic. Earlier styles did not adapt well to the New Look, although some local dressmakers were very clever at lengthening skirts. In spite of the protests, the New Look, at all levels of society and sophistication, was adopted so thoroughly that ten years passed before the silhouette changed again. Deprived wartime couples were determined to have their share of the good life.

Actually, some fashionable Canadians fared rather well during the war years. Holt Renfrew in Montreal carried Canadian designer Marie-Paule's gowns, suits, and coats. After the war, Holt Renfrew and other department stores resumed copying Parisian haute couture models for their clientele. These copies now included a label of design origin.[7]

CANADIAN RESISTANCE

Dior's New Look show was in February 1947 and by summer the Canadian reaction to it was news in most of the big daily papers. While many fashion-hungry young women considered the longer, fuller skirts dignified and elegant, the opposition was challenging the New Look in editorials and by organized protests. The *Ottawa Citizen* spoke out against "the absurdities of dress makers and stylists," and although the writer saw "signs that Canadian women do not intend to surrender easily to the latest foreign style improvisors," nevertheless questioned whether they would "have the courage and individuality to resist the new trend which so called fashion centres are trying to impose for their own commercial gain."[8]

The *Montreal Gazette* devoted a column and a half to an article headed, "New Longer Look Brings Rebellion from Office Girls Who Let Down Hems in Evening."[9]

A sinister note was struck in a report from New York published in the *Montreal Gazette:* "The new long skirts give shoplifters greater opportunities to conceal stolen articles. The fashions have brought back a once out-moded device consisting of an elastic band fastened above the knee with hooks attached. Stolen articles are swept under the long skirt and hung on the hooks."[10]

The *Toronto Star* reported a Protest Parade against Long Skirts down Yonge Street on 13 September 1947, organized by the National Federation of Labour Youth. The CCF (Co-operative Commonwealth Federation) youth movement in Ottawa urged its members to picket stores displaying the fall fashions: "We protest the high-pressure campaign of the big fashion magazines to bully women back to the fashions of the past,"[11] declared a spokesman.

A *What's Your Beef?* show on CBJC radio in Toronto suggested the formation of a Society for the Prevention of Longer Skirts for Women which was supported by more than 1,500 angry letters from women across Canada: the long skirts hindered them when rushing for streetcars. The full skirts take up too much living space in small flats (remember the housing shortage). Men thought them "awful . . . horrible!"[12]

On 1 December 1947 four male students of the Ottawa University French Debating Society, debated the proposition: "short skirts are more suitable than long skirts to women's personal charm." The affirmative side won.

Some Canadian organizations took a stand regarding skirt lengths for their uniforms. The St. John Ambulance Brigade

Nursing Division decided, "after considerable discussion . . . to recommend that the present length of sixteen inches from the ground—a little below the knee—be retained as smarter and more practical than the fashion trend towards longer skirts."[13] The Red Cross opted for an inch or so longer; the Toronto Transit Commission chose sixteen inches for their guides; and TCA stewardesses wore their skirts one-and-a-half inches below the knee. But the Salvation Army's rule that skirts should be fourteen inches from the floor (this length was established thirty years previously) made it the leader in the New Look uniform fashion parade.

Not all the claims of economics, politics, law and order, health and safety, or even lovers, husbands, and fathers could hold back the tide. Long skirts were in for a number of years, as the consumer fell into line with the manufacturers' moderate interpretations of the New Look. Mr. Sam Farben of the Montreal Dressmaker's Guild summed it up in the *Globe and Mail* of 4 May 1947, albeit somewhat chauvinistically, "I suppose the New Look is here to stay . . . but the idea should have been introduced slowly. If there had been a gradual dropping of the hemlines no one would have noticed the difference, not even the men."[14]

MODERN FOR EVERYONE

As an aftermath to the war, full-skirted crinoline dresses and the bustle revival of 1948 reflected people's nostalgia for Victorian and Edwardian elegance. Nostalgia also partly accounted for the popularity of traditional ballet on stage and in such films as *An American in Paris* (1951), a popularity that created a fashion for full, airy, calf-length cocktail and evening dresses.

The early fifties were a curious blend of nostalgia for the past and a passion for the new and modern. The New Look echoed Victorian romanticism, but the faster tempo of life and a search for basic fundamentals of form in many of the arts encouraged designers to begin to simplify. Many of the elements of 1950s modernism actually began in the years immediately following the war. New kinds of visual symbols were turning up in advertisement illustrations, magazine graphics, and packaging, as well as in designs on textiles. Textile designs were either large-scale, super-realistic floral motifs showing an English influence or they took advantage of the tendency towards dynamic, free-form abstract shapes in the lighter, brighter colours, seen increasingly in the new plastic products. Asymmetrical, moulded shapes appeared in modern jewellery, hats, shoes, and bags.

70 DRESS

A one-piece dress in navy viscose-rayon crepe with chartreuse rayon accents, a fashionable colour scheme in the early forties. With no closure system, it simply pulls on over the head. The collarless bodice front has two navy over-panels giving the more important look of a bolero jacket. The design of this dress aims to create the maximum of function and interest with a minimal amount of fabric and notions.

The Suddon Collection

71 SUIT (jacket and skirt), *about 1942*

A two-button, single-breasted daywear or business suit in charcoal grey pinstriped wool. Throughout the years of World War II the man-tailored suit was an appropriate fashion for the involved Canadian woman. This authoritative jacket has broadly cut squared shoulders, further accented by the angle of the wide peak lapels. The long vented sleeve is trimmed with three buttons. Darts and seams mould the lines to the figure. The jacket is fully lined in black with inside pocket. The unlined skirt is crisp but roomy with a central inverted pleat both front and back. A stitched false hem in black lining fabric keeps lines neat and costs down.

The Suddon Collection

72 EVENING DRESS WITH BOLERO

A navy, rayon crepe, halter-necked dress with bolero jacket in navy-and-white crepe. The dress is shaped to the figure with a sweetheart bust draped above a fitted ribcage and a long, narrow sarong-styled skirt. A metal zip closure is inserted down the left side (no seam). The bolero's padded shoulders and sleeves are accented with white braid, beads, and sequins for a fanciful naval look.

The Suddon Collection

73 COAT

A full-length coat with Persian lamb collar and lapels. The semifitted front has princess seaming and overlaps to fasten asymmetrically with three self-covered buttons. Shoulders are padded and the coat is lined in green satin. A generous Canadian winter coat in spite of wartime rationing and shortages, worn here with fur-trimmed carriage boots.

Label: Bromleigh, John Northway and Son Ltd.　　*The Suddon Collection*

74 AFTERNOON DRESS

A summer day dress in coral rayon "linen," trimmed with edging in beige-and-white stripes. Elbow-length sleeves are both pleated and padded at the shoulders. Tailored styling is offered in front only using a minimal amount of fabric—the pleats are only one-half-inch deep. Pintucks, small pockets, buttons, and edging economically provide visual richness. The built-in cummerbund ties apronlike in the manner of a young girl's dress of the period and suggests more innocent styling than does the front.

The Suddon Collection

75 SUIT (jacket-blouse and slacks)

A two-piece slack outfit for casual wear in green cotton and acetate poplin trimmed with brown-and-white windowpane-checked cotton sailcloth. The use of two contrasting fabrics continues to be popular. The straight-legged slacks have a standard waistband and a low crotch. No zippers during the war years means a buttoned fly closure on the left.

The Suddon Collection

76 UNIFORM, *1943*

A Canadian Women's Army Corps (CWAC) uniform in khaki wool suiting. The single-breasted jacket closes with four brass buttons by United-Carr, showing the insignia of Athene, the Greek Goddess of War and Wisdom. Smaller similar buttons close two large hip pockets, expandable in the style of a poacher pocket. The jacket is neatly fitted to the torso with darts and seams and the slightly padded shoulders are accented with buttoned, brown wool epaulettes.

The unlined, six-gored, khaki skirt has a standard waistband, metal Lightning zipper (Made in Canada) in left seam, very wide seam allowances, and a false hem in brown wool crepe.

The CWAC was established in 1941 in response to the need for assistance in the war effort. Women were trained as non-combatant clerks and as technicians for radio, telephone, and automobile operations. They were integrated into the Canadian Militia in 1942. More than 21,000 women served before its dissolution in 1946.

Jacket Label: Jacket size I, Height 5'0 and 1, Waist 25"-26", Breast 33"-34", Sterling Cloak Co. Ltd., Winnipeg, Canada, 1943.
Skirt Label: Size 2, Waist 25", Hip 38"
Worn by V.M. Scott. The right sleeve shows that V.M. Scott was a telegraphist with rank of sergeant and two years' service.
The Seneca College Collection

77 SUMMER DRESS, *about 1944*
A short and snappy dress for cycling, tennis, or other summer sport in a creamy beige rayon fabric. The front-buttoning shirtwaist style has shirring detail for ease of movement and short sleeves with five darts at the sleeve head giving width through the shoulders. A metal Talon zipper is fitted into the left seam through the waist. The six-gored skirt is trimmed with flaring vertical rows of nearly matching piping, adding richness of texture to a fairly skimpy skirt.
The Suddon Collection

78 DRESS, *about 1948*
A short, glamorous dress in rayon faille with a bustle effect. The print is a very stylish sketchy-drawing motif in navy, rose, green, and tan on an aqua ground. The shirring and draping at the back was one of the themes of 1948, in keeping with the interest in bustles emerging in Paris just after the war.
Label: Laurie, Toronto, Canada   *The Suddon Collection*

79 TWO-PIECE DRESS, *about 1949*

An afternoon dress in black wool. The bodice is fitted with long waist darts and the slim raglan sleeves create a natural shoulder. The unusual shawl collar closes asymmetrically.

A long and very full permanently pleated skirt fits tightly at the waist over a black silk lower portion of the bodice. Stitched to the inner waistband is a full, double-layered, black tulle petticoat. All seams are handfinished. Black patent leather belt.

Designer: Christian Dior, Paris
Worn by Mrs. Dora Matthews   *Royal Ontario Museum*

80 GOWN

A full-length evening gown in printed rayon faille and black rayon sheer. The bodice is of black faille printed in a bold, impressionistic floral motif in red with ribbon motifs in bright green. The double-layered skirt comprises the black sheer scattered with floral appliqués over black taffeta. The bodice is cut and shirred to create a curvaceous torso, and the short sleeves are padded at the shoulder.

The Suddon Collection

81 GOWN, *about 1949*

A dramatic one-piece gown in brown embossed satin with brown net panniers and overskirt. The strapless and boned bodice closes centre back with a metal zipper and is trimmed with opaque berry-and-leaf-shaped glass pink-and-brown beads. The browns of the two fabrics do not match. (Fath made popular the combination of blue and green, previously considered a clash of colours.) The hourglass silhouette is accented by the pleated panniers formed over buckram supports. The varied hemline in eveningwear at this time leads to the longer and more luxuriously full skirt of the 1950s.

Designer: Jacques Fath, Paris
Worn by Mrs. John David Eaton   *Royal Ontario Museum*

82 COAT, *about 1950*

A lightweight, fitted coat in grey-and-white slubby ottoman. Superb fit is achieved with double princess seaming front and back. Dolman sleeves give softly rounded shoulders. Self-covered buttons taper to a tiny waist. Here is the postwar silhouette in all its glamour. Luxurious detailing includes buttoned pockets worked in at front waist, bound buttonholes, and the intricately tiered skirts, as well a considerable amount of handstitching.

Designer: Cornelia, Toronto   *The Suddon Collection*

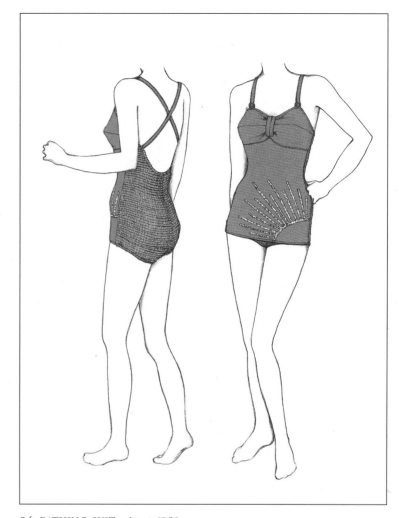

83 SUNDRESS, *about 1947*
A halter dress for resort wear in printed cotton. The hibiscus print on white ranges from navy blue through turquoise to light aqua. (Exotic Hawaiian and Mexican prints were very popular in North America in the forties.) The fitted bodice has elasticized shirring on each side and a boned bustline. The sarong skirt is a natural here.
Label: Alfred Shaheen, Honolulu
Worn by Mrs. Silverman   *Royal Ontario Museum*

84 BATHING SUIT, *about 1950*
A periwinkle-blue bathing suit in cotton and rayon faille. The suit is lined in matching acetate tricot and trimmed with silver glitter. The elastic shirring through the entire back creates a fitted suit with a nonstretch fabric and no closure system. Straps hook in front.
Label: Pedigree product, Made in Canada, 36"   *The Suddon Collection*

a *Afternoon elegance of the early 1950s.*

• T H E •
1950s

IN 1945/46, RETURNING SOLDIERS AND REUNITED COUPLES WERE THE catalyst for a new era. The natural desire to sort out one's life again and to re-establish family ties was the order of the day. A rash of delayed domesticity broke out and this period saw the biggest increase ever in births, a boom that was to have a great impact on marketing by the late 1950s. Popular culture, as expressed in films and women's magazines, stressed family togetherness. Most women's lives now centred around nurturing this lifestyle in the new suburban developments that sprang up in an effort to meet urgent housing needs. The media portrayed the Canadian woman as the happy homemaker and stylish hostess.

In spite of some weak sectors, the 1950s saw impressive economic, physical, and cultural growth in most parts of Canada, and many households were better off than they had been at the start of the war. An article in *Mayfair* on the state of the 1951 economy claimed, however, "with Canadians' income at an all-time high, inflation is the concern of every citizen . . . But until they hear the 'action stations' rattler, Canadians will go on consuming at a rate undreamed of outside North America . . . at a rate hardly dreamed of by Canadians themselves a generation ago."[1]

Urban population far outnumbered that of rural Canada by this time. The greatest expansion took place in the dozen or so largest metropolitan areas, which grew by half of their former size in ten years. Planned developments, such as Don Mills in Toronto, led the way with a collection of amenities for attractive city life: schools, a community centre, theatres and a shopping plaza. Tourism increased greatly, and the thirty-five hour work-week enabled people to travel to cottage country or, at least, to entertain in their backyards around barbeques. New drive-in movie theatres proliferated throughout the countryside.

By the mid-fifties, the lifestyle of most Canadians centred around the house in the suburbs, children in the house, and a flashy American-styled car to take them all anywhere they wanted to go. Often they wanted to go to the nearest shopping mall. North American consumerism was being invented and born-to-shop people got a head start in this decade. Their children would grow up to be labelled yuppies.

SHOPPING CENTRES

The marketing concept of finding out what the customer wants and then selling that to her, although it started in the 1930s, now began to be used as never before. Until the development of the shopping centre, stores in most cities and towns were on the main commercial stretches of downtown streets; parking cars near shops became a problem as populations increased rapidly. In the small stores or in the dress departments of the large stores, salespeople waited on customers and personal service was an important part of sales.

To expand your clientele beyond a certain point depended upon automobile access. With crowded conditions, city-centre transportation became a challenge. Street parking and thorough-fares and city transportation systems were improved when possible. In Toronto in 1954 Canada opened its first subway which brought shoppers downtown along Yonge Street. Down-town shopping in Montreal was thriving so much that in 1957 Eaton's on St. Catherine Street expanded its facilities and became the largest department store in Canada. Times were so good that in addition to all the downtown action, suburban malls in most cities were developing rapidly.

In the 1950s suburban growth radically changed the Canadian landscape and life began to centre around the plaza. The earliest were strips of retail businesses with attached parking lots. Canada's first shopping centre, the Northgate Shopping Centre in Quebec, was built in 1949 and followed the next year by one in Dorval and the Park Royal Centre in West Vancouver. Toronto's Sunnybrook Plaza, built in 1952, opened with seventeen stores and was promoted as following a modern retail merchandising trend which had already made a deep impression in America. A mother could shop for all her family needs without leaving the centre.[2] Much larger suburban plazas or malls soon followed the Sunnybrook Plaza, but these centres, still exposed to the elements, were only the beginning.

Yorkdale, an indoor shopping mall, opened in North Toronto in the early sixties. Yorkdale was, at the time, the largest and most spectacular indoor shopping mall in Canada, and Eaton's and Simpson's were both under the same roof there. In the 1980s, Toronto's Eaton Centre and Montreal's Place Ville Marie each combined downtown office and retail space and revitalized the city cores. Alberta's 1988 megamall, the West Edmonton Mall, took the concept even further with some 800 stores mixed with recreational and community space in a controlled indoor environment.

Enclosed malls became favourite places to stroll and window-shop, especially in bad weather. By the fifties in-store layouts and window displays in Canadian shops were becoming more sophisticated. Lightweight, fibreglass display mannequins began to replace the heavy plaster models, which made handling and dressing much easier. The shapes of the 1950s female manne-quins reflected the girdled figures of the era.

CITY GIRLS

The female counterpart to the business executive, the "man in the grey flannel suit," began to emerge in urban centres at this time. Greater numbers of young women found careers in areas other than teaching and nursing, in particular, as office account-ants, stenographers, secretaries, and typists. They were often referred to as career girls.

Even Hollywood was putting women into the corporate workplace. A number of popular fifties films made heroines of women executives dressed in highly fashionable business wear. Katherine Hepburn played the role in *Pat and Mike*, and Nina Foch, Barbara Stanwyck, and Shelley Winters in *Executive Suite* in 1954.

White-collar workers, as well as the affluent nonworking wife, paid great attention to fashion news from Paris. The front-page coverage of Parisian style news in most Canadian daily papers heightened women's impression that they were powerless to rebel against Paris dictates.

The conservative early fifties city suit was made in traditional menswear suiting fabrics (wool worsted, flannels, small checks, subtle plaids, fine tweeds, gabardine, duvetyne). English tailoring was a favourite with Toronto women. Holt Renfrew at Yonge and Adelaide promoted collections in the early fifties as showing

b
The cut of coats in the early 1950s often demanded a stylish cinched waist.

combined the career woman and suburban mother when it featured "grey menswear flannel to suit mothers-to-be."[3] Dark and neutral colours for fall and winter were required immediately after Labour Day, regardless of the weather. Charcoal to medium greys, black, dark tweed mixtures, coffee brown and beige, and, on occasion, navy blue, wine, mulberry, or even rich red were worn. Jackets were usually long and figure fitting, but shorter, less formal styles appeared by 1953. Different shapes of tailored pocket flaps and lapels **[85]** created a minimal amount of variety.

With long straight sleeves and turned-back cuffs, the most elegant versions of women's suits were so moulded to the figure that one couldn't wear a blouse. Necklines were filled in by pearl necklaces or scarves often held with sparkling pins for a dressy look.

Clothes were fitted over a highly stylized form created through controlling underwear. The waist was always small, belted or not, and the peplum of the long jackets often padded or darted to enhance rounded hips. Of course, the padded or "pencil-sharpener" bra helped with the shapes on top. Even the soft cashmere sweater was always draped over a stiffened bra. The way to look sexy in a suit was for it to have a well-fitted, buttocks-revealing, long sheath skirt, kick-pleated at the centre-back hem. The sheath, as opposed to the full skirt, was at once professional looking and alluring. The skirt was fitted to the figure, but not the wearer's figure, so panty-girdles were essential. No well-dressed woman in the 1950s ever jiggled or bulged in the wrong places; conventions were too rigid to allow for that kind of honesty.

Gloves, high-heeled pumps, and a hat were still essential daywear for any really stylish woman. For the cocktail hour a tailored afternoon suit could be dressed up with a small but entertaining hat, gloves, and a glitter pin or pearls, with perhaps a fur stole. The perennial little black dress was indispensible for occasions of undefined formality; it was sophisticated and yet neutral and could be dressed up or down.

the smart look of London. Other leading shops—Morgan's, Ogilvy's, Eaton's, and Simpson's—also carried ready-to-wear suits and coats by fine English tailors, such as Lachasse, Dereta, Hardie Amies, Charles Creed, and Peter Russell.

Canadian-made fashions were often in imported British wools. A brown-and-beige English wool gabardine Bromleigh coat and suit were advertised in 1951 by Northway and Son at 240 Yonge Street in Toronto. Holt Renfrew advertised in 1952 that they had an original Hardie Amies of London suit and also eight Hardie Amies outfits that they had reproduced in English-bought fabric, these offered at great savings.

Brown and beiges were popular, but the grey flannel look was everywhere. A maternity fashion ad in a 1950 *Vogue*

One idea in the 1950s about being well-groomed was that the hemline of skirt and coat should line up perfectly, with the exception of casual car coats and toppers. Even the three-quarter-length coat wasn't the right length anymore when Paris decreed a hemline change of so many inches.

Some coats, either full-length or short, and described as a pyramid style, flared full in back and often had wide-cuffed, three-quarter sleeves [90]. *Mayfair* magazine in 1951 ran a Holt Renfrew ad for a reversible pyramid number in plain coatings and muted plaid tweeds.[4] Creeds in Toronto was clearing some stylish pyramid coats with very full sleeves in 1952 when they were getting ready for the big move to 27 Bloor Street West. The chesterfield coat style with velvet collar was considered very chic throughout this decade.

DESIGNER FASHION IN CANADA

After World War II, French couture quickly reestablished itself to its former level of worldwide prestige, even while its actual clientele was shrinking in numbers. In order to survive financially, some couture houses expanded their operations to include a broader market, not by producing ready-to-wear, but by allowing easier copying. Stronger links with North American manufacturers made it possible for designer copies to appear quickly in Canadian shops.

The best stores, such as Morgan's and Holt Renfrew, regularly took full-page photo-ads in *Mayfair* advertising afternoon dresses, suits, and gowns by couturiers such as Dior, Dessès, Grés, Balenciaga, and Fath. As well as originals, Holt Renfrew and Morgan's also carried and promoted their copies of couture clothing and described them as made in the custom manner at a fraction of the costs of the originals.

Morgan's and Holt Renfrew also regularly advertised in local newspapers, particularly the *Globe and Mail*. A Morgan's ad in 1952 illustrated a copy of an original by Fath, a silk organza blouse in gold or grey, with picture-frame collar and full sleeves, plus a full black bengaline skirt. This style of blouse in organza was the prototype used in the mass production of nylon blouses for the middle market. Not all style leaders came from Paris. Holt Renfrew advertised an Italian copy of a stylish suit but no designer's name was mentioned.

The House of Dior reigned supreme in the early fifties. There was an almost built-in obsolescence as Christian Dior's creative genius provided something new each season to please everyone —couture clients as well as retail store buyers and wholesalers who were buying copyrights. In Dior's 1954 collection he began to make silhouette changes to the severe hourglass so firmly locked in since 1947. For the next three years his haute couture lines eased away from the New Look styling. His sudden death in 1957 helped to launch his assistant designer Yves Saint Laurent as a new star.

Jacques Fath created sexy daywear and evening gowns. He was known for slender lines and a strong preference for angles and points. His unusually inventive approach to colour helped to loosen up rigid ideas about what "went" with what. For example, he combined blue and green in one outfit, while most designers were following the rather dull colour rules of the era.

Other important Paris couturiers at this time were Cristobal Balenciaga, Nina Ricci, Pierre Balmain, Jean Dessès [95], and Hubert de Givenchy. With the films *Funny Face* in 1957 and *Breakfast at Tiffany's* in 1961, Givenchy's crisp avant-garde designs for Audrey Hepburn helped to establish her elegant gamine image. By the late decade Pierre Cardin was also one of the leading names of the avant-garde [96].

Change was in the air in 1954. Both Balenciaga and Dior were introducing a straighter silhouette to their haute couture lines, but not quickly enough for Coco Chanel, who had closed her doors in 1940 and who had been watching Dior's influence with disgust. Chanel decided to stage a comeback because she felt women were ready again for her simpler and more functional approach to dress. In her seventies at the time of her reopening, she met considerable success, if not with the press with North American sales. The style message of her smart suits spread from high fashion to mass production.

American designers began to make an international name for themselves during World War II and were highly regarded in Canada. After the war an editorial in *Mayfair* said, "Now that quota restrictions on imports have been lifted, we may expect a greater selection of New York designer fashions."[5] The same issue of *Mayfair* showed a blue silk shantung cocktail and dinner dress by Hattie Carnegie, polo-belted pedal-pushers in royal blue cotton duck by Tina Leser and various fashions by Nettie Rosenstein, Pauline Trigere, and Adele Simpson. The innovative designer Claire McCardell, as well as Ann Fogarty and Norman Norell were other notable American designers throughout the forties and fifties.

Canadian designers in the 1950s were relatively unsung. In Montreal there were a number of couturiers who supplied clients with elegant suits, coats, and gowns, usually very much in the Parisian style of the day.

Raoul-Jean Fouré was a Frenchman who married a Montrealer, Margaret Mount, and settled there in 1927. His specialty was bridalwear for Montreal society. He moved his studio de couture from Sherbrooke West to a four-storey townhouse at 1748 Cedar and in 1951 took on an assistant, Jacques de Montjoye.

In 1954 Fouré founded the Canadian Association of Couturiers. With fourteen members the association was sponsored by the textile industry and was to promote Canadian textiles and designers at home and abroad. That very year, the couturiers held the first all-Canadian fashion show outside the country in the Hotel Pierre in New York and made a creditable start at educating American buyers who had been expecting a "woolen-minded"[6] collection. The association lasted nearly ten years and

c *Cornelia of Toronto created this collection of glamorous gowns using the finest European silks and trims.*

included D'Anjou, Jacques Michel, France Davies, Philippe de Sève, Louis Berai, Bianca Gusmaroli, and Marie-Paule Nolin all of Montreal, and Frederica, Tibor de Nagy, and Cornelia of Toronto.

Marie-Paule Nolin left Holt Renfrew in Montreal when the store began to carry Parisian copies after the war. Nolin worked out of various Westmount addresses through the fifties until she moved her business to Bousecours Street where she remained until her retirement in 1973. Women of the Bronfman and Desmarais families were among her clients, and she designed both private and theatrical fashions for Quebec actress Jeanine Beaubien.[7]

Cornelia of Toronto, one of the city's important couturières, opened her salon at 232 Bloor West in 1947. She brought her Hungarian-born talents to the art of couture and dressed both the Toronto career girl and fashionable socialites from far and wide. Her specialty was glamorous and dramatic eveningwear, using the finest luxury fabrics from France and from Canada. She employed fourteen workers, including Frederica, before Frederica opened her own salon. Although Cornelia did produce one line of ready-to-wear for Morgan's in the early fifties, a refined fit and the distinctive look of couture were her passions. The Wool Bureau of Canada and the *Globe and Mail* sponsored a special showing of her designs in Miami, Florida, in 1959.

In Toronto and area, other couture names of note were Georges Couture, Marie Cluthe, Chez Madame, Simon's Gowns and Wraps, and Beube's Coats and Gowns, all on Bloor Street, as well as Tibor de Nagy, who specialized in elegant dresses of softly draped fabrics, and Olivia of Hamilton. Ruth Frocks in Sunnyside was one of the first specialty bridalwear shops in Toronto. The Ruth Frocks shop was managed by Maude Burgess and owned by Adam Eckerd, who, in about 1960, purchased John Northway's a couple of years before its bankruptcy. Some Canadian sportswear design houses were Lou Ritchies, Pedigree, Irving, and Lore Maria Wiener of Vancouver.

New advertising methods produced wider markets for brand name fashion lines. The Frenchshire and Blackshire labels in dresses, suits, and gowns were particularly successful throughout much of Canada in these years. Full-page illustrated ads in *Mayfair* magazines in 1951 invited readers to write to Montreal for their Frenchshire style books. The style book featured highly sophisticated black-and-white photographs of their lines.

The Fashion Group Incorporated, a New York-based international organization to promote cooperation in fashion businesses, industry, and education formed regional associations in Montreal and Toronto. These groups have sponsored special events and fashion shows regularly ever since and have had a considerable impact on the development of fashion awareness in Canada.

COCKTAILS AND EVENINGS

Throughout the 1950s traditional formal evening dress continued as an integral part of women's wardrobes and was essential for dances, balls, the theatre, university and high-school proms, and bar mitzvahs. The shorter, full-skirted, semiformal styles, sometimes called the ballerina length, were more popular than full-length gowns for all but the most formal occasions. Long or short, the romanticism of postwar styles continued to be expressed in skirts spread as full as those of the Victorian period. In fact, there were many nineteenth-century ideals at the foundation of fifties society and the skirts were an obvious symbol [87]. Crinolines kept skirts spread wide. Eaton's had double-skirted petticoats of stiff nylon net for about twelve dollars in 1952.

Long and short lace, tulle, or net gowns in pastels were favoured by debutantes and other young ladies. The 1951 Ottawa debs presented at Rideau Hall along with the Honorable Rose Alexander, daughter of Governor General Viscount and Lady Alexander, were all gowned in pastel lace and tulle, off-the-shoulder or strapless, with the requisite corsage. Similarly dressed debs could be found all across the country from Victoria to Halifax. For the more mature, satin or taffeta gowns had a sophisticated air. Evening drama was created with plunging necklines, bare shoulders, spaghetti straps, or strapless bodices. Shapes were sculptured and controlled, never drapy or languid. The red evening gown or the black cocktail dress always presented a dramatic contrast to the fluffy pastels [88 and 94].

...and how it works

The Count of Fourteen originated in the fashion world of Paris in the last century and its principles are used by smart women everywhere today. The rule was that to be really chic, "no woman should have *more* than fourteen points of interest visible in her costume."

In other words everything that *shows*, counts 1 point or more, depending on how elaborate. A *simple* hat, even though wildly smart—1 point. A hat with much trimming *and* a veil—up to 4 points. Plain pumps—1 point: with a bow—2 points, and so on.

Look at the two extreme examples at the right. Our girl is going out for a special evening—cocktails or dinner or a party. She has a very smart dark dress with a pretty neckline and matching jacket. Trying to feel "dressed-up" she adds everything but the kitchen sink—fussy hat with veiling (4 points), dangly earrings, fancy shoes and gloves, until she ends up with 25 points—and looking like a bargain counter. Below she's dressed with taste and charm—her total count . . . 10 points.

So before you go out, look in the mirror—and when in doubt—*SUBTRACT*.

TOTAL 25

TOTAL 10

21

d *A 1950s lesson in good taste from* Career Girls' Wardrobe Guide. *Jean Miller, Canada's leading fashion illustrator in 1958, helped create this booklet for the Wool Bureau of Canada. A graduate of the Ontario College of Art, Miller also illustrated many ads for Simpson's, which appeared in the* Toronto Telegram.

A cocktail dress was less formal than an evening or dinner gown, but dressier than street wear. Designers were often intrigued by the challenge of converting office wear into cocktail dress by the removal of a jacket and adding accessories. Frenchshire offered in one of their style books: "two complete outfits [in one] . . . On the slim sheath dress, a bodice of self-dyed wool lace backed by nude marquisette. The long roll collar softens the figure-following jacket"[8] that matched the dress and turned it into a business-suit look.

THE NEW FABRICS

Before the Second World War all dress fabrics were made of natural fibres—silk, wool, cotton, and linen—or of the early artificial fibres—rayon and acetate. In the 1950s various kinds of fabrics of artificial fibres were used in clothing, including nylon, the first truly synthetic fabric. Silks, especially sturdy shantung, Moygashel Irish linen, and Viyella, a washable combination of wool and cotton, were favourites, but new fabrics with easy-care qualities soon widened the range of choices.

The crisp, smoothly sculptured lines of the fashion silhouette demanded firm materials and often plenty of starching and ironing. No wonder servantless, middle-class Canadians, concerned about looking correct and neat, accepted the easy-care fibres with enthusiasm.

The early use of nylon fabrics for clothing began with men's shirts and stockings and slips for women, but other fashions soon followed. In 1951 Creeds of Toronto advertised in the *Globe and Mail* "white nylon blouses for every wear. Dainty, ultra feminine wardrobe pet—billowy push-up sleeves, tiny tucks . . . $11.95."[9]

Quick-drying nylon blouses were practical to a degree, but so sheer that camisoles or slips were needed to cover brassieres. The popularity of these nylon garments declined because they were uncomfortably warm to wear and yellowed fairly rapidly.

Nylon floral-printed sheers were used in the common shirtwaist dresses of the period, and nylon was also made up in textured seersucker and plissé for summer outfits. In the early years of the decade, Simpson's featured many variations of the light and feminine shirtwaist, mostly from New York. By 1952 fashion designers were using DuPont's Orlon (acrylic) and the new textured nylon fibre, Banlon, to produce easy-care pullovers and popular sweater sets. Orlon woven to look like shantung was advertised by Simpson's as nearly wash and wear, and cotton denim was used in colours other than indigo and combined with the new fibres for sportswear.

The wash and wear qualities of polyester were demonstrated by Cary Grant in the 1963 movie *Charade* when he wore his polyester suit while taking a shower. Canada's television singing star Joyce Hahn promoted polyester Terylene blouses in a 1957 issue of *Mayfair*.

Polyester was offered in a sixty-five–thirty-five percent blend with cotton as a new fabric that combined the crispness with easy care. Orlon and cotton blends were used in summer sundresses. Blends offered easy washing, no discolouring, fast drying, wrinkle resistance, and little or no ironing.

Triacetate, an easy-care relative of the older cellulose acetate, was also introduced in the fifties. Acrylics were being promoted as sturdy, warm, and washable fibres that competed well with wool for pullovers and cardigans. Lycra appeared in 1959 and because of Lycra's great stretch control, the swimwear and undergarment industries were revolutionized.

New fibres don't tell the whole story of fifties fabrics. A palette of pastels, derived from colours seen in the new plastics, showed up in textiles as yellow, chartreuse, mint, aquamarine, turquoise, rose, pale pink, and salmon. Pinks and certain greens, aqua, and turquoise were favourites. Even the sophisticated world of couture was affected: a *Mayfair* ad for Morgan's showed a Christian Dior of New York dress in "turquoise linen with a 'hand-span' waist."[10]

Black was still important, turning up in the black turtleneck, the little black dress, capri pants, and eveningwear. Classic Dior red was another dramatic alternative, which emerged as a favourite by the later decade.

Textile designers in the 1950s produced some new looks in prints. Patterns were straightforward in their repeat, motifs usually set out on a solid background. The motif, more often than not, was an abstract shape reminiscent of the ameoba, the artist's palette, a boomerang or fins, or some other fast-moving form, all sculptural shapes with rounded corners. The English influence showed up in realistic florals, and even those tended to be suspended in an orderly manner [89].

STATUS ACCESSORIES

Most accessories in the fifties were geared towards a status image. The exception was the developing teenage market. No one took plastic poppet beads seriously, although they were very popular with young women for several seasons. Costume jewellery most often imitated expensive, precious jewels, particularly diamonds in traditional settings. Cheap rhinestones were everywhere, in necklaces, earrings, and the ubiquitous scatter-pin and were even applied directly onto sweaters. Rhinestones were part of people's concern with status.

In an era that was anything but spontaneous, one often saw matching sets of necklaces, earrings, and pins. Sometimes styles were based on the speed-crazy fifties technology and other times traditionalism prevailed in such motifs as flowers, animals, swirling stars, snowflakes, and, of course, ballerinas. Pearls and jewelled or fur collars might finish the necklines of angora or cashmere sweaters.

The mink coat or jacket was perhaps the most sought-after

ACCESSORIES

Hats – 4
    2 in basic colour and
    1 summer, 1 cocktail
Gloves – 4 pr.
    1 basic colour
    1 evening, 2 light
Handbags – 3
    1 basic, 1 summer
    1 cocktail – evening

Shoes – 6 pr.
    2 basic, 1 summer
    2 dressy, 1 walking
Stockings – 6 pr. (1 colour)
Scarves – 2
Belts – 2
Jewellery – 3 sets

e *Accessories of 1958 as drawn by Jean Miller for the Wool Bureau of Canada.*

fur piece. Canadian furs continued to be tops. Some Toronto furriers of note were Holt Renfrew, Eaton's, Sellers-Gough, Stan Walkers, and Colquhouns. The fur department of Creed's carried designer furs such as those by Ben Kahn. Ranch or wild, mink's prestige was rivalled only by chinchilla.

For those who couldn't afford a whole jacket, a fur stole was the ultimate in simple display and became an international symbol of fashion status. Stoles served no functional purpose and even needed both hands to keep them on.

Hats showed signs of disappearing as early as the fifties, but most stylish women had some—flat sailor styles and Bretons, cloches, little caps, pixie shapes, and turbans. The hat disappeared in sections: first it became smaller, then lost its brim altogether (the popular pillbox) or was a brim without a crown, and eventually melted away to a mere hairband holding a small veil. By 1960 hair was more important than hats. Fifties hair styles were as firmly sculpted as the dress, although a softer, more casual, Italian shaggy cut appeared as an alternative.

The 1950s glamour face had strongly defined eyebrows, shaded eyelids, and boldly sculptured lips. All this drama might have been framed by a little cocktail hat. A wardrobe of coordinating gloves was also needed, including white summer shorties in cotton or nylon, longer leather gloves for fall suits and coats, and full-length, multibuttoned ones for formal dress.

Shoes changed greatly through the decade although some early styles kept a thick-soled chunkiness left over from the forties. Pumps, cut fairly high on the instep, with rounded toes and sturdy high heels, were worn with chic daywear. Emily Post, dictator of etiquette and proper dress, stated in the mid-fifties that open sandals with evening dress were too vulgar to mention.[11] They persisted, however. Stockings were more often seamless now. By the later fifties, the Italian influence in shoes was producing a predominance of ultra-narrow stiletto heels and more pointed toes. Flat Capezios were considered essential for casual dress for beatniks and teenagers, but the latter might also wear canvas running shoes, loafers, or saddle shoes.

A look at fashion of this time period would not be complete without a mention of the fifties bra. The underwear needed to create the ideal uplifted shape could be nearly as restrictive as that of the Edwardian period. In addition to the girdles, still used for hose support as well as for shaping the figure, the fifties bra was essential for the high, pointed, and even separated, uplift that fashion demanded. Many bras were underwired or padded, and even the simplest were of stiffly stitched sturdy fabrics, such as woven cottons, rayon, or satin. The one-piece combination bra and girdle was worn by some women for a smooth line under sheath dresses.

FIFTIES CASUAL

Casual dress at this time was considerably more formal than it is today. Most Canadians still seemed to agree with Emily Post that slacks were only proper on a boat, at a picnic, or perhaps to play golf. Shorts were to be worn only at the beach or on the tennis courts. Never would you be seen on city streets in shorts.[12]

Acceptable dress for country or suburbs was based on the shirtwaister dress **[86]** or separates. Comfortable skirts in wool or cotton, often gathered or pleated, were paired with pullover sweaters, preferably imported cashmere by Braemar or Lansea, or tailored cotton blouses. For the complete prep-school look, the formula involved kilts, grey flannel skirts, classic pumps, loafers, espadrilles, Oxford cloth shirts, polo-necked T-shirts, Fair Isle sweaters, sweater sets, tennis pullovers, and cable-knit cardigans, as well as polo coats in camel's hair, and Burberrys.[13]

Fifties traditionalism included a great surge of enthusiasm for country music, dance, and dress. Fiddle music and square dancing were an important part of Canadian popular culture. *Don Messer and His Islanders* was a countrywide institution on radio and, later, on television. The program's dancers wore full-skirted country fashions for some performances, and, at other times, richly decorated ethnic dress.

By mid-decade there were already signs of a shake-up. As the more relaxed suburban lifestyle predominated and travel increased, women were offered a greater variety of pant styles which then began to cross clothing barriers. Mannish slacks were replaced by slim-fitting pants whose names varied with the season and the crop point on the lower leg—matadors, toreadors, capris, slim-jims, and pedal-pushers, all with side or back closures and usually worn with flat shoes like Capezios and crisp, tailored tops **[91]**. Eaton's carried sweater blouses and cotton T-shirts with new styling from Milan in 1952. These T-shirts were neater and more formal than the later variety.

f
Casual pants in the style of the late 1950s. Illustration by Jean Miller.

Just-above-the-knee Bermuda shorts, especially worn with knee socks, had become so respectable for both men and women that a few daring Canadian men copied the American rebels who wore them to work in New York during the heat of the 1952 summer. Certainly this kind of sportswear helped to bring men's and women's dress closer together. For any woman feeling a little hesitant about the acceptability of pants, there were culottes trying to be the best of both worlds.

A casual style favoured by the young was the jumper, sleeveless and scoop-necked with full or sheath skirt, and worn over a blouse or sweater. An eccentric or arty look in dress was identified as beatnik—pony-tails, peasant blouses, turtleneck sweaters, tweedy jumpers, black tights, wooden beads, and desert boots. The early Audrey Hepburn image glamorized the look and added a touch of ballet—black turtleneck, soft skirts or slim pants, and flat slippers.

Most summer sportswear at this time bore the stamp of New Look glamour. Bathing suits were mainly one-piece with an excessive amount of boning and lining. In 1952 Simpson's showed fitted suits in striped Lastex, and skirted bathing suits in rayon satin, as well as playclothes by Cole of California. Iona Monahan's editorial feature in a spring 1957 *Mayfair* showed sturdy maillots and tank suits in cotton and other knits by Rose Marie Reid and Jantzen, and a Rudi Gernreich suit with "minimum coverage," although it only differed from the other suits by a slightly raised legline. The original bikini was a relatively modest two-piece suit, not accepted in North America until the 1960s.

THE TEENAGE MARKET

The growing prosperity of North America put buying power for the first time into the hands of a young generation. Teenagers became a target group for advertising and marketing strategies. Although many young women never considered rebelling against the rules and were only too eager to adopt the grown-up style of the time, others sought novelty. The gap between the generation of the depression and the war years and their offspring was very great.

Fashion for the tuned-in Canadian teenager was a blend of mainstream styling from Paris, England, or Italy and the young looks that came from the United States. The Americanized teenager was much discussed and worried over, just as the flapper had been before her. Teenagers were the centre of such corruption as horror comics, bubble gum, automobile madness, and rock and roll. Elvis Presley was an American sex symbol

of new variety. The popular music and dance of the era, particularly jive, sometimes flung the girl high over her partner's back, making the most of skirts that allowed peek-a-boo titillation.

New ideas were travelling farther and faster via television, American fashion magazine like *Seventeen* and *Mademoiselle*, Hollywood movies, popular music from rock and roll to love ballads, and *Life* magazine. All this now seemingly innocent pop culture was expressed in young people's dress of the era. The small waist and bouffant skirt appealed to the romantic young and combined conformity and nostalgia for nineteenth-century elegance. The more layers of crinolines spreading a skirt the better and, as for the small waist, the elastic cincher belt was effective and stylish. Shoes were flat—oxfords, bucks, or saddle shoes often worn with white ankle socks. Even for teenagers, the ideal look was both neat and new. Blue jeans, worn only for informal occasions, were straight legged, loose fitting and normal waisted.

TRANSITION

Signs of social change for women were appearing by mid-decade. Barriers that women who wanted to work had previously encountered began to be lowered, and there was greater acceptance of the working woman. Factors that hastened changes were improved birth control, more training available for women, and reduced working hours per day and per week.

The year 1957 seemed to mark the actual beginning of the end to the fifties. The Russians launched Sputnik, the first earth-orbiting satellite, and the space age began. To express such an expansion, dress had to change radically.

There were signs of a change in women's silhouette several years earlier, but primarily with couture. Balenciaga and Dior made simple suits with jackets that were figure skimming instead of figure hugging, skirts only several inches below the knee,

Glowing Colour and
Studied Ease...
The Exciting Essence
of Fashion

EATON'S FALL FASHION PRESENTATION 1957

g   *Eaton's 1957 fall presentation was right on top of the new, easier silhouette of that year.*

collars away from the neck and sleeves from the wrists [92 and 93]. Chanel's tweedy cardigan suits were an instant classic in North America where functional dress was especially valued.

Paris designers knew women were no longer obsessed with the waist, so they were experimenting to anticipate the new direction. Couturiers such as Givenchy, Cardin [96], and Yves Saint Laurent for Dior were changing the silhouette even more radically.

The Parisian chemise of 1958, a loose and fluid garment, did not translate well to mass marketing. The silhouette change was too abrupt for women who had not perceived the subtle adjustments of previous seasons. *Vogue* magazine considered the situation an emergency: "too many women are plunging into chemises without knowing how to wear them. They haven't found the winning combination in chemise techniques."[14] *Vogue's* recommendations for success with the chemise included: shorter hemline, fabric snug under the arms, and some taper from bosom to hipline but a snug fit through the hips.

Retailers who were well stocked with chemises that season promoted them enthusiastically. Simpson's carried spring lines in Dacron with cotton and in linen by Toronto manufacturer Miss Sun Valley and promoted the garments in a somewhat defensive way, claiming that a subtly fitting chemise could do wonders for a girl's figure. Lack of fluidity in some manufacturers' fabric choices for the chemise did not work well with the shape and people believed at the time that it was the men's veto that killed it. The most extreme versions of the chemise came to a puff below the derrière and were ridiculed [99]. Many manufacturers who had bet on the new styles went out of business.

The experiments with the chemise shape did lead to a major silhouette change eventually and within a few years simple chemiselike silhouettes were the norm. In the meantime, full skirts became even fuller, an example of the extremities to which a fashion often goes just before it disappears [97]. Two things were clear, hems were shortening and styles were simpler [98].

By the later half of the decade, in keeping with the space age, many round and compact forms became long and pointed in such products as lamps and other furniture, automobiles, eyeglasses, and shoe styles. In 1959 Naturalizer ads referred not only to the stiletto heel but to the stiletto toe. Things Italian were very much "in" all over North America, especially Sophia Loren and Gina Lollobrigida, espresso coffee bars, and Italian love songs.[15]

An unusual entry into the worldwide fashion scene was that of Finnish designer and business woman Armi Maria Ratia who founded the Marimekko company which produced a distinctive line of bright and bold cottons in the supergraphic style. Through the late fifties in Finland and sixties in Canada her women's fashions offered a refreshing and avant-garde variation on mainstream styling.[16]

In 1957 Doris Anderson as the new editor of *Chatelaine* began to make subtle changes in the magazine to reflect and appeal to women's new outlook. The changes kept *Chatelaine* vital to Canadian women. *Mayfair*, on the other hand, represented an era gradually fading and was no longer published after 1959.

85 SUIT (jacket and skirt)
A two-piece grey flannel suit. The single-breasted, princess-seamed jacket is side darted and slightly padded for a curvy torso. Sleeves are fashionably cuffed. The long, slim skirt flares below the knee with three kick pleats front and back, each with an extra pleat.
Label: Travers Fox Ltd., Toronto, Canada
Scots Grey, Worsted Flannel, Made in England, Styled by Auckie Sanft Inc.
Montreal   *The Suddon Collection*

86 SHIRTWAISTER

A classic cotton shirtwaist dress in gingham, large checks of blue on white. Characteristic details of this popular fifties look are the small neat Peter Pan collar, the self-fabric belt, the darted bodice, and the long, very full skirt often worn over crinolines.

Label: An Original Miss Sun Valley by Morris Watkin. Zoussac de P—. Laver comme soie ou laine, wash like silk or wool. Size 14.

The Suddon Collection

87 COCKTAIL DRESS, *about 1952*

A full-skirted cocktail dress in off-white taffeta printed with a small, black floral motif. It has a pleated sweetheart neckline framed under the bust by a band which served as shoulder straps and collar in the back. The band is trimmed in front with black floral beadwork and sequins. The fitted bodice accents a full skirt gathered in pleats in the front around two vertical slot pockets. Light buckram petticoat attached.

Purchased in Florida and worn by Ruth Mount   *Private Collection*

88 EVENING SEPARATES (halter top and skirt), *about 1954*
The halter top in black velvet has seven satin-covered buttons that close centre front with two more at the back of the neck. The bodice, darted with both waist and side darts for an accented bosom, could be teamed with an evening sheath or a full crinolined skirt.

A very full circle skirt in white taffeta flocked with black lines and swirls. It is seamed only centre back and along the sides with a metal zipper at left waist. The wide black elastic cincher waistband is also flocked.
Label: [*halter top*] *Val Hughes, Montreal, 14*   *J. Walford Collection*

89 GOWN
This formal gown is in ivory peau de soie, machine embroidered in red silky threads imitating a couching technique. The floral vine motif is interspersed with rhinestone studs. The huge bow in back that snaps off on one side to expose the centre-back zipper closure is lined with red peau de soie and firmly interlined. The bodice is supported by nine bones sewn into the bodice lining, and the bustline is shaped with bust pads. The skirt is supported by an attached four-hooped crinoline plus a tulle petticoat.
Label: Julian Rose, London   *The Suddon Collection*

90 COAT

A light chartreuse yellow spring coat in wool twill. The seven-eighths length flared silhouette fastens just below the neat shawl collar. Fairly full raglan sleeves are three-quarter length with large turned-back cuffs. Hand-done topstitching is in brown thread. Huge turned-back sleeves, worn with long gloves, were stylish features in coats of this period.
Label: Ls., Chatsworth, by Lurie and Saunders [*Toronto*]

The Suddon Collection

91 SPORTSWEAR

LEFT: COTTON OUTFIT
A front-buttoning blouse of printed cotton in bold stripes of circles, squares, and stars in yellow, chartreuse green, orange, and taupe on white. A Peter Pan collar and short set-in sleeves are classic. The bright orange cotton pants close with a side metal zipper and are cut slim and tapered.

The Suddon Collection

RIGHT: DENIM OUTFIT, *about 1952*
Top and pedal pushers in pale blue cotton twill. The pullover top is laced at the neck and on the sides with white shoestring ties. Seams are finished with white topstitching. The cropped pants are only slightly tapered and are styled after men's jeans with a centre-front zip.
Label: White Stag

Royal Ontario Museum

92 SUIT (jacket and skirt), *about 1956*

A dressy afternoon suit in pale grey green wool flannel. New features for this season are seen here in the shorter, less fitted jacket, the cuffless sleeves, and larger collar. Fifties glamour is expressed in the draped neckline, the sculptured rose, and the rhinestone buttons.   *The Suddon Collection*

93 AFTERNOON DRESS, *about 1958*

A pale dusty rose dress in contrasting textures of slubby linen and satin. The waistline is disappearing—Cornelia does it with princess seaming and tucks. The tucks release as pleats below the intricate satin hipline motif. A nylon zipper closes centre back. The dress has its own specially designed slip in pink china silk sewn inside out with a white lace brassierelike top.

Designer: Cornelia, Toronto   *The Suddon Collection*

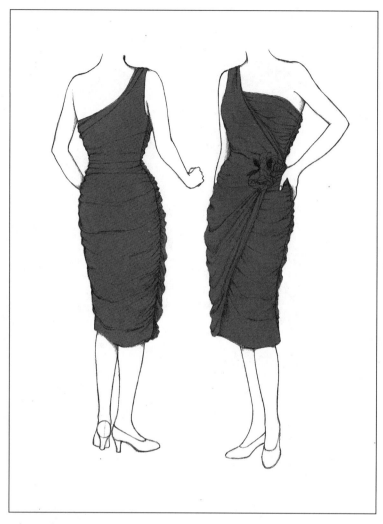

94 COCKTAIL DRESS

A draped and fitted number in scarlet rayon crepe. Rounded hips and the colour made this dress just right for cocktails. The horizontal draping from gathered side seams is overlaid by diagonal lines which form one shoulder strap and curve up from the hem in a sarong effect accented with two scarlet self-fabric poppies at the hip. Closure with long metal zipper down left side.

Label: René Original

The Suddon Collection

95 GOWN

A formal gown in draped aqua silk chiffon over blue taffeta. A basket-weave effect is created in the front with intricate pleating and stitching by hand. The bodice front is shaped inside with four long bones, the waist held by a narrow inner waistband. The slim-fitting skirt is scalloped at centre-front hem and opens centre back with a long vent underneath the separately cut fishtail train. A metal zip closes centre back.

Designer: Jean Dessès, Paris

The Seneca College Collection

96 COAT, *1958*

A sandy beige textured wool coat. The fully circular, finely pleated collar is formed in one piece with the rest of the coat. The pleats then release to a bouffant skirt. The short, plain sleeves are cleverly set in amidst the pleating. A reverse fly centre-front closure works with six, hidden self-covered buttons. The entire coat is lined with a fine taupe beige silk taffeta.

Designer: Pierre Cardin, France
Label: Holt Renfrew and Co. Ltd., by Pierre Cardin, Paris
(Made in France)
                      The Suddon Collection

97 SUNDRESS WITH BOLERO, *about 1958*

A summer day dress in green-and-white printed cotton broadcloth, and a bolero in avocado green linen. The dress is piped in avocado green matching the spaghetti straps. The gathered skirt is fairly short and very full, but the waist is only semifitted. In these years the full skirt often flared to extremes just before disappearing in the early sixties.   *The Suddon Collection*

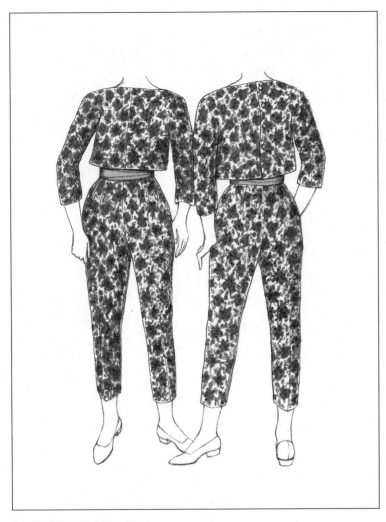

98 PANTS AND TOP, *1957*

A sporty, three-piece outfit in printed cotton piqué comprising pants and top with a cummerbund in light blue cotton broadcloth. The print is a bold splotchy floral in two tones of blue. A Talon metal zipper is on left side of the pants. Garment shapes are simplified and shrinking with tighter fits and more body exposure.

The outfit made up for a Torontonian after a cover photo of Harper's Bazaar, *May 1957.*

The Suddon Collection

99 SACK CHEMISE, *about 1958*

A Paris-influenced sack dress in black crepe. Emphasis on the waist was fast fading in these years; this dress shows the fashionable puffy silhouette in back below a shoulder yoke. The front is gently moulded to the figure with a centre-front seam and long bust darts. The sculptured shape includes short dolman sleeves. Completely lined in black silk, closure is centre back with a metal zipper and three large self-covered buttons with bound buttonholes.

J. Walford Collection

· T H E ·
1960s

ENGLISH FASHION HIT A HIGH POINT OF INFLUENCE IN THE SIXTIES. Throughout the 1950s, a lively set of rebels—writers, artists, musicians, photographers, and just plain eccentrics—created a stir in the seedy, bohemian Chelsea area of London. These creative people were the source of the goods that later would be snapped up by the postwar English baby boomers, the mods, with money to spend and an appetite for novelty.

In this period, a small group of style-conscious young men called teddy boys spent large sums on maintaining their pseudo-Edwardian images; female counterparts of teddy boys often wore the English version of beatnik dress—black sweaters and long clinging skirts with black tights. This first beat generation sowed the early seeds of discontent and change, which were later nurtured by the rockers, followers of the rock and roll cult developing in the United States.

Soon the mods joined into the life of the Chelsea area. They developed their own style message on the streets and in the shops and coffee bars along the King's Road. This renaissance of English fashion resulted partly from the influence of art- and design-school students, and partly because young people had money to spend. The mods' anti-establishment look wasn't cheap, and the new fashions were essential to their identity.[1]

By the 1960s all London was jumping to the sounds of the Beatles and then the Rolling Stones. A new society whose leaders were artists, fashion photographers, hairdressers, and models had developed. *The Avengers* television series and the movies about James Bond promoted the English mod look to a world-wide audience. Mary Quant nurtured the look when she opened her first Bazaar boutique back in 1955 and became known for dressing the Chelsea "birds" in everything from pinafores and knickers to simple A-line dresses. Both the original Bazaar and the second one in Knightsbridge stopped traffic with their wild and witty facades.

Quant's market continued to be the young mods for whom status in dress was a matter of having the right look, not necessarily a rich look. In 1962 Quant began designing wholesale collections for the J.C. Penney chain in the United States; in 1963 she started her Ginger Group line [106]; by 1964 she was designing for Butterick Patterns, and in 1965 for America's Puritan Dresses. Obviously Quant was the major source of mod design in North America.[2] Dress silhouettes were simple and bold, as were the details: large buttons, crude lace, big daisies, diamonds, checks, and other graphics. The mod look quickly influenced American and Canadian designers, and soon it was the only way to dress. Quant's hot pants of the later sixties were not seen in Canada, however, until about 1970 [114].

"The Look," as Quant called it, was reinforced by crisply smooth, childlike haircuts by Vidal Sassoon, not unlike the bobs of that other era of liberation, the 1920s. Not everyone went for the short, neat cut but everyone did want straight, shiny hair. Even the long styles had to be smooth and some young women took to ironing their hair.

Quant wasn't the whole picture however. Other London designers of note from this era were: Tuffin and Foale, Frederick Stark, John Bates who designed for Diana Rigg in *The Avengers*, and Ozzie Clarke for Quorum.

Barbara Hulanicki's Biba boutiques were also a significant part of the swinging London scene. Starting in 1964 with her first Biba, Hulanicki gave a new twist to sixties fashion with cheaply priced but interesting designs fabricated in dusky art nouveau colours. Her dresses were skinny, flared, with high armholes and narrow sleeves. Her large new Biba store, opened in 1973 at the peak of the nostalgia craze, combined art deco with Rennie Mackintosh, Gaudi, and Warhol pop in an atmosphere-doused interior. People came to look but didn't buy and Biba was soon closed.

Jean Shrimpton and Twiggy (Leslie Hornby) were two of Britain's most sought-after models. They appeared on magazine covers all over Europe and North America. Twiggy's thin face, large darkened eyes, and boyish haircut were perfect with miniskirts and shorts that exposed her bony knees. *Vogue* magazine claimed that she was called Twiggy because she looked as though a strong wind would blow her away. Twiggy's face was the ideal of the sixties: "bony, pale-skinned, big-eyed, vulnerable, laquered with a stony stare of arrogance." *Vogue* claimed "the look of arrogance is a happy accident. Twiggy wouldn't know what arrogance means."[3]

WOMEN'S LIB AND UNISEX

Popular fashion in the late 1950s was a curious blend of innocence and sex appeal, perhaps best summed up by French film star Brigitte Bardot in her gingham bikini—a woman's figure

a
Simple, little-girl styled dresses of the 1960s provided comfort and freedom.

dressed in a child's fabric. Fashion models now had baby faces, dark-lashed eyes with pale lips, and as the sixties styles developed, childlike bodies growing rapidly out of their clothes. Like most adolescents, the sixties woman was to become a relatively liberated creature or at least one concerned with freedoms and bearing a certain resemblance to the flapper. Like the young twenties woman, she had money in her purse and she related to the image of strength and independence of her male counterpart. Unisex, however, was still in its infancy. There were only isolated touches of sexual equality visible in dress at this time. As early as 1957, *Mayfair* magazine published a piece, "He-and-She Trend, Equality of the Sexes," that was about the matching bulky sweaters of the Italians, raincoat duets by the Swiss, French cashmere topcoats for either sex, and "such Canadian horrors as matching pyjamas and swimsuits."[4] These unisex clothes were merely amusing and experimental, they did not yet express a deep-rooted social phenomenon.

By the sixties the shortening skirts provided physical comfort and psychological freedom, at least in theory. The fairly sudden public leg exposure made some women nervous, but the easing away from a nipped-in waist was a comforting compensation. As the decade progressed, women abandoned first their girdles and then their bras. A compromise was to wear the minimal, less-constructed bras in the elastic fibres that were developing to meet the needs of the times and a panty girdle or no girdle at all. A little bosom bounce became perfectly acceptable in contrast to the rigid body language of the fifties.

Mary Quant has been credited, along with André Courrèges, as the inventor of the miniskirt, but perhaps of greater significance is the introduction of what would eventually become widely marketed pantyhose. By mid-decade the hemline began to rise above the knee to establish legs as the new erogenous zone. Stockings were suddenly important, available in Britain with bold textures, bright colours, and patterns. Early Canadian mini wearers had to contend with the problem of garter gap or wear the less sexy, usually opaque black tights only available as dance wear or for the small beatnik market. Lacy fishnet tights came only in black or white and were not easy to find. Designer Pat McDonagh remembers looking desperately for tights in Toronto in 1966. By the late sixties pantyhose in natural and even bright colours were being mass-marketed at reasonable prices throughout Canada.

Although *unisex* was never a 1920s term, the flapper's boyish shape expressed a similarity between the sexes. In the latter part of the 1960s, sexual similarities were symbolized by various popular unisex styles: shorter hair for women and longer hair for men; youthful, flat-chested lines in women's dresses, tunics, and jackets; women's hipster jeans and other pants with front-fly zips; jumpsuits; and more body exposure for women with see-through garments, cut-out areas (often at the midriff), and topless styles.

American designer Rudi Gernreich became internationally known in 1964 over his topless woman's bathing suit, cut-out fashions, and transparent blouses [115]. His topless bathing suit was a long way from the modest double-knit nylon bikini shown by Sea Queen for Canadian women in the summer of 1967, and even that amount of exposed midriff could cause gasps on the beach. It was about this time that a few adventurous Canadian designers started to raise the legline a little on their swimwear and also began to present more avant-garde daywear.

In 1969 a new unisex boutique opened in the Fairweather's store in the Yorkdale Mall in Toronto. The boutique was called Big Steel. Designers Suzie Kosovic and Roger Pettet's matching sets of mod fashions for men and women shown at its opening hit the right note for the time.

FRENCH HAUTE COUTURE

Even before 1960 women's dress was being stripped of all its non-essentials, thanks, in part, to such Parisian designers as Balenciaga and Chanel. Suits and dresses were often collarless, and the short, semifitted tops were either sleeveless or had plain short or three-quarter sleeves without cuffs. Trim was minimal and even the large buttons were used sparingly. Tailored skirts were narrow and hemmed just at the bottom of the knee [100].

Fashion was favouring the soft, light colours of youth, and shoes were childlike with lower, sometimes sturdy, heels. The shirtwaist dress and the crinoline were definitely doomed, as design metamorphosed out of the last of the fifties New Look. All the changes seemed to be expressing a conscious or subconscious effort to return to the essence of things, to turn, in fact, towards youth.

b

The sixties revolution took on a special significance in France where the business of fashion had for centuries been based on the trickle-down effect, from haute couture for the elite, to copies, and, eventually, to clothing for the masses. The dressmaker long remained important in France, and prêt-à-porter (ready-to-wear) was a relative latecomer. Nevertheless, as economic pressures increased on the couture industry, houses such as Givenchy, Balmain, Nina Ricci, and Yves Saint Laurent expanded into ready-to-wear. Other young French designers launched their careers in ready-to-wear and were highly competitive with the established designers. Ready-to-wear developed its own stars: Sonia Rykiel, Dorothée Bis, Kenzo, Paco Rabanne, Cacharel, and Daniel Hechter, among others.

Chanel was selling her ideas of functionalism to the fashion elite and happily seeing her designs widely copied by manufacturers. Her new reputation was built heavily on her coats and classic suits—textured but neat and narrow skirts with matching boxy jackets simply edged in contrasting braid. Jackie Kennedy wore a Chanel suit on her tragic trip to Dallas in November 1963. The suit is now in the costume collection of the Smithsonian Institute.

In his fall collection with the House of Dior in 1959, Yves Saint Laurent shortened hems to the knee [102]. Saint Laurent opened his own house in 1962 and began a period of rich, yet simple, semifitted elegance and timely experimentation, essentially in tune with his generation. His Mondrian dress became a milestone, as did his pop art dresses of the following years.

Pierre Cardin's 1959 collection already showed the kind of sculptured geometry that would characterize the top French lines of the sixties. Ungaro, by the later decade, was creating avant-garde, cut-out, body-exposing mini outfits in silver or white, sometimes trimmed with such bold sixties motifs as the daisy. Later Ungaro moved on to develop his reputation for dynamic brightly coloured prints, still his trademark.

André Courrèges launched an extremely influential collection in 1964. His designs, along with those of Cardin, were labelled the space-age look and were developed for a number of following seasons. Firm fabrics, often in white or pastels of double-faced wools, sculpted, curved edges boldly topstitched into a harmony of simple forms, and accessories of white vinyl boots and helmetlike hats completed the look to perfection. Pale colours, silver, bold abstractions in black and white or red and white, see-through vinyls, cutouts, high-tech details like the industrial zipper, all were components of the French space-age look that lasted until about 1971 [113].

BOUTIQUE SHOPPING

Boutiques grew out of the idea of having all the right fashions and accessories for the latest look immediately to hand and at an affordable price. Like country fairs, the casual and colourful atmosphere of boutiques had entertainment appeal. Department stores could be rather middle-aged and dull, most specialty shops too limited and expensive. Fun and relaxed, boutiques began opening in centres across Canada. As with any retail situation, location was important. Most desirable were areas where young people gathered to talk and drink in coffee houses, to listen to music, and to have lunch in cafés that were cheap and cheerful.

In the late fifties, Gerrard Street Village was the small beginnings of such an area in Toronto. There, Karelia Studio represented the best of Scandinavian design, and casual, colourful Mary Johns restaurant gave great value in comfort food.[5] Their dark-laquered walls plastered with posters set the sixties tone, and Sir Ernest and Lady McMillan were among the regulars who enjoyed their ninety-five cent specials.

Designer Marilyn Brooks and friends from the United States opened the Pot Pourri boutique on Gerrard Street in 1962. The next year marked the inauguration of Brook's Unicorn boutiques, one on Gerrard and another on Cumberland Street in the then undeveloped Yorkville area. They were an irresistible hodgepodge of everything either camp or pop, alongside outlandish Unicorn-created fashions and accessories.

Susie Kosovic's Poupée Rouge opened on Gerrard in 1964 in a pink-painted house that rattled to the sounds of the Tijuana Brass [110]. Her brightly coloured mod-inspired designs appealed to hip young women with a strong sense of style. A couple of years later, the cover of *Maclean's* magazine featured her "rich, simple styles that propelled her to the forefront of Canadian design."[6] Kosovic became a designer for Big Steel and, in the seventies, a partner in John Alexander in the Manulife Centre on Bloor Street.

c   *Bold but feminine styles in bright colours marked the Susie Kosovic look of the mid-1960s.*

Yorkville by the late sixties was a midtown meeting place for the emerging Toronto hippie population. Scruffy Victorian houses, restaurants, and coffee houses—the Purple Onion, El Patio, Mousetrap, the Mynah Bird, the Riverboat, and others—were havens for the city's young people, some into communal living, poetry, and folk songs. The hippie style of dress was making an impact on mainstream fashion. At the same time Yorkville had some of the most interesting boutiques in the city. Marie Cluthe's formal and bridalwear shop on nearby Bloor Street was owned by Mrs. Heit who also owned many of the Yorkville coffee houses. Here, too, were Shelagh's Boutique, Two Bizarre, Zoe Limited, Récamier, and others.

Yorkville was just the beginning in Toronto's boutique development. By 1967 even the more sedate specialty shops such as Jean Pierce's on Eglinton Avenue were adding boutiques aimed at the junior customer.

Boutiques blossomed in Montreal, too. Designers such as Leo Chevalier and Marielle Fleury pioneered the fashionable boutiques of Crescent Street where Fleury created her typically Québecois styles, sometimes in handwoven fabrics. Leo Chevalier's shop Cheval, with its elegant art nouveau interior was well established on Rue St. Mathieu in time for Expo 67. John Warden's boutique on Crescent was trendsetting and fun, and not far from Jacques de Montjoye's A La Fleur Des Temps. Anne-Marie Perron's Masculin-Feminin was at 2130 Crescent, and La Boutiga on Sherbrooke Street started designer Elvia Gobbo's fashion career.

Traditional retailing chains and department stores were also changing. Bigger companies were buying up smaller, older businesses. In 1951 the long established R.J. Devlin Company in Ottawa had become another Morgan's. By 1960 in Montreal the Hudson's Bay Company acquired ten stores in the Morgan's chain and then began national expansion as the Bay.

Most of the department stores across Canada adjusted to the competition of the new boutiques by setting up in-store boutiques in various departments. By the late sixties, Eaton's in Montreal had more boutiques than any other department store in North America.

CANADIAN DESIGNERS

The sixties provided a surge of energy into the Canadian fashion industry. By the spring of 1961 the International Ladies' Garment Workers Union had gained sufficient stature that their first label was sewn into Canadian-made garments. The following September the union launched fashion shows in Montreal, Toronto, Winnipeg, and Vancouver, and these manufacturers' shows continued annually into the 1970s. At Place des Arts in Montreal in 1967, a gala centennial version of the union's annual national show was a great success.

Montreal's fashion industry also expanded its exports to Britain in particular because the British liked the new miracle fibres that Canadian designer-manufacturers were using for their stylish, well-made garments. New designers took advantage of the trend towards simple but experimental fashions. For the first time some Montreal manufacturers considered the abilities of Canadians. In 1964 Auckie Sanft hired American-trained Canadian designer John Warden, and a few years later Jack Margolis of Bagatelle hired English-born Margaret Godfrey to design under her own name. That same year Margo Dress hired Canadian Hugh Garber, back after a two-year apprenticeship in Rome.

A new generation of trained designers was emerging in Canada. In Montreal Leo Chevalier began designing in 1960. With a B.F.A. from École des Beaux Arts, Chevalier spent some years in display and sales before he opened his couture boutique Cheval. But by 1970 he had phased out the couture side of the business and was concentrating on his very successful ready-to-wear.

Michel Robichaud was established as a Parisian-style couturier in Montreal by 1963. He designed the Air Canada uniforms the following year. In 1969 he opened his ready-to-wear boutique and also presented a capsule collection in Europe.

One of the highest profile Canadian designers was John Warden who opened his women's boutique in Montreal in 1966, and another for men a few years later. He designed uniforms for a number of the pavillions at Expo 67, where Canadian fashion was presented in an outdoor show to a large international audience [112].

d *This evening coat in white-and-gold brocade with cuffs of dark ranch mink by designer Irene Morson, won an EEDEE award for David E. Rea in 1966.*

In 1962 the Ontario government began to back the fashion industry in the province in an effort to increase exports. With government support, the Apparel Manufacturers Group (Highland Queen Sportswear, David E. Rea, Norman Rogul Furs, Elen Henderson, Ruth Dukas, Claire Haddad, Allenby Fashions) began to promote their lines in the United States. Some years later the Ontario Fashion Institute initiated the EEDEE award for excellence in Ontario fashion design.

Other Toronto designers were making their names known. Jean Pierce, who opened her store on Eglinton Avenue in Toronto in 1955, hired display designer Everett Staples as house designer in the early sixties. Couturier Rodolphe in Yorkville was already a name since the 1950s, as was Tibor de Nagy on Balmuto Street, well known for chic and feminine draped styles in chiffons and jerseys, and David E. Rea, known for special creations in bridalwear and evening gowns. Marie Cluthe, long established at 95 Bloor West, Frederick's Lingerie, Helmar of London on Yorkville, and Sarah Couture on Cumberland were other Yorkville area names. In these years Maggy Reeves and Angelina were noted for their simple elegance, and Ruth Dukas for her luxurious beading and embroidery on dressy gowns and cocktail dresses [108].

Swinging boutiques aimed at a younger clientele created a truly sixties flavour. In 1962 David Smith opened at 44 Avenue Road and the next year Marilyn Brooks was offering wild and wonderful items at both her Unicorn boutiques. Pat McDonagh came from mod-inspired England to Toronto in 1966 and met the Gerrard Street Village crowd, including Winston Kong who opened his first boutique there in 1967 [111]. McDonagh returned a second time to Toronto to open a series of boutiques in the 1970s, and to create collections of designer fashions for various manufacturers as well as for her own labels [122].

Toronto manufacturers of note in this period were: Allenby Fashions, Better Blouse Company, Diamond Tea Gown, Highland

Queen, Mr. Leonard, Lurie and Saunders, Murray Kates, Dorothea Knitwear, Percy Lindzon, Miss Sun Valley, Jack Posluns, and Sea Queen, among many others.

The Fashion Group of Toronto opened the 1966 season with a meeting and fashion show under the direction of Dora Matthews, Olivia of Hamilton, and Chairman Raoul-Jean Fouré (also President of the Association of Canadian Couturiers). Held in the King Edward Hotel, the fashion show featured zingy hot pinks and purples, space-age lamé, velvets for day and evening with fur trim and leopard-print gaiters. Designs were by Tibor de Nagy, Maggy Reeves, Everett Staples, Robert Irwin, and Frederica, among others.[7] At that time designer Ruth Dukas was doing such space-age looks as stretchy white jumpsuits teamed with a beaded poncho or a slinky long gown in white silk organza with a cutout hemline.[8]

The Canadian fashion industry was coming of age. In 1968 the federal government's Department of Industry, Trade, and Commerce sponsored presentations of Canadian fashions in New York which were very successful in stimulating interest and sales. In January 1971 the *Financial Post* was able to report that, "Canada exported an estimated $53 million worth of garments to the United States, up 23 percent from 1969 and a whopping 342 percent over 1967."[9]

FASHIONS FOR THE YOUNG

The styles of the 1960s reflected the influences of a number of factors. Where the women's movement and its struggle towards social freedoms indirectly affected fashions, the general counterculture revolution by the young affected it directly. The relatively good economy allowed the baby boom generation to have a dominating impact throughout the decade. The generation gap meant a rejection by the young of stuffy, middle-aged styles, expensive elitist garments, and couture. The young people played by their own rules and their dress reflected this attitude. There was a breakdown of the idea that certain kinds of outfits were only acceptable for specific occasions, places, or times of day. Youth became so influential, that, as Dora Matthews said when commentating an Alta Moda Italiana show at the Royal Ontario Museum in 1965, "There are no old women anymore. There are just some who are younger than the others."[10]

Early in the decade, the fact that women were wearing pants for a broader range of occasions is in itself an indication of the narrowing of the differences between men and women. Pants were plain and narrow, even slightly tapered in towards the ankle and with a central crease. They were already favourites for casual daywear or sportswear, perhaps worn with a mohair sweater, but now they were sometimes part of a dressy afternoon or evening outfit [101]. A little later in the decade a young woman's trendy pantsuit might copy the English mod style with a wide-lapelled skinny jacket and low-rise pants with a flare.

Most often women still wore suits or dresses in the early decade. Skirts were usually the simple just-below-the-knee-length sheath; tops and suit jackets had plain, shortened sleeves and straight lines stopping near the waist, or perhaps slightly blouson to the hips. The neat, stiff little waistless shift, often sleeveless, perhaps collarless and narrow, or with an A-line skirt, became standard. Details might include patch pockets and Peter Pan collars set a little away from the neck. Nothing was very complicated in the way of design, although high-fashion followers of the Balenciaga style might have a wide, bias-cut, shaped collar.

Classic checks, bouclés, paisleys, clean solid colours in black, moss green, wine, and blues were soon followed by lighter colours, whites, and pastels as the space-age look took hold. After mid-decade there was a wonderful colour explosion and large-scaled floral prints or supergraphics in combinations of bright colours were often seen: aqua plus moss, yellow plus blue, bright red plus lilac, and combinations of clashing blues and greens.

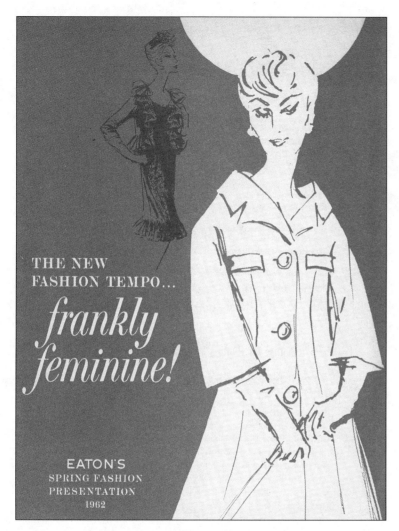

THE NEW
FASHION TEMPO...

*frankly
feminine!*

EATON'S
SPRING FASHION
PRESENTATION
1962

e *By the early 1960s lines were semifitted, often with princess seaming, sleeves were shortening, and collars stood away from the neck.*

Coats followed the evolving silhouette with ever-shortening hemlines and exposed Canadian legs in knee-high boots for the winters of the late sixties. Coat styles favoured were simple classical reefers, sometimes the neat Rajah coat or even tent shapes **[104]**.

Hats in simple styles—helmetlike shapes, Chanel's Bretons, and the traditional pillboxes favoured by Jackie Kennedy—were worn in the early decade as a complementary statement to the formal, tailored ensembles and pared-down suits. By the later years, however, hats had essentially disappeared as the younger fashions took over.

Early sixties eveningwear was relatively austere and surprisingly modest. The strapless fifties gown gave way to more covered, classical, and narrower lines, often in solid colours in finely draped chiffons or simple styles carved in crisper fabrics such as rich brocades. Décolletage and sometimes even the bustline hardly existed. Neat jewelled edgings and bands were used, often as part of the high-waisted neoclassic style. Evening separates of long skirts and various tops were an acceptable formula.

As usual, popular dance and fashion went hand in hand. Chubby Checker's landmark recording of "The Twist" produced a new disco dance in which partners took to the floor and did their own thing without touching, in complete equality rather than leading or being led. Instead of being locked together in unison, how one looked facing one's partner was now part of success on the dance floor. Short and sexy, sometimes fringed, dresses very like those of the twenties, were revived and helped to speed up the shortening of everyday hemlines.[11]

Crisp synthetic fabrics in light colours, whites, silver, or the brights were favoured, often in mini form but with some longer lengths appearing. A much more casual attitude was developing about what constituted being dressed up and by 1969 women wearing minis, mixed with women wearing long evening skirts and separates at almost any given social event. The most

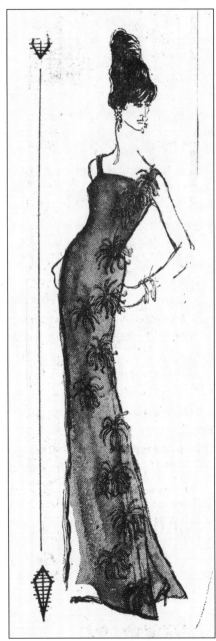

f
*Fashionable formal dress
was narrow and classical.*

characteristic evening outfit from this period was the tunic and pants in evening fabric, often a synthetic. Along with the synthetic dress fabrics, women wore obviously false eyelashes and false hairpieces. Unreal was where it was at.

The fashionable Canadian hemline began to move up the thigh about 1967; miniskirts proliferated from then into the early seventies. David E. Rea offered miniskirted bridal gowns in 1967, one an empire-line gown of cotton lace over taffeta with a long court train.

Colourful decorative motifs became bolder and were used more often. Stasia Evasuk, fashion editor for the *Toronto Telegram* reporting a Toronto Fashion Group show in November 1966, described evening outfits "out of the Arabian Nights . . . in a chiffon print of shocking pink, blue, pink and burnt orange," and another as "red, blue and green. Designed by Ruth Dukas, it was beaded and had floating panels that looked like butterfly wings."[12] Many evening outfits featured bare midriffs, harem pants, cutouts, and see-through fabrics.

By the late sixties large Afro haircuts in all colours balanced the new, bell-bottom trousers. Work clothes and fantasy clothes were part of street fashion and denim was especially popular; particularly admired were creatively patched, embroidered, and appliquéd jeans. Young women wanted to be seen as doing their own thing. In this period of anything goes for day- as well as evening-wear, some conservative people were shocked by what was sometimes worn to the office.

The do-it-yourself approach to dress meant that the whole existing system of fashion marketing was in a state of flux. Manufacturers had to make low-priced garments quickly in order to compete with homemade efforts, treasures from secondhand stores, and the fashions of the new designers of ready-to-wear in the boutiques. All these sources provided acceptable, even fashionable, dress that competed with and replaced expensive high fashion and couture sales.

OP, POP, AND OBSOLESCENCE

The Hungarian painter Vasarely, with his geometric arrangements of tone and colour that produce a kinetic effect in his colour-rich and precise optical art of the late fifties, might be considered the father of the op art movement. He believed that all the plastic arts form a unity and that there was no need to split them into fixed categories such as painting, sculpture, or graphics.[13] It was not surprising then, to see textile and fashion designers in the mid-sixties, using some of the simpler effects of op art, just as designers had already been influenced by the colours, forms, and textures of abstract expressionism.

Intricately programmed black-and-white graphics, in the manner of the fine art works of Bridget Riley, were printed as designs on fashion fabrics. Cruder, bolder copies and spin-off designs were pieced or appliquéd like quilts and used in garments. Many of the effects were like designs of the pioneer coverlets produced on jacquard looms in nineteenth-century Ontario. Op art and graphics could be abstracted to a simple combination of stripes and polka dots, in one timely minidress, for example. Contrasts of two boldly opposite colours were an important part of the sixties fashion statement. As psychedelic colour schemes took over, op art moved from severe geometry to Peter Max-type romanticism.

As well as influences from op art, fashion absorbed and reflected the pop art movement of the period. The consumer society had steadily escalated since the 1950s, and affluent America was by this time well and truly in the grip of the marketing and advertising industries. The trend now was, as the pop artists demonstrated, not to economize but to consume at a rate that would keep up with production. Little thought was given to the problem of waste. Obsolescence was built into everything from furnishings to fine art.

Clothing was an obvious area in which to accelerate turnover. Although there had been some experimenting in New York with paper dresses in the 1920s and the Scandinavians made children's wear out of paper during World War I, it was not until 1966 that disposable clothing was fairly widely available. That year the Scott Paper Company introduced low-priced instant fashion in dresses made of nonwoven tissue strengthened with mesh, printed in brightly coloured patterns. In spite of being easily damaged by liquid spills and nonwashable due to fire retardent, these dresses were advertised as good for four or five wearings. They came in four sizes. In 1966 Scott received orders for 500,000 dresses.[14]

In the United States, J.C. Penney and other stores carried a line of paper goods printed in paisleys, op art, and space-age silver. The Royal Ontario Museum stocked two prints, which one could order by mail. In the spring of 1968 David E. Rea and Everett Staples produced a line called Paper Things, which included bridalwear.

Toronto fashion journalist Joyce Carter suggested that the disposable wedding dress made a lot of sense: "You don't need an attic to store it for some daughter you may never have. You don't have to go through the agony of having some dressmaker try to hack it into something useful for you. And you don't have to pay much for it."[15] Prices were about forty dollars. Carter was bothered by their fake look, however, and this may have been one of the factors against them, considering the bridal desire for perfection.

Paper was used not only for dresses, but also jackets and jumpsuits. The interest in disposable clothing died as quickly as it was born. There was a sense of vulnerability in wearing disposable dress, and although Andy Warhol suggested that maybe it just wasn't marketed correctly, grass-root feelings were emerging that were against new, experimental dress ideas.

THE NEW PROPORTIONS

The almost exclusive use of photography in fashion magazines of this decade affected the way women saw themselves collectively. Whenever fashion illustration still did appear, however, it was evident by the late sixties that there were new body proportions. Upper torsos were small and the lower limbs stretched out like taffy, reminiscent of art nouveau illustrations from the turn of the century. The figure's erogenous zone was the legs, the longer the better. As hemlines rose, the viewing angle for fashion photography changed. With the camera at floor level, women's legs appeared stretched, waists raised, and shoulders nearly disappeared—the best shape for an A-line minidress.

Bodices became even smaller with tight armholes and raised waists. The neoclassical silhouette with its raised waistline had a revival, but instead of being completely narrow as in earlier versions, skirts favoured the A-line of perspective. Even as the hemline dropped these shapes and proportions remained in the yoke-topped dresses, spare bodices, halter necklines, and tight sleeves, which were teamed with the elongated A-line skirt.

The eventual dropping of the hemline caused controversy and did not occur as rapidly as the North American industry would have liked. By 1969 some European designers were promoting the new long-skirted midi at the high fashion level, but the hemline change took several years.

ROMANTIC NOSTALGIA

The sense of fun and freedom that the sixties economy, the youthful energy, and the women's movement promoted encouraged the attitude that women would no longer be dictated to by the fashion industry. This idea largely disregarded an industry geared towards survival in some form or other.

The baby boomer had grown from a rebellious teenager to

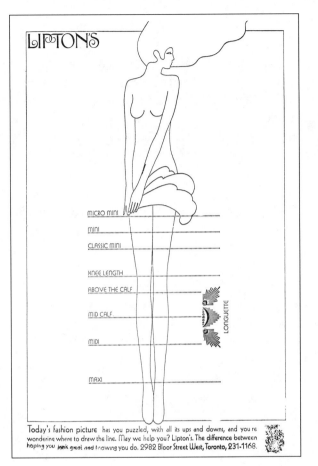

g *Lipton's illustration by Toronto graphic designer Theo Dimson, about 1969, shows the hemline controversy most effectively on a figure with art nouveau influences.*

a young woman in a romantic search for her roots. There was a great surge of interest in the fabric arts all over North America: weaving, macramé, embroidery, and appliqué. Many weavers and designers in fabric, along with their contemporaries as consumers, rejected the drip-dry fabrics of the previous generation.

By the late sixties, being interestingly dressed was more important than being correctly dressed. Wardrobes were a collection of costume pieces mixed and worn in a rather casual way. Hippie fashions were visible in many urban centres, especially Vancouver where styles were already more laid-back than in other Canadian cities. Western jeans, T-shirts, North American Indian dress blended together, but not just in the west and not always casually. In 1968 Everett Staples produced a collection using screen-printed textiles of Arthur Shilling's designs based on Ojibwa art.[16] Staples's collection marked the beginning of an ongoing interest in the art of Canada's native people.

For many young women the informality of hippie styles combined with folkloric and granny looks created a softer femininity. The granny or pioneer look of long, full-skirted styles in old-fashioned, traditional daytime fabrics, was popularly worn, in hippie to mainstream fashion versions.

Periods of romantic dress always thrive on looking back instead of to the future. Designers return to earlier times for basic themes of decoration and structure and to other cultures for exotic twists. The fabrics for this late sixties indulgence were ethnic designs in the stripes and geometrics of primitive weaving, and the handcrafted looks of textured wovens, knits, and crochets. There were details such as laced closures and fringes in Indian buckskin, shawls and wraps, calico florals, plaids and ginghams, East Indian cottons, mid-Eastern vests, cossack shirts, tie-dyes, gypsy headscarves, peasant blouses, caftans, ponchos, and accessories such as tied cincher belts, sashes, bead necklaces, and blunt-toed, chunky-heeled boots. Appropriate to the times, structures were simple: kimono-sleeved pop tops, dirndl skirts, wraps. An ethnic European shoe in the form of wooden-soled clogs emerged to be worn with these trendy clothes. Even the Fashion Group of Toronto took advantage of the nostalgia craze to raise money through their first flea market at Casa Loma in 1968.

The look was eclectic, rich with colour and mixed patterns. Contemporary textile designers were influenced by ethnic motifs and the way traditional cultures combined patterns and also by the psychedelic graphic art out of California. Many contemporary textiles were offered in zingy bright colours—hot pinks and scarlets, acid yellows, rich purples, bright green and turquoise, either alone, in simple combinations, or in large-scaled, lush floral prints. Pucci prints with their multicoloured, hard-edged graphics were extremely popular, recognizable, and influential.

As well as the arty, boutique-generated look in the streets, the ethnic statement crept into high fashion. Claire Haddad, Canada's best-known loungewear designer showed Eastern influences in her robe designs. Haddad started her company in 1964, on Spadina Avenue in Toronto. Through the sixties she won the Canadian Cotton Council Award, two EEDEEs, and the coveted Coty Award for her innovative, feminine, and often exotic leisure wear. By the seventies, as loungewear styling merged with the increasingly casual evening fashions, Haddad's lines were widely marketed across Canada and the United States.

Nostalgia was not only affecting the clothing industry and fashionable dress. European and North American store mannequins for display also began to broaden out from the longtime caucasian image into every race and colour, as well as high stylized and abstract human forms.

Not only was there a good deal of dipping into other cultures, but also a new past was officially discovered in the late sixties. English author Bevis Hillier in his book *Art Deco* named the style of the 1920s and 1930s as art deco and helped to create a strong revival in North America.[17] The theatre, films on late night television, and even contemporary first-run films were all reviewing the 1930s [103]. Art deco influences were turning up everywhere and eventually produced, among many other manifestations, a run of geometric textile prints for both men's and women's fashions in the early seventies. Art deco motifs inspired designs for jewellery, scarves, and bags and were used effectively in the graphic design of the visuals that promoted them.

100 SUIT (jacket and skirt)

This two-piece suit in pale blue wool bouclé shows the ubiquitous short boxy jacket of the early sixties, with a wide Peter Pan collar plus single button, plain, three-quarter length sleeves, and unusual pocket details. Jacket front closure is held with dome snaps. The new shorter sheath is lined and multi-darted for a smooth fit and has both a waistband and a Petersham waistband.

Label: Made in England expressly for Creed's of Toronto, by Frederick Stark, London

The Suddon Collection

101 PANTSUIT

A pantsuit in coarse black lace, completely lined with black lining fabric. The fitted pants are without a waistband, with a zip closure at the centre-back seam. They are cut slim and tapered to the ankle. The sleeveless top is loose cut and hip-length with three buttons closing the curved back trimmed with decorative black edging.

Labels: [*Top*] *PANT-MATE by Len Wasser, Made in Canada.*

[*Pants*] *PANT-MAN by Len Wasser, Made in Canada.*   *J. Walford Collection*

102 COCKTAIL DRESS, *1959/60*
A cocktail dress in black silk chiffon trimmed with black velvet ribbon bands, bows, and silk flowers. Yves Saint Laurent's collection for this season featured a more natural waistline and skirts shortened to knee length. The bouffant gathers of soft chiffon contrast subtly with the rich black velvet. Snaps and hooks at centre-back closure.
Designer: Yves Saint Laurent, Paris
Label: Christian Dior, Paris (Made in France)   *The Seneca College Collection*

103 GOWN
An evening gown in the thirties style of chartreuse yellow chiffon over taffeta. Two more layers of chiffon cut in full gores form the skirt. The seams are covered with silvery beads and sequin clusters; the full spread of the skirt accented with pale yellow ostrich plumes recalls Ginger Rogers's costume for one of her dances with Fred Astaire in *Top Hat*.
Designer: Rita Dennis, Toronto   *The Seneca College Collection*

104 COAT, *about 1965*

A knee-length, princess-seamed spring coat in muted aqua wool twill, very much in the style of the French designers of the early sixties. This semifitted, double-breasted reefer with plain three-quarter sleeves and neat collar is a classic of its time. The large buttons are smoky mother-of-pearl.

Label: Carol Carter, Ft. Lauderdale, Florida   *The Seneca College Collection*

105 SUMMER DRESS

A sleeveless A-lined dress with princess seaming in silky printed acetate twill. The print is a very painterly rendition of hot-pink roses and sketchy green leaves. The fully lined dress has a scooped neckline trimmed with nine three-dimensional self-fabric roses. Centre-back nylon zip closure.

Label: Reproduction of Pierre Cardin, Modes Paris   *The Suddon Collection*

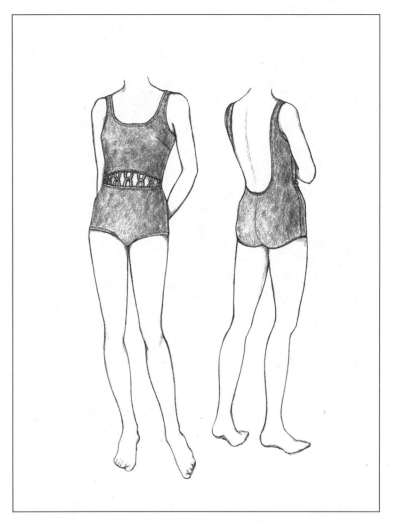

106 SHIFT, *about 1964*

A sleeveless, barely knee-length jumper in black-and-heather-grey wool jersey. Here shown with black turtleneck and tights, the severe geometry of this shift is characteristic of the avant-garde design out of London and Paris at the beginning of the decade. A time lag of a couple of years meant the very short London mini had not caught on yet in Canada but was on its way.

Designer: Mary Quant, London

Label: Mary Quant's Ginger Group. Made in England, 100% Wool, 13

The Suddon Collection

107 BATHING SUIT

A maillot-styled swimsuit. The unlined suit is in a heavy synthetic knit dyed with variagated shades of ochre. Loops of self-fabric open the waist in front. The back is low cut. Stiff white bra cups are fastened to the inside facing.

Label: Piege. Marque et Modèle Déposes, 42, Made in France.

The Seneca College Collection

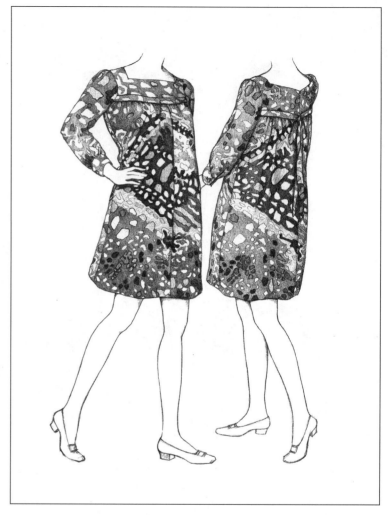

108 SUIT (jacket and skirt)

A dressy, soft-skirted suit in a putty-coloured textured fabric with matching trim. Interesting synthetic fabrics were now being accepted by the best designers. The silhouette is semifitted, the collar youthful. Knotted satin buttons match bound buttonholes and jacket edging.

Designer: Maggy Reeves, Toronto   *The Suddon Collection*

109 SHIFT or CHEMISE

A long-sleeved chemise in blue-and-gold printed silk. The painterly fabric design is totally nonobjective and random in its repeat. The structure of the shift is as simple as a traditional little girl's dress, the sophistication all in the fabric.

Designer: Guy Laroche, Paris
Label: Modele Guy Laroche, Paris Diffuse par Maria Carine, Made in France.
Simpson's St. Regis Room   *The Suddon Collection*

110 MINIDRESS, *about 1968*

A minidress in rich purple suede. The empire line together with the shortened hem create that extreme proportion relationship of the period: the small top with the long-legged body. Worn with gold ciré knee-high boots, the thighs become the erogenous zone. The bodice is covered with large metal eyelettes, a subtle version of the sixties "see-through" obsession.

Purchased from Susie Kosovic's Poupée Rouge boutique, Toronto and worn by Diane Meaghan   *Private Collection*

111 MINIDRESS, *about 1970*

A pert yet elegant evening minidress in gradated tiers of lustrous cotton shantung. The top two ruffles and the straps are pale pink, the next two, slightly longer, are brighter pink, and the last and longest ruffle is hot pink. The look is both youthful and romantic. Centre-back zipper closure.

Designer: Winston, Toronto   *The Suddon Collection*

112 COAT, *about 1966*

A spring coat in cavalry wool twill. Here is a sixties version of the double-breasted trench coat with the lapels, the belt, and the detailing in back. Strongly emphasized outlines through widely spaced topstitching on patch pockets and lapels recall designs by Chanel, Cardin, and Courrèges.

Designer: John Warden, Toronto

Label: Haute Couture by John Warden   *The Seneca College Collection*

113 MINIDRESS

A body-exposing summer mini in bright red and white striped cotton matelassé. Shoulder straps each include two large white plastic rings matching the four which link top to skirt. The entire dress is lined with thin cotton muslin. The top closes in back with four self-covered buttons and bound buttonholes. The centre-back zipper was put in by hand.

Labels: [1] Luris-Mari, Nice, Côte d'Azur, Made in France

[2] Mr. Roberts Shop

J. Walford Collection

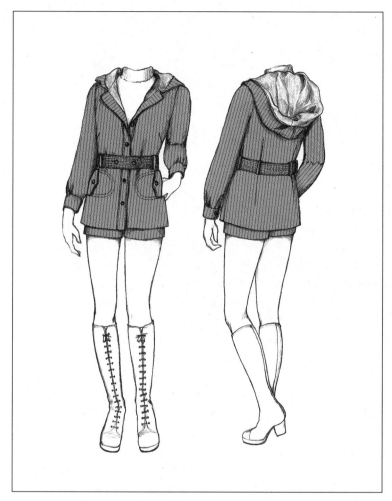

114 SUIT (jacket and hotpants)

This two-piece suit is in a novelty checked wool fabric in greys and browns. The semifitted jacket and large hood are lined with rust-coloured satin. The multi-stitched self-fabric belt is loop bound and buttons centre front. Hip-level semicircular pockets have buttoned flaps. The short shorts lined in rust satin fit over the hips with many darts. There are two semicircular pockets in the back and a zip closure centre front.

Purchased from Susie Kosovic's Poupeé Rouge boutique, Toronto, and worn by Diane Meaghan *Private Collection*

115 DRESS, *about 1965*

A slinky side-slit dress in black-and-putty diagonally striped wool knit. Large daisy-shaped appliqués in op art herringbone of black and putty double knit create a very sixties statement. The diagonal neckline and the one cap sleeve are edged in light orange over wider bright red wool braids. Left side Talon zipper. Gernreich pioneered the use of these heavy knits in lean silhouettes in the early sixties.

Designer: Rudi Gernreich, United States
Label: Rudi Gernreich for Harmon Knitwear *The Suddon Collection*

THE

1970s

THE YEAR 1970 SAW FASHION IN A STATE OF MAJOR TRANSITION ONCE more. Neat geometric designs, often in double knit, which evolved from Courrège's tailored space-age clothes, were still seen, usually as miniskirts, but also as pantsuits or long, sculptured dresses. Few Canadian women were wearing the new midi length, introduced the season before in the European collections. Once again, as with the 1958 chemise, the midi length was too drastic a change from minis and pantsuits for most women to relate to immediately.

The fashion trade newspaper *Women's Wear Daily* (now called *WWD*) declared 1970 "the year of the Midi in North America." However, 1970 turned out disastrously for many manufacturers who committed 100 percent to the midi because the newly independent consumer resisted it both in Canada and the United States.[1] Although fashion journalism and advertising promoted the new hemline length, women were reluctant to give up the sex appeal of short skirts and adopt such a radical and sudden change to their image [117].

The eclectic, free-form wardrobes of the late sixties continued to please at all levels. Antique and secondhand clothing shops had an air of chic instead of thrift, and shops in Toronto, such as Amelia Earhart, Quality Junk Shop, Paraphernalia, and the Cabbage Town Curiosity Shop, sold nostalgia in the city's liveliest shopping areas. People were putting together recycled dress items in new, inventive ways that reflected the hippie lifestyle.

Hemlines were all over the place. The romantic, long-skirted granny look for young women continued well into the seventies. Prints by England's Laura Ashley were favourites for this look. Women who revelled in fashion extremes tried a Canadian winter in maxi coats over miniskirts, but most took refuge in pantsuits. Microminis were so short now that some women merely added pants to make up a suit.

The young body fit of the 1960s continued into the seventies, indeed, was exaggerated. Jackets and coats were body-hugging with narrow sleeves and very wide lapels; there was no ease through the bust and shoulders; armholes were small in both woven and knit garments. Knits were structured to mould to the figure in everything from poor boy sweaters to long skinny knit dresses. Woven fabric garments were cut with small top proportions, often made smaller by a somewhat raised inverted-V waist seam, sewn to a narrow A-line skirt (a variation on the Directoire style). Halter tops were another popular variety of the small top. Sleeves, nearly always set-in, were tight near the head, any fullness was on the forearm.

Synthetic fabrics were prevalent: sturdy double knits, crimplene, various polyesters, including polyester-denims, Ultrasuede, and the softer Arnel and Qiana jerseys. In the opening years

By 1974 softer lines and longer hemlines introduced a period of romanticism in dress, as seen in this sketch of a Tom d'Auria design.

illustrations, already in a pseudo-art-nouveau style and a spin-off from psychedelic, elongated the lower body even more in relation to the top.

In 1973 the most common daytime skirt stopped just below the knee, and hemlines continued to drop. A short-skirted version of the World War II look in day dress was part of the eclectic scene. This leggy, body-revealing silhouette similar to the one of early 1940s (a tarty look with padded shoulders and skimpy, drapy skirt worn with ankle-strapped platform shoes and, perhaps, seamed stockings) was labelled the retro style. Retro-forties was the early fashion statement of the singing group the Pointer Sisters.

WEARING PANTS

As a result of unisex clothing in the late sixties plus the hemline hulabaloo, pants for women were accepted as never before in our culture. Pant styling followed the same shape as the dress silhouette in spite of being bifurcated. Loose-legged and sometimes floppy about the lower leg, pants were increasingly fitted through the thighs and lower torso. As though compensating for the loss of peek-a-boo skirts, the way to look sexy in pants was to wear them low-rise and moulded to the crotch and buttocks; at its most extreme this erogenous statement had very little subtlety. Tight pants were often teamed with the popular skimpy battle jacket or clinging, ribbed sweaters.

A logical development from the micromini were city shorts, known more popularly as hot pants. Their acceptance in Canada was somewhat delayed to the late sixties and early seventies. Worn with high-heeled shoes or high boots, hot pants were considered too vulgar by many and lasted only a couple of seasons [124]. In 1971 *Chatelaine* featured a middle-of-the-road Canadian mid-thigh version, mostly covered by a long jacket in jersey knit by Pat McDonagh/Re In-Vestments, headlined as

of the decade, large-scaled and colourful prints were still making a strong statement, but smaller, neater art deco-type repeats would soon win out. Knits of all kinds were becoming a dominant part of women's wardrobes, even for evening wear.

Gradually, from 1970 to about 1973, people's perceptions adjusted to lower hemlines and to layered clothing. Knee-length vests and tunics were worn with skirts or pants. The popularity of pants soon served to drop many hems to the ground where they spread like roots anchoring the figure and providing a long overdue stability [119]. Both skirts and pants flared wide, although they remained fitted through the body; shoes were very heavy with platform soles and chunky heels. Bottom-heavy figures made possible the later fad of leg warmers. Fashion

b
Fall 1975 outerwear by Nicola Pelly for Bagatelle: fur-lined quilted corduroy jacket with toggle fastenings plus big sweater, tight jeans, and bright accessories.

to an arty European look and their styling spread into jackets, [120] skirts, shorts, hats, and shoes.

Next in popularity to blue denim were beige and khaki. Cool and tough looks for women included army looks, work clothes, and safari styles. Seventies romanticism included the illusion of escapist travel and "real" living.

Pantsuits were avant-garde in the sixties when designers such as Yves Saint Laurent put their blessing on them. Now pants and mannish-styled shirts and blazers were becoming a more dominant part of women's wardrobes. Stylish collars were large and lapels very wide, often with rounded points. The more masculine jackets might be in wool flannels and gabardines, but synthetic knits and softer double knits of all kinds were worn [116].

With varying degrees of formality pantsuits became a wardrobe mainstay and appeared at every price level and for all occasions. They were worn to work and to parties and, with a little initial friction, gained entrance to high-class restaurants. There were dressy styles that looked more like knee-length dresses teamed with matching pants, and at the other extreme, suits with a very mannish air. Unisex lived on for a few years, the name changed to the menswear look and later to androgynous.

DESIGNER NAME DROPPING

As the young French prêt-à-porter designers entered the fashion scene in the late sixties, their influence quickly spread to North America. Their ready-to-wear lines had nearly as much prestige in Canada as haute couture, but at much better prices. By the 1970s labels such as Kenzo, Sonia Rykiel, Daniel Hechter, and Dorothée Bis were selling very well in the international market and creating excitement in fashionable Canadian urban centres. The ready-to-wear lines of high-profile couture names, such as Yves Saint Laurent, Pierre Cardin, and Givenchy, along with the

"the zippy new leg-baring shortpants for summer."[2] Hot pants and skimpy tops were being shown by other designers, for example, Lilly Dee and Elvia for Luv, in Montreal.

While hot pants were perhaps the most idiosyncratic statement of the seventies, knickers and especially jeans were the most popular. Blue denim was the fabric of the decade. There were so many jean manufacturers that sometimes they couldn't get a supply of denim. Faded and worn with an old T-shirt, jeans expressed rebellion, stylishly cut with the latest label, they reflected the growing phenomenon of designer fashion. Even people who knew nothing about fashion knew about designer jeans. Jeans were presented in every way from classy cowboy strictly ready-to-wear designers, began to broaden Canadians' awareness of top fashion names. By the eighties Cardin could be said to have saturated the market.

The designer label as a motif was a phenomenon that helped Canadians to start recognizing designers' names. Previously, the maker's label on a garment was carefully hidden inside; sometimes fastidious women even removed labels because they were too commercial. Now labels began to appear as signatures on accessories such as scarves or bags. Marketing-conscious manufacturers realized the power and prestige of brand name designers. Logos moved from discreet to blatant. They developed into the repeat for a textile or were blown up and featured on everything from cars to fur jackets. In 1973 the House of Dior featured its name in bold letters at the hemline of a full-length white mink coat.

Designers of note were not only French. In England there were Jean Muir, Zandra Rhodes, John Bates, Bill Gibb, Ozzie Clarke, and Laura Ashley [121], among others. Important American designers at this time were Bill Blass, Geoffrey Beene, Mary McFadden, and Oscar de la Renta, all known for dressy day- and eveningwear, and Halston, Anne Klein, Ralph Lauren, Calvin Klein, and Perry Ellis, all known for elegant and wearable sportswear with a mix of restraint and trend-setting styling.

In the seventies Canadians also discovered Italian designers —Armani, Versace, Krizia, Missoni, Valentino, and Biogotti. The best Italian design had a look that was sombre but elegant, professional, and authoritative, in new and beautiful textures and colours.

The Canadian fashion consumer was label-conscious for other reasons, too. Newspaper and magazine fashion reporting and fashion advertising paid more attention to designer names in Canadian manufacture. The industry might despair of any substantial recognition for their designers, but it was slowly happening. Canadian designers were especially good at creating the smart and wearable fashions increasingly demanded by the Canadian consumer at the same time as prices of imported fashions were rapidly escalating.

In spite of a poor economy and rapidly rising prices, consumer spending increased, particularly on top-of-the-line goods. Fur designer-manufacturer Norman Rogul of Toronto was quoted in 1976, "Prices are phenomenal, incredible, but so are sales. I don't know where people are finding the money." Toronto retailer Eddie Creed said on the same occasion, "I'm amazed the way sales are booming."[3] By the end of the decade the yuppie (young upwardly mobile) customer had been identified, defined, and targeted as the consumer of every new luxury item imaginable. Status dressing was completely reinstated, and the "me" decade was off to a great start.

THE CANADIAN INDUSTRY

In the 1970s the Canadian fashion industry geared up its efforts to become more competitive, to present a stronger, more unified message to the world, and, in some cases, to gain greater recognition for its designers. The federal government was prepared to assist in a renewed drive to sell Canadian fashion to the American market. Fashion Canada was formed in 1969, under the direction of Lissa Taylor, to institute a federal fashion and textile promotion program.

One factor that affected the Canadian fashion industry in the seventies was the formation of fashion design and production programs at many of the new Ontario Community Colleges, including George Brown, Seneca, Sheridan, and St. Lawrence. Programs already existed at Ryerson, the Ontario College of Art, École Alyne Larin in Quebec, and the Academy of Fashion Design in British Columbia, among others.

Fashion Canada offered an apprenticeship program, scholarships, and bursaries to promising students. Winners in

1973 were Wayne Clark and Linda Lundström of Sheridan and Barbara Semrick of Seneca. By the mid-eighties Toronto would add more competition in the form of a new private fashion school, The Academy of Merchandising and Design.

Training for a position in the fashion industry in Quebec was also available on a broader scale. By the eighties there were over a dozen private colleges and institutions in Montreal alone, among them College Lasalle, College Marie-Victorin, and École Vincent d'Indy, as well as government-controlled schools with art and design programs that could lead to a career in fashion.

In 1972 the government-sponsored Montreal Mode was formed to promote the Quebec industry. Aimed mainly at the American press, Montreal Mode's annual shows were showcases for the talents of designers John Warden, Michel Robichaud, and Leo Chevalier, among others.

The Fashion Designers Association of Canada was founded in 1972 with Mary Stephenson as executive director. She dealt effectively with the problems created by the rivalry between Quebec and Ontario and by the isolation of the west. She organized semiannual shows in Montreal and Toronto and toured the country, showcasing the best works of the association's members. Founding members in Montreal included the high-profile John Warden, now designing for such top firms as Auckie Sanft, Beverini, and Molyclaire; Michel Robichaud, designer for Auckie Sanft and others; the well-established Leo Chevalier for Montroy and others; Marielle Fleury for Rainmaster; Elvia Gobbo; Hugh Garber for Margo; and Tom D'Auria for Modes Bilboquet, among others. Toronto founding members included Pat McDonagh and Claire Haddad [132]. Later members included Lilly Dee, Malcolm Pearcey, Nicola Pelly, Bernard McGee, Peter Skibinsky, Alfred Sung, and Colin Watson. Vancouver designers Gabriel Levy and Christopher Ryan were also members. The Fashion Designers Association of Canada floundered in the eighties and no longer exists.

Marilyn Brooks, Claire Haddad, Pat McDonagh, Elvira Vali, and Everett Staples (house designer for Jean Pierce) were some of the designers represented by the Fashion Group of Toronto. Jean Pierce's store on Eglinton carried Everett Staples's originals along with imported fashions in an Art Nouveau Room. The Gallery boutique, featured Pierce's young Canadian designer collection—works by recent design-school graduates. Wayne Clark and Linda Lundström were two of these graduates, who later would be instrumental in establishing the Toronto Ontario Designer's Association.

Lundström, a Sheridan College graduate, started her own business in the mid-seventies when she returned to Toronto after studying abroad on a scholarship. Wayne Clark designed for Aline Marelle through the seventies and established a reputation for glamorous and glitzy evening confections.

Husband and wife team Bernard McGee and Shelley Wickabrod began their fashion careers in the early seventies in Toronto, he as a Fashion Canada winner and designer for Aljac, she as fashion editor for *Miss Chatelaine*. McGee and Wickabrod's Clotheslines began with their shop in Mirvish Village and quickly developed into a high fashion house with a reputation for trendy classics. By the eighties one of the items Clotheslines was best known for was their trench coat—fine quality fabric, generous cut, and interesting details.

Alfred Sung, originally from Hong Kong, studied at the Chambre Syndicale in Paris and Parson's School of Design in New York City before coming to Toronto. Sung worked with Lindzon Limited in 1972, and also illustrated fashions for *Style* magazine for a number of years. Building on his reputation for clean, classic design, Sung opened his own boutiques in the late seventies.

Marilyn Brooks, Claire Haddad, Marni Grobba, Luba, Michelle Lloyd, Pat McDonagh, Edith Strauss, and Winston were other important fashion designers in Toronto in the seventies.

Montreal's fashion industry in the early decade was well catalogued by *Elan Image*, the trade magazine of the Montreal Dress and Sportswear Manufacturers' Guild. *Elan Image*, first launched in the late sixties, by about 1980 was Canada's only trade magazine for men's and women's fashions. Some well-known labels in Montreal were Auckie Sanft, Irving Samuel, Bagatelle, Modes Bilbouquet, White Stag, Joseph Ribkoff, Molyclaire, Van Essa, Margo, Tiki, Mic Mac, Elvia for Luv, and Donald Richer.

Designers such as Chevalier and Robichaud were producing very marketable collections built around suits, ensembles, and simple figure-skimming shifts in luxury natural fabrics. At this time Chevalier began designing classic coat styles for Montroy, feminine loungewear and lingerie for Van Essa, as well as designing for Brodkin and Dalie. He also consulted on uniforms for Air Canada and the Toronto Transit Commission.

Designer of the Year for 1973, John Warden produced designs for eleven independent knit manufacturers in that year. In 1974, Chevalier, Robichaud, Warden, and Marielle Fleury formed a team for the prestigious job of designing the official uniforms for the Montreal Olympics. Warden also designed accessories for Canada Belt and Bag, as well as costume jewellery, loungewear lines for Molyclaire, and, later, western and other looks for Baron Leathers.

Some new names were emerging on the Montreal scene. Peter Skibinsky, who worked with Chevalier on couture in the late sixties, did four productive years with Irving Samuel in the seventies and went with Joshar in 1979. Other designers were Jean Claude Poitras, Gordon Griffin, and François Guenet. Simon Chang, a Vancouver School of Art graduate, began a partnership, Simon Chang for International Typhoon in 1976. The Nicola Pelly–Harry Parnass design team started their trendsetting new wave sportswear company, Parachute, in 1978.

Noted Vancouver designers of the period were Scottish-born Christine Morton, whose charming way with antique laces and delicate fabrics still produces the ultimate in feminine, romantic tops and exquisite lingerie selling in the finest stores in Canada and the United States and Lore Maria Wiener, whose haute couture house on West 41st Street was a veritable institution throughout the decade. Other names of note were Trish Keating, Eveleen Hill, and Yolanta Tang of Tango Garments.

Local papers and magazines increasingly featured Canadian content for their readers. Lillian Foster, fashion editor for the *Toronto Telegram* wrote about fashion in the fifties and sixties. Eveleen Dollery as fashion and beauty editor of *Chatelaine* and *Miss Chatelaine* in the sixties and seventies provided the average Canadian consumer with basic information on fashion and sometimes included information on Canadian labels and designers. In the seventies the daily papers provided more up-to-the-minute fashion news from a variety of talented journalists: Iona Monahan for the *Montreal Star* and later the *Montreal Gazette*; Wini Rider also in Montreal; Penny Rubin for the *Vancouver Province*; Sybil Young for the *Canadian;* Joyce Carter for the *Globe and Mail*; and Joan Sutton, Marina Sturdza, Signy Stephenson, and Vivian Wilcox for *Style*, to name a few.

In the later seventies new and sophisticated Canadian magazines were published to inform trendy readers of the latest amenities. Many of these magazines regularly carried fashion articles, for example, *City Woman, Calgary, Vancouver, Vancouver Life, Montreal, Calendar,* and *Toronto Life. Toronto Life Fashion* started in 1977.

Flare was Canada's first national monthly fashion magazine. Launched in 1979, *Flare* developed out of *Miss Chatelaine*, published since the mid-sixties and aimed at the younger fashion market, the baby boomer as teen. *Flare*'s target was the working woman, the same teen now grown up. *Flare*'s emphasis is on fashion and beauty, but the magazine also covers careers, sports, sex, entertainment, food, and women's roles.

DRESS FOR SUCCESS

Compared to the Canadian economy of the 1960s, the seventies suffered rapid inflation and considerable unemployment. Incomes did not keep up with rising costs. More women now worked mainly for economic reasons. Because of the uncertain economy the mood of fashion in the seventies was a conservative one. No more flashy new synthetics, experimental was out, and the highly stylized design of the sixties began to give way to what was being called a return to nature, or at least, to the natural order of things.

A female version of the long-established businessman's suit was called "investment dressing," conservative, long-lasting, and in sympathy with the male image. Pinstripe, flannels, gabardines, and other traditional menswear fabrics, usually in grey, were favoured. Styles moved towards that of the IBM corporate image.

In 1971 when casual and colourful dressing was infiltrating IBM offices, the chairman of the board directed all IBM managers to see that the dress of their employees was "far behind the leading edge of fashion" because too many were "beginning to exceed the bounds of common sense in their business attire."[4] Severe conformity of dress in the workplace was still recommended in 1977 by author John Molloy in *The Woman's Dress for Success Book.*[5]

Some thought that the standard blazer and shirt worn with pants completed the long journey to dress equality for women. Seventy-five years since cycling bloomers, women had finally arrived. No sooner were they into the entire man's suit, however, when they began to decide that female dress was really more fun. In any case, most institutions continued to support the traditional view of pants for men and skirts for women. By about 1973 pantsuits were starting to be traded for skirt-suits as the state of the economy deteriorated.

c   *Theo Dimson's illustrations for Lipton's took on a more geometric quality in the seventies.*

By mid-decade there was a more relaxed attitude about business dress. *Chatelaine* continued to encourage this attitude with such comments as: "the neutralizing male way is not the only way. And the new woman—purposeful, self-confident—feels no need to look like an imitation man in a skirt."[6] Women seemed to be comfortable with the blend of femininity and professionalism in the period's dresses and skirted suits, which were much more mature in styling than they had been less than five years earlier. Suits often had the new longer skirts, pleated or softly gathered, by the end of the decade. The Italian designers did these fashions best, in beautiful but sombre fabrics. As ever in the world of fashion, the menswear look, although set aside for the time, would return again.

REVIVAL LOOKS

The decade began with a strong interest in art deco. People related to the bad economic times of the thirties and young designers were also excited by the decorative geometry of "early modern." Deco-printed wools and synthetics were used in skinny dresses, shirts, and blouses.

Synthetics had a determined final fling with such fabrics as crimplene and the "wet look" in ciré. Matte jerseys were also big in wild-cat prints and toned-down psychedelics. Prints were being scaled down and colours were neutralizing considerably. Natural fibres soon gained favour, especially in designer lines. In 1974 Everett Staples used deco-printed wool challis in a ready-to-wear collection for Jean Pierce. His line was mass-produced for the first time, in an effort to keep down costs. That year the art deco revival peaked on the fashion scene; John Warden, for example, used black and silver in a lounge- and sleepwear line for Molyclaire that echoed thirties glamour.[7]

Retro styling was reviving the forties with sweetheart necklines, padded shoulders, shirring, and gathering. Unisex was still strong and the press was also talking about the layered look (they had yet to see the bulky silhouette of the late seventies). Altogether there was a definite turning backwards for inspiration, rather than expressing the unquieting present.

A longing for the exotic usually accompanies romantic revivals. Much was made of an oriental theme in 1975, as part of the ethnic mood, as well as mideastern looks in harem trousers by Nicola Pelly and old European looks in Pat McDonagh's peasant blouses.

The menswear look for women used both skirts and pants in the 1975 season. The new chemise styles, often in the form of a smock, were loose and swingy, best in soft knits. Fitted bodyshirts were fashionable and most pants were still flared, but cigarette pants offered a stark contrast for the very trendy. Indian cottons were seen more often, a low-cost ethnic look.

The big skirt with the Russian tunic-top had had a relatively high profile in Canada as early as 1974. By 1976 the hemline had completely dropped and the silhouette changed to set the stage for even more romantic looks in dress. The longer, fuller skirt was worn with turtlenecks or long pullovers, as the figure disappeared under protective layers of clothing.

By 1976 Montreal and Toronto designers were doing lots of Canadiana: Nicola Pelly's Hudson's Bay stripes, Marielle Fleury's updated Red River coat and Tom D'Auria's North American Indian motifs. Toronto's Rita Dennis, who in 1973 was hired as a designer of loungewear and lingerie by Kayser-Roth, produced acrylic knit accessories with Indian designs. On the market there were also horse-blanket ponchos, mideastern caftans, Claire Haddad's Persian prints, Peruvian looks, leg warmers, and lumberjack, suede and duffel coats. Nostalgia was big for ethnic styling from near or far.[8]

The folkloric flavour continued for several more seasons with knit and crocheted shawls, Moroccan influences, peasant blouses [126], tartan skirts, blouson battle jackets, and Marielle

d *Claire Haddad's handwoven look in a narrow caftan for her, with a matching robe for him, 1975.*

Fleury's Belle Québecoise looks. In 1977 Fleury did two versions of the Hudson's Bay coat and in 1978 Nanook of the North.[9] Many international designers were exploring African, Chinese, Guatemalan, Greek, and Tibetan cultures for fashion themes. Yves Saint Laurent did the ultimate ethnic looks in richly fabricated layered outfits for day and evening.[10]

In 1979 the first issue of *Canada Fashion/Mode* showed high-styled samples of genuine ethnicity: Eskimo parkas by Central Sportswear of Winnipeg, Cowichan sweaters [145], and Hudson's Bay coats, along with other leathers and furs. The Kalpakian Knitting Mills of Vancouver sold the Cowichan sweaters to a growing Japanese market looking for a western Canadian image.

Canada was becoming part of the worldwide fashion business. The Salon International du Prêt-à-porter opened in 1978 at the Olympic velodrome in Montreal. For the first time in Canada, fashions from around the world were brought together with those from Canadian firms and presented to salesmen and store buyers in an effort to become a more important part of the international trade.

CHEMISES AND OTHER SHAPES

By mid-decade the silhouette was starting to change. The tight, small bodice was disappearing. Knit fabrics had helped to give some comfort to skimpy cuts, and the casual T-shirt shape had been lengthened to create the T-shirt dress. The fit gradually became more generous at the same time as the shoulder line started to move out a little. Softer, loftier knits with a more handmade look were gaining favour, as an expression of "natural."

By the late decade minis began to appear again but only as a side show to the main spectacle. The dominant feeling was now loose, long, and full. The layered look began to over-power the figure with tunics, vests, and jackets worn with long

e
A jumpsuit, zipped and elasticized, with snapped expansion pockets, by Lilly Dee, 1973.

This period saw an even broader reaction against synthetic fibres. Young people who shopped in the secondhand thrift stores discovered the comfort of presixties cottons and woollens [129]. Designers were also using more natural fibres in high fashion collections. Colours were very muted and neutral [125]. Real silk in various forms was more widely available and handpainted silks and silklike synthetics were moving from the craft scene into ready-to-wear fashions. Paula Zoubek of Ottawa created original handpainted fabrics for Claire Haddad for some seasons after leaving Sarah Clothes of Ottawa and Toronto. Synthetics stayed strong only in the middle market.

The chemise silhouette was even worn as an overdress with slim pants and heels. When the bulky silhouette reached its limit, it began to narrow down to enhance the broad-shouldered look that was developing. Many skirts were shortened to just below the knee, and the look became more classical, even rather dull.

The long and straight chemises hid figures for a few seasons, but not for long with designers such as Paris-based Azzedine Alaïa creating his innovative and influential body-clinging looks. Shorter hemlines were becoming more prevalent. Women had new reasons to stay fit as fashions increasingly revealed body shape.

By the mid-seventies, when the baby boomers entered their thirties and began to worry about their figures and declining fitness, jogging was their solution. The fitness movement was generated partly through the efforts of the government-sponsored Participaction, encouraging Canadians to become health conscious. At first the fashion industry provided standard leotards and tights and the early forms of the tracksuit in heavy cotton/polyester knits or velours. Soon these garments began to be adapted into fashionable sportswear.

The active sportswear market expanded rapidly with such items as cotton jersey jumpsuits, two-piece summer jogging outfits of shorts and tops in velours and cotton knits. There

calf-length skirts and high-heeled indoor boots. A blouson effect was popular in jackets, sweaters, and tops; pants were either cut straight or fuller through the hips to taper towards the ankle.[11] As a fuller, looser chemise style developed soft drapy fabrics were favoured: fine, clinging matte jersey, Qiana, and other thin, supple synthetic knits, as well as light gauzy knits, challis, satin, georgette, chiffons, lightweight linens, crepes, and velours.

were sportswear items of all kinds—sweatshirts and long pants in acrylic triple knits, nylon rainsuits, tank tops, cotton terry short shorts for cycling and squash, and cotton or nylon-lycra bodysuits for running and aerobics. Tennis wear was often a semifitted micromini dress in a synthetic material.

Lilly Dee first made her name in active sportswear. Czecho-slovakian by birth, Dee studied design in Toronto, and then moved to Montreal where she worked for Lady Utex and Susan Van Heusen through the sixties. In 1969 she went to Bilbouquet where she developed her own label, Activi-Dee, collections of interchangeable separates for tennis, golf, sailing, cycling, and other sporting activities. Using polyester and cotton blends in poplins, denims, and terry cloth, Dee updated sportswear with the latest design details: tunnel-waistlines, fancy snaps, big zips, drawstring control, and well-placed expanding areas. In 1977 her own new firm, Lilly Dee Creations of Canada, expanded into other lines of sportswear and contemporary women's fashions.

EVENINGS

The decade began with eveningwear mainly in mini form of micro shortness in silvers and whites or brights. Seventies discos were much more spectacular than the earlier variety, with pulsating checkerboard floors, fog machines, and dazzling visual effects, as dancers did the Hustle or the Bump. Sexy space-age looks or shiny hot pants made the most of the erotic dances. Sometimes both long skirt and short shorts combined in a compromise as in [124]. English designer Ozzie Clarke's halter dress [119] illustrates a reluctance to give up the mini. But soon the long dress looked newer, especially for more intimate, quieter scenes, and fulfilled the wish for romantic evenings.

As psychedelic prints faded, a simpler, almost neoclassic look prevailed and the empire line was explored with a new variation. This version involved the raised and angled waist seam and a flared rather than gathered long skirt, more in keeping with 1930s and 1940s lines. Fabrics were at first fairly crisp and firm, even heavy, and many were synthetic. About mid-decade more light crepes, chiffons, and textured knits appeared. Fabrics were gathered to create soft lines and rich textures. Solid colours, prints with smaller motifs, and lacy, lofty textures were in, often glowing and multicoloured as in the beautiful Missoni knits.

The rich costume quality of Yves Saint Laurent's colourful 1976 Russian collection and his 1977 Spanish gowns created a sensation and a long-time influence [127]. Other later-decade evening looks were skinny pants outfits and wrapped skirts in sexy silk charmeuse, crepe, georgette, or polyester satin, worn with high-heeled sandals. The chemise translated for evening into narrow, low-cut, elegant classics [128]. Black lace and sheers were important, also velvets, taffeta, lamé, and glamorous touches of sparkling sequins. By the end of the decade, total glitz was well on its way.

PUNK AND STREET FASHIONS

The most revolutionary aspect of dress in the 1970s was seen in the punk movement which first appeared in London. Punk combined sex, violence, and kitsch. By the time punk was labelled a fashion movement, many young people in Canadian urban centres were adopting its symbols, totally or in part.

Imitations of rock stars' outlandish dress produced a look both revolutionary and inventive. Safety pins, studded collars and belts, zips in black leather, and torn, skintight jeans showing lots of ankle, were topped with brightly coloured hair in explosive cuts or shaved head styles.

For young women involved in the punk movement, it was a revolt, among other things, against the conventional stereo-typing of women, the growing materialism of the period, as well as a statement glorifying alienation. The ethnic revival mood of the 1970s along with the poor economy and rapidly rising prices created the perfect conditions for recycling clothing—a defiant mix-and-matching that provided entertaining tongue-in-cheek chic on city streets, in areas like Toronto's Queen Street. The secondhand shops provided the wherewithal for punk and other kinds of eclectic street ensembles, including the 1978 Annie Hall romanticized menswear look.

Punk trickled up from the street to high fashion. In 1978 models wearing Parisian designer Claude Montana's broad-shouldered studded black leathers marched down the runway to great applause, and so began a period of hard chic, a remarkable fashion theme that was popular in the early eighties along with the theme of utter chaos, from such designers as London's Vivienne Westwood and Parisian Jean Paul Gaultier. The more stylish postmodern looks incorporated some of both these themes.

THE NEW WAVE SHOULDERS IN

Nineteen seventy-eight was the year of the film *Annie Hall*. Actress Diane Keaton's fashions by Ruth Morley blended little-girl romanticism and traditional menswear items. She played with the tweedy country-casual styles for men and turned them into dress-up and costume for women. Although *Annie Hall* started a fad, women couldn't take the look very seriously. Women's fashions had already quite naturally incorporated a power message that truly belonged to them. They were carried into the eighties with the broad shoulders of their own dress, in new sophisticated and modern fabrics.

At first, shoulders had a little widening via pleats and gathers, small shoulder pads, epaulette trim, or just full-cut bodices with full-cut sleeves. Soon extremely large shoulder pads were used in everything. Padded anoraks, coats, and jackets added more shoulder width to an already bulky silhouette. Jackets expanded and pants were looser and softer.

Chunky-textured handknits, mainly pullovers and jackets, hit the heights of fashion by the end of the decade. Designer Norma Lepofsky pioneered the knitwear trend in the seventies from her Yorkville boutique in Toronto. Designers Lola Leman, Vivienne Poy, and Gundi followed in Norma's footsteps. Styling seemed to grow more rococo with each progressive season. Feathers, sequins, beads, and appliquéd glitzy fabrics added crusty details and glowing colours. Even fur was knit. Norma's market spread to Calgary and to major fashion stores in the United States, Europe, and Japan.[12] The rich textured look of handknits also spread into many popular mass-produced knitwear lines. Designs by Hilary Radley for Splend'Or of Montreal, like the Adrienne Vittadini imports, for example, featured wearable lush knits in beautiful colours and forms.

While yuppie women in the later decade were busy trying to look like executives in their unconstructed jackets, other women were dressing somewhat androgynously, often more an intellectual look than a sensual one, a manner of dress influenced by the fashion-conscious popular music scene.

As punk faded, new wave emerged, simpler and cleaner, a look based on spiky hair, pointy toes, black leather jackets, and jeans or leather pants. The jackets with new proportions and in solid colours were a style akin to chic and reflected a look back to the sixties. Now began the reappearance of vinyl minis, bold black-and-white mod, hard-edged fashions that would help to form the eighties style. In Toronto Gerald Franklin's Hot Couture had the look and in Montreal Assez, Pur Hasard, and Parachute.[13] Popular singer k.d. lang dressed in a western version of new wave fashion.

116 SEPARATES (tunic and pants), *about 1972*
A sleeveless wool tunic-top "homeknit" worn over a cotton knit pullover and teamed with flared double knit wool pants. Comfortable knits and more formal knit pantsuits became a wardrobe mainstay by the early seventies. The top is in heathered moss green with decorative borders of knit patterns in mauve, terra-cotta, and tangerine. A tangerine stripe finishes the neckline and armholes, which are squared at the front and back side seams.
Label: Ulla Heathcote, London
Worn by Caroline Routh   *Private Collection*

117 DRESS, *1973*
A sporty dress, unlined, in heavy aqua cotton sateen. The style is typical of Courrèges's by then established space-age look, using the centre-front white plastic industrial zipper as a design statement. The collar is detachable, held in place by eleven tiny dome fasteners stamped "Flox (A. Raymond RG)." The belt is stitched into place.
Designer: André Courrèges, Paris
Label: Courrèges, Paris, Made in France, cotton 100%, Creeds, Toronto
Worn by Françoise Rioux   *The Seneca College Collection*

118 SHEATH

A long and narrow sheath in printed silky jersey. The characteristic abstract print is screened in mainly pastel colours (pale peach, salmon, mint, mauve, and pink, with bold touches of orange and black) outlined with a fine black line and scattered with tiny "Emilio" signatures. Closure is centre back with a V-neck and seven, self-covered buttons plus loops. The border-printed panels are seamed horizontally front and back through the black stripes at bust level.

Designer: Emilio Pucci, Florence
Label: Emilio Pucci, Florence-Italy, Made in Italy,
Purchased in Paris and worn by Lois Morantz

The Seneca College Collection

119 GOWN

An evening gown in moss crepe. The empire line is carried a step further in bareness with a bikini-like top printed in red, green, black, and cream. The black seven-gored skirt echoes the 1930s and 1940s with a front-buttoning, form-fitting shape that flares towards the hemline. The gown is transitional in that it shows a reluctance to give up the seductive appeal of the leg.

Designer: Ozzie Clarke, London

The Suddon Collection

120 TWO JACKETS AND A CAPE

LEFT: DENIM JACKET
Denim was increasingly used in fashionable styling of designer goods.
Label: SOS and IB Drasbek Design Purchased in Denmark and worn in Ontario about 1970

MIDDLE: WOOL JACKET
Cream textured wool jacket lined in cream satin.
Label: Cuddle Coat, New York

RIGHT: WOOL CAPE
Unlined, double-layered, chocolate brown wool cape with a hood. All seams and darts are beautifully finished inside and out to create trapuntolike edgings and details. One thread-covered large hook and eye closes front neckline.
Label [1] André Laug, for Audrey S.R.L.
Roma, Made in Italy
[2] La Belle Boutique, Toronto
Worn by Toni Stoneham
The Seneca College Collection

121 SUMMER DRESS

A high-waisted and full-skirted dress in the Laura Ashley milkmaid look of floral printed cottons in pink and blue. This romantic pioneer image in calico and ruffles was picked up in the early seventies by young women in England, the United States, and Canada.

Label: Designed by Jacqui Smale for Spectrum, London, Eng.

The Suddon Collection

122 ENSEMBLE (jacket and dress), *about 1970*

A long clinging pull-on dress and matching jacket in black wool knit. The raised waistline is covered by an appliqué tree design in dark green wool knit with a rust "trunk" loop over a gather of pumpkin orange wool knit. The skimpy, unlined jacket has two patch pockets in bright purple with appliqués of a rust house on an orange hilltop. This was a period of strong interest in the fabric crafts.

Designer: Pat McDonagh, Toronto

Label: McD

Worn by Diane Meaghan *Private Collection*

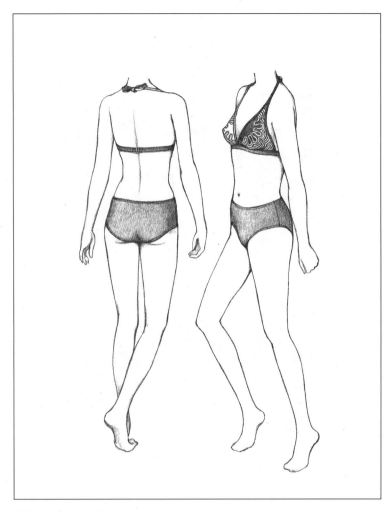

123 BIKINI, *1973*
A blue-and-yellow printed, relatively modest, bikini swimsuit. The simple low-rise pant is in bright blue stretch knit of eighty-five percent nylon and fifteen percent lycra, for fit, comfort, and quick drying. The halter-tied top in the same fabric blend is mainly yellow (with some blue) on one side and mainly blue on the other. The bright blue, two-millimetre-wide, elasticized band hooks centre back with a blue plastic hook.
Label: 8 (Huit)
Purchased in Paris and worn in Ontario   *Private Collection*

124 HOT PANTS DISCO OUTFIT
A one-piece outfit for disco dancing in black and orange synthetic crepe. The fitted scoop-necked top zips up the back and has long, slim, set-in sleeves. A "skirt" of twenty-one long bands in black and orange crepe, slightly tapered to the waist seam, hangs over short shorts. The black and gold plastic belt in rectangular units hooks with a coarse chain.   *The Suddon Collection*

125 CHEMISE

A soft and swingy chemise in unlined wine heather wool. Fullness in body and sleeves is gathered to saddle shoulder yokes. Six bone buttons close centre front. Two large welt pockets are worked in at hip level. Here accessorized with a long Missoni knit scarf of gauzy silk in shades of wine, rust, mauve, and grey green.

Label: Krizia, Made in Italy. 40"
Purchased at Browns, South Moulton Street, London and worn
by Claire Becker   *The Seneca College Collection*

126 PEASANT BLOUSE AND JEANS

A peasant-styled, Romanian-made blouse of cream cotton gauze, hand-embroidered and smocked with light and dark blue and silvery white threads. The neckline is smocked in dark blue and the centre-front opening is edged and tied with the same blue, as are the wrists. Bands of cross-stitch worked in the two tones are centred on the front and on each sleeve, interspersed with narrow bands of white embroidered florals. The seams of the raglan sleeves, the side seams, and the armhole gussets are blanket-stitch edged in dark blue, and all seams are beautifully finished inside with white blanket stitching.

Bought in France and worn by Caroline Routh   *Private Collection*

127 GOWN, *about 1980*
A glowing full-length evening dress of unlined light moiré taffeta in emerald green. The folkloric look is evoked through the crisp full skirt, the ruffles, and the low-cut square neckline, but the broadened, padded shoulders are new. The fitted bodice closes centre front with snaps and five self-covered buttons with machine-stitched buttonholes. Here the waist is accented with a black pleated silk sash tied with a front bow.
Label: [*1*[*Michel Goma, Paris* [2] *La Belle Boutique, Toronto*
Worn by Toni Stoneham  *The Seneca College Collection*

128 CHEMISE, *1979*
An evening chemise in black velvet. The low V-neckline and straight lines work well with the burst of ruffled sheer at the hemline. The dress is fully lined. The sleeves are vented at the wrists and close with a black satin-covered button plus loop. Worn here over a lacy black camisole.
Designer: Sybil Casey, Toronto
Label: Sybil Casey Collectables
Worn by Claire Becker *The Seneca College Collection*

129 LEFT: SUMMER DRESS
A simple, pull-on, one-piece summer dress of cotton gauze in purple and light green. The gauzy fabric somewhat softens the colours. The strapless top and the waistline are worked with a band of elasticized shirring and the skirt is slit at left hem.
Label: Fiorucci   Made in France   *The Suddon Collection*

RIGHT: OVERALL
Romanticized dungaree styling in beige cotton gauze. The airy one-piece garment is cut very full and gathered to elasticized ribbed cuffs at the ankles and to the narrow yokes of matching cotton voile which tie at the shoulders. Slot pockets at hips.
Label: Catherine I Salvet Pour Phillipe Salvet.   Made in France
The Suddon Collection

130 SHORTS AND TOP, *about 1980*
A two-piece sportswear outfit in aqua velour. The pop-on top in aqua with white stripe has short kimono sleeves and an elasticized waistband. The figure-hugging shorts are bound in white with a drawstring waist and curved vents at the sides. Velour and stretch terry shorts were popular at this time for casual summer wear.

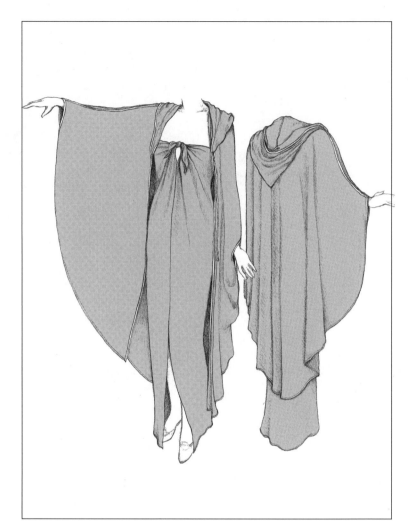

131 SKI SUIT

A ski suit in three variations of green. The hooded jacket in two layers of dense cotton poplin is a reversible construction. The front zipper works from both top and bottom, and the cut is loose enough to be worn over a sweater. The sleek fitted shape of the pants is darted to a narrow waistband with side zipper. Straps underfoot keep the line snug.

Label: Hettemarks
Made in Sweden *The Seneca College Collection*

132 LOUNGEWEAR, *1977*

A two-piece lounging outfit in lapis blue Qiana (100 percent nylon jersey) comprising gown and caftan. The narrow, straight-cut, strapless gown pulls on and ties at the breast; the neckline is secured with a fine encasing of elastic. The only seam is centre front down to a generous vent at the hem. The hooded caftan is trimmed with bright gold jersey piping, binding, and ties. The batwing sleeves add fullness to the wrap.

Designer: Claire Haddad, Toronto *The Seneca College Collection*

THE
1980s

IN THE EIGHTIES CONTEMPORARY DESIGN EXPRESSION WAS SO SELF-AWARE that it was served up already labelled postmodern. Unlike the 1920s and 1930s, this decade didn't need later historians to explain and define it; it obviously reflected an attraction to, and an evolution beyond, the modern design statements of the 1950s. Design journalism, as well as marketing promotion and advertising, was so fast-moving and sophisticated by now that everyone knew what was happening as it happened.

One of the early expressions of postmodernism was the Italian design association, Memphis. It grew out of a development of a collection of prototype furniture designs by small specialized companies in and around Milan in the late seventies. The radical philosophies of the designers, who came together for the 1981 Milan Furniture Fair, helped to produce a new direction for the applied arts, internationally. Inspired by pop motifs, bad taste, and punk and street fashions, the designers were reacting against the anonymous neutrality of institutional design, much as fashion designers were reacting against the corporate styles of the seventies. Some leaders of the Memphis school were Ettore Sottsass and Michele De Lucchi in furniture and Nathalie du Pasquier in textiles.[1]

Memphis first shocked and then helped to revolutionize the development of design in the eighties, with obvious ties to both the period of art deco and fifties modern. The Memphis designers like many ready-to-wear and couture designers, turned their inspirations into something more individual, playful, and inventive than fifties or art deco design had ever been. Forms and structures were aggressively asymmetrical and unconventional; there was a tongue-in-cheek humour in the escapism of postmodern design [138].

The link between art and fashion was strengthened in the eighties, no doubt as an antidote to the powerful mass marketers. Wearable art was a term used to describe handmade neo-baroque designs with decorative trim, or later in the decade, colourful and usually chaotic geometrics on sweatshirts, T-shirts, and other knits [148].

Palettes combined brights and pastels in luminous television colours, gold, scarlet, fuchsia, violet, pinks, blues, and greens. Synthetic and natural materials were put together in a new way. Designers in various media around the world produced work that was joyful in colour, highly patterned, and even eccentric. Postmodernism reinforced and extended the creations of new-wave artists, craftspeople, and jewellery and fashion accessory designers, whose work was headed in a similar direction. In spite of references to the past, postmodern design was exciting and experimental.

Early eighties postmodernism in dress absorbed much of the highly stylized punk themes of the young street culture, and

a *Postmodern illustrations were geometric and highly stylized in 1984.*

three stages of sixties revival to be found in the postmodernism of the eighties: first, the mod revival as a subtheme of punk; secondly, the rather belabored fashion industry's sixties revival through the mid-decade; and finally, the matronly Pucci-like reruns of the late eighties, when the baby-boomer generation was thirtysomething at least.[2]

Out of the whole history of women's dress, the decade of the 1960s was a short period of relative liberation. Its fashions expressed the youthfulness and hope for the future that people in the eighties did not feel. Recycling sixties fashions was inevitable in the troubled eighties, but the decade also expressed its own particular values: more blatant, aggressive sexuality and more ostentation. Dressing for evenings, for example, involved pulling out all the stops in an attempt to have it all: colour, rich fabrication, décolletage, hourglass shape, bouffaut skirts, and legs, too.

The mid-1980 daytime version of postmodern dress blended assertiveness and sex appeal in the masculine, inverted-triangular, broad-shouldered power jacket atop those newly exposed legs. Rarely was dress simple or functional; the problems caused by extreme shoulder pads were enough to ensure a lack of function. The television poise and self-confidence that severely modern dress required was not seen often in real life where the urge to embellish in all areas remained strong.

The ever-increasing technology of the computer has remodelled our systems for designing and producing goods and services. Computerization has affected the work process enormously in terms of time and the ability to see all the possible alternatives in the design process. The freedom afforded designers by computers should push the explorative, creative urge to new limits when other factors don't interfere to cancel out the benefits.

Computers have turned up in fashion in other ways, for example, as the microcomputer fitted to Adidas's Micropacers, which allow the running wearer to keep track of performance and caloric combustion.

punk-inspired terrorist chic offered similar trendy touches— black leather with chunky zips, short spiky hair, streaks of colour on hair and eyes, fifties-type sunglasses, and metal-studded, anti-establishment jewellery.

Canadian fashion writer David Livingstone defines all modern dress as functional, free of decoration, and with broad appeal to the public. Further, he says, it must express its own time. In his search for modernity of dress for this century, he refers to

JAPANESE FASHION DESIGNERS

In the 1970s there were only two Japanese designers making their mark in the Parisian fashion world: Hanae Mori, working in the traditional methods of French haute couture, and Kenzo Takada, who successfully blended East and West in his whimsical ready-to-wear lines. It wasn't until the early eighties, however, that a Japanese style created shock waves in the world of fashion. Issey Miyake, Rei Kawakubo, and Yohji Yamamoto were the leaders of this fashion revolution.

Issey Miyake apprenticed with Givenchy, Laroche, and American designer Geoffrey Beene. He experienced the anti-couture era of the late sixties and was left with an over-riding desire to start again from the beginning to define the nature and role of dress today. Miyake set up his own company in 1970 in Tokyo and pioneered the way for a new approach to garment design—a Japanese artisan's version of dress for the Western world, marketed out of Paris.[3]

Miyake integrated the forms of traditional Japanese working clothes and crafts, into such fashion items as his cotton denims and woollen coats. He developed his own methods of draping fabrics on the body that produced rich, totally unconventional structures in dress, sometimes with the simplicity we associate with ancient cultures, but showing modern sensitivities and imagination of form.

Following Miyake's lead, a wave of Japanese-designed styles arrived in Paris in 1982. The esoteric philosophies of Rei Kawakubo and Yohji Yamamoto, in particular, created enormous controversy. Not only were their clothes revolutionary, but also their sales pitches. Kawakubo's Zen-garden inspired shop, Comme des Garçons, appeared as empty spaces of stone and glass, puzzling most shoppers who were used to the traditional retail store and conventions of Western business culture.

Kawakubo's Comme des Garçon collections expressed an androgynous look extolling the beauty of self-sufficiency and freedom from materialism—enveloping, sometimes narrow, always big, asymmetrical, ripped, randomly wrapped and tied, dark colours—clothing totally opposite to Western conventions in dress: "fabric sewn and folded into shapes that shift on the body like shadows. Colours that seem to come from the shaded sun-dried underside of the spectrum."[4] The look might have amazed, even stunned, but to many in 1982 it seemed also to speak volumes, as pessimism about the economy and quality of life mounted.

Americans linked the look of the Japanese designs to the bag-lady look and it turned up glamourized in 1983 as torn sweatshirts showing a sexy shoulder, a look derived from the movie *Flashdance*. Trendy urban Canadians hunted out the look from design firms such as Parachute and Zapata. Broader effects on mainstream fashion design produced a trend toward asymmetry, disjointed joinings, traditional Japanese motifs, and long loose lines [133, 134, 137].

INTERNATIONAL FASHION TRADE

The narcissism of the eighties was nurtured by the influential new music videos. Heroes and heroines of the pop scene were studied in great depth, not just for inventive visual expressions of their music but for every detail of their appearances. Fashion videos were produced by mid-decade by such firms in Toronto as Shooters, Schulz Productions, and Cabbagetown Productions. The ready-to-watch fashion era was quickly ushered into Canada with weekly television shows such as City TV's *Fashion Television* with Jeanne Beker, *Flash Mode Québec* on TQS, and later *Fashion File* with Tim Blanks.

Through videos, films, advertising, fashion magazines, and coffee-table books on fashion, the fashion consumer in the eighties was highly aware. Newspapers published many more excellent fashion articles written by journalists such as Iona Monahan for the *Montreal Gazette* and Monelle Saindon for *Le Journal de Montréal*. The *Globe and Mail* and the *Toronto Star* published weekly fashion sections, with top-notch fashion journalists Joyce Carter, David Livingstone, and Marina Sturdza.

Haute couture designers in Paris tried to make it quite clear that the ascendancy of the ready-to-wear designers in the seventies had faded and that couture was number one again. Strong fashion statements continued to be made by designers who had stayed on top through two decades or more: Yves Saint Laurent, Ungaro, Dior, and Cardin. But it was Karl Lagerfeld, designer for Chloé for twenty years, who in 1982 took on the formidable task of refurbishing the Chanel couture collection. Lagerfeld blended eighties class and humour for a highly successful postmodern version of Chanel which had an enormous impact on fashionable dress for many seasons and made him internationally known.

Some French designers were responding to the success of the Japanese invasion of the intellectual with even more than usual flamboyant sexuality. Designers such as Thierry Mugler, Claude Montana, and Jean-Paul Gaultier staged increasingly entertaining fashion theatre—at the most marketable, emphasizing a clean lean line, or a clean voluptuous line, and, at the most bizarre, displaying undergarments for streetwear.

Eighties tastes for costume and fantasy quickly made a star out of Christian Lacroix who in 1987, after six years with Patou, wowed the fashion press with his audacious couture and with his ready-to-wear. Lacroix led the way in fifties-inspired eveningwear.

Tunisian Azzedine Alaïa emerged on the Paris scene about 1982 with his own distinctive approach to fashion design. He had perhaps the strongest influence of any designer on late eighties styles with body-defining clothes in knits and leathers that showed off female curves. His bold shoulders of the early decade gradually became smaller as the years passed. Some other designers with a somewhat similar spare chic were Romeo Gigli and American designer Donna Karan, much admired for her distinctive and liberated eighties dress.

London, as a leader of the earliest and most extreme expressions of punk, through the eighties had a reputation for eclectic eccentricity springing from its colourful street fashion. Eccentricity is a quality highly valued by a society permeated with long-established rules and conventions. The revolution of British youth moved onto the fashion runways, where wild, sometimes witty, creations celebrated the romance of poverty, not unlike Rei Kawakubo in Paris. The look was nurtured by such designers as Zandra Rhodes and Vivienne Westwood in the seventies, and by the English design team Body Map.

Westwood was the champion of English fashion rebellion. Her Punkature of 1983 gloried in intentionally twisted seams, bad cuts, unfinished hemlines, and uncoordinated colours. Westwood's fashion statements, like Peter Pan, revelled in childhood and her images of bumbling youth appealed to romantic natures. Westwood continued her childlike images through the eighties, for example, her short and puffy neo-fifties crinolines.

American labels of fashionable clothes from sportswear to eveningwear still included Bill Blass, Geoffrey Beene, Oscar de la Renta, Perry Ellis, Calvin Klein, Ralph Lauren, Norma Kamali, and Anne Klein. Klein employed designers Louis Dell'Olio and Donna Karan. Karan later set up on her own with great success. New names added in the eighties were David Cameron, Carolyne Roehm, John Anthony, Michael Kors, Stephen Sprouse, Isaac Mizrahi, and Carolina Herrera, among others. The admirable Halston career that ended mid-decade was commemorated with two shows in New York at the Fashion Institute of Technology, where the designer's nonreferential, truly modern approach to dress stood as an exception to the over-indulgence of many high profile eighties designers.

EIGHTIES SILHOUETTES

Early eighties postmodernism was an eclectic blend of new wave fashion, Hollywood glitz, Japanese-influenced design, and fitness mania. There was a heavy dose of androgyny in all, and in the traditional menswear look that was promoted for fall, 1982 as part of the investment dressing for difficult economic times. The cost of clothing production was rising rapidly; consumers resisted the high prices and bought carefully. Some manufacturers saw a partial solution in shorter skirts, narrower lines, and less detailing, practical reasons to relive the sixties. By mid-decade shorter hemlines were competing strongly with longer lengths [140].

The pared-down tailoring from new wave, along with the poor economy, helped to produce simple mainstream daytime fashions —collarless dresses and jackets sometimes parti-coloured like jester's tunics. As far as possible from the sombre Japanese statement were conventional evening numbers: sequined sheaths and gowns with emphasized shoulders, in shiny metallic fabrics, some styled on the lines of television programs such as *Dynasty*. Wayne Clark's Alexis dress was a best-seller in 1981 and the gown [136] by Linda Lundström illustrates the look, somewhat toned down.

Fitness was a new status symbol. Fitness centres sprouted up all over the country, and some women even took up body-building in an effort to shape up into the sexiness of a champion athlete [139].

Closer goals for men and women in many sporting activities plus the status of a sleek and fit body shape created a market for active sportswear with similarity of design for both sexes. (Unisex sportswear only showed more clearly the differences between the sexes.) This sportswear with its bold colours and modern fabrication, for example, various knitted structures with omnidirectional give, held great appeal as fashion items [147, 148]. Real active sportswear was still a relatively small part of

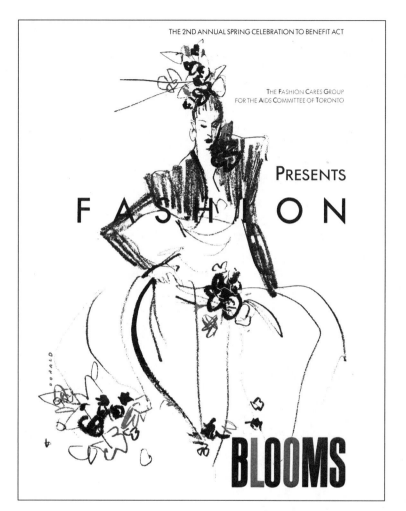

b *The 1988 program cover for Fashion Blooms, with Donald's avant-garde illustration, showed a softer, more romantic mood.*

the market; the impulse behind most purchases was fashion.

Active sportswear spread beyond its boundaries into dress for everyday leisure wear and even merged with the new sexy look in dress clothes. Post-baby-boomer customers took enthusiastically to the short and unforgiving clinging dress silhouette, which called attention to the small round derrière and the bust.

Knitted tops featuring off-the-shoulder styling recalled the late fifties, but real cleavage, officially rediscovered by mid-decade as part of the neo-fifties look, meant evening gowns that "were clinging or low cut or strapless, or all three."[5] Taken even further, the bustier turned up for daywear as well as evening, and extreme, costumelike fashions from some of the most avant-garde designers made much of the artificial breastplate look by 1990. Straplessness was only part of the late eighties message in eveningwear [143]. Brightly coloured fabrics, often rich and luminous taffetas, ruched and puffed into short and sassy full skirts, set off a leggy look. Barbie doll sales boomed.

By 1987 severe postmodernism had softened; the newer fashion illustrations, for example, were less geometric, less simple, less bold. Not surprisingly, they took on a character similar to 1930s illustration. Many fashions dressed the figure in softer lines, with a more generous use of fabric as in the full, swinging coats of the late decade. Still, the broad variety in styling indicated the ongoing independence of the consumer and her right to a range of choices.

SOME CANADIAN STARS

In the eighties a new sense of entrepreneurial pride created an atmosphere of world-class competition in Canadian fashion. Although stylish designer clothes were only a small part of the apparel industry here, nevertheless this designer clothes chutzpah came at a time when a flagship of fashion was needed. Competition with American-manufactured goods is so difficult that some Canadian manufacturers work hard to maintain growth in Canada. Those Canadian firms with something special to offer made efforts through the eighties to expand into the American market: Irving Samuel, Mr. Jax, Dominic Bellissimo,

c   *High-fashion design from Zapata. Karen Gable and Nancy Young formed a creative partnership in their student days at Seneca College in Toronto. Their distinctive 1990 collection was built on subtle colours and richly detailed forms.*

d *Elvira Vali's fall 1990 fashions for girls were romantic and right in tune with grown-up styles.*

Debora Kuchmé, Mr. Leonard, Alfred Sung, Tom d'Auria, Bagatelle, Hilary Radley, Parachute, Stephan Caras, and Thalie, to name a few. The names slowly changed through the decade as old guard designers such as Chevalier and Warden moved on to make room for a new generation of influence.

The big Canadian cities all have their fashion designer stars; some stay local, some are briefly popular, others endure. Fashion retailing is also often in a state of flux. In the early 1980s the Queen Street area near the garment district in Toronto was redeveloped and shops such as Koochee, Metropolis, Atomic Age, Fab, Harlequin, Boomer, Club Monaco, and the latest Marilyn Brooks were established. Other parts of the city had Finishing Touches, Sportables, Chez Catherine, Roots, Dorrit, Creeds, Holt Renfrew, Ira Berg, and Cotton Ginny.

Toronto's Spadina Avenue also changed. The Ontario Fashion Exhibitors, an organization of manufacturers' agents established in 1990 at King and Peter Streets, along with the other new merchandising marts nearby, updated the look of the city's garment district.

In 1985 the Festival of Canadian Fashion, under the direction of Steven Levy, opened in the new Metro Toronto Convention Centre and until the end of the decade sold fashion hype and the semblence of unity in the Canadian fashion industry to sell-out crowds. The later productions included "FASHION TECH" displays and the Festival Trade Forum, a program of seminars addressing current industry concerns.

Throughout the eighties, fashion-conscious people in Toronto were talking about Steven Schacht, Zapata, Tim Jocelyn, Loucas, Robin Kay, Clotheslines, Paul Cornish, Dean and Dan, Selina, Gerald Franklin, Leighton Barrett, Shelly Walsh, Donna Stephens, Emily Zarb, Edie Johne, Babel, Colin Watson, Bent Boys, Sunny Choi, Brian Bailey, Fiona Duncan, Roger Edwards, Franco Mirabelli, Hoax Couture, Tu Ly, Lida Baday, and others. Two big names in fashions for girls were Elvira Vali for Petite Originals and Elen Henderson.

It was in the mid-eighties that Peter Nygard moved his international company from Winnipeg to its headquarters in Toronto. His labels—Tan Jay, Bianca, and Alia—have been aimed at the large middle market since the late 1960s when he first began to market to price-conscious Canadian women who avoided minis and built their wardrobes in polyester. Twenty years later sales to women still avoiding minis have created an empire with production and distribution centres in Winnipeg and Los Angeles, and research and design facilities in New York, Montreal, Europe, Hong Kong, China, Indonesia, and Taiwan.

Various Canadian government ministries and agencies continued in the eighties to support and promote our top designers and manufacturers to American buyers. Struggling beginners were not forgotten. As a result of a strengthening liaison between Toronto's fashion industry and the city government in the eighties along with federal support, the Fashion Incubator on Richmond Street was formed under the direction of Carol Outram to help young Toronto designers establish businesses. One of the names launched from the Incubator is D'Arcy Moses, an Edmonton-bred Cree Indian designer who blends the imagery of his culture with exciting fashion statements. Another is James Yunker, a Ryerson graduate who won the City of Toronto's Most Promising New Designer Award in 1990.

In the eighties Alfred Sung became Canada's first big fashion star, our best-known designer label. In 1979 the shy and reserved designer joined forces with the entrepreneurial talents of Saul and Joseph Mimran to form the Monaco Group. Madly methodical and detail-obsessed, known as Mr. Clean for his correct, classic separates, wearable feminine suits, and preppy sportswear, Sung continues his search for perfection. Monaco expanded the Sung label into sunglasses, belts, hats, luggage, and designer fragrance. Club Monaco stores are chained across Canada, and expanded into the United States. Subsequently, Sung left the Monaco Group.

e *Comrags, 1992.*

f *Winter glamour Canadian style by Linda Lundström. Her choice of "no-tears fur" reflected a growing reaction against real furs.*

The witty and well-made clothes from Toronto's Comrags express the successful design liaison of two Ryerson graduates, Judy Cornish and Joyce Gunhouse. They blended fifties fantasies, body consciousness, and new wave to create high fashion for their followers in Toronto, Vancouver, Montreal, and New York. In 1987 Cornish and Gunhouse won the Festival of Canadian Fashion's Gold Award for their fashion video, "Road to Utopia," and the following year they were one of five Canadian competitors in Le Club Creation for the Maison du Lin. Their garments for the competition are now part of the Royal Ontario Museum collection. In 1991 Comrags was in the Hong Kong show for Festival Canada, and Cornish and Gunhouse were selected as Designer[s] of the Year for the City of Toronto.

Designer Linda Lundström hit a new stride in the mid-eighties with her highly successful LaParka [144], a coat combination of wool duffle and a showerproof outer shell that can be worn over it or separately, as the weather dictates. Lundström's enthusiasm for Canada's cultural heritage expressed through its native people, coupled with her recognition of the problems of northern climates, led to the development of this beautiful and truly Canadian fashion statement. Available in many colours and with the option of a variety of decorative native motifs, the coats sold very well.

Vancouver had enormous growth in the eighties, and its fashion manufacturing and retailing grew in part because of more tourists. The Pacific Centre, Robson Street, including the elegant Robson Fashion Park, South Granville, and the newly restored Sinclair Centre are the city's best shopping areas, carrying everything from the world's most prestigious labels to those of new west-coast entrepreneurs. Leone, one of the designer boutiques, supported a fashion design award program, sponsored in part by the Western Canadian Designers and Fashion Association, to encourage local young designers.

More designer names drew attention to the west coast. Christine Morton and Zonda Nellis were well established by the eighties. New designers were graduates of the private school training for the industry, the Helen Lefeaux School of Fashion Design on Abbott Street, which joined the Vancouver School of Art, the British Columbia Academy of Fashion Design, and the Emily Carr College of Art and Design, as well as Capilano College in preparation for a fashion career.

Some Vancouver designers are known internationally. Zonda Nellis, creating gloriously rich colours in handwoven, high-fashion lines of dresses, separates, coats, and accessories, is selling in prestigious shops worldwide, and she has expanded into a ready-to-wear sport collection. Julie Shilander, Catherine Regehr, Abby Kanak, Van Osch Design, Rosemarie Ceuvas, Dana Clelland, Elly Johnston, Neo Romantics, Neto Leather, and jewellery by Martha Sturdy are some of Vancouver's design names. The large Vancouver-based firm Mr. Jax, with a good-looking, fashionable line of sportswear, did extremely well in the eighties under the direction of Louis Eisman and as a result of their aggressive marketing plans and highly computerized production operations.

Montreal changed greatly over the 1980s, too. The city's downtown redevelopment transformed the look of St. Catherine Street shopping from the magnificent Les Cours Mont-Royal just north on Peel Street, through Place Montreal Trust, the Eaton Centre, and the Promenades de la Cathédrale under St. Patrick's. Ogilvy's, renovated in 1987, has elegant boutiques and other luxurious amenities which still celebrate its historic Scottish heritage.

The very competitive fashion industry of Montreal by the eighties had arrived at the point where clothing accounted for more than forty percent of all manufacturing jobs in the city. Although some designers had gained acceptance and, consequently, big orders from the department stores, most continue to sell in low volume from their own boutiques, many located

g *Award-winning designer Poitras creates womenswear and menswear fashions that sell in Canada and the United States.*

in the colourful district of the Plateau Mont-Royal, the old residential and commercial quarter that sprawls east and south of Mount Royal. On St. Denis Boutique Revenge, for example, exclusively promotes Québecois designers, and nearby, the eclectic St. Laurent Blvd. offers everything: avant-garde fashions,

h *A quality eighties look by Irving Samuel.*

retail bargain stores, and expensive shops, as well as supplies for garment manufacturers. At the north end is Chabanel Street and a major part of the city's garment district, where manufacturers and their reps open doors to the public on Saturday mornings, on a cash-only basis.[6]

The fashion names continue to evolve in Montreal. Longer established labels such as Debbie Shuchat, Hilary Radley, Simon Chang, and Parachute have been joined by Alain Thomas, Lorraine Beauchamp, Edwin Birch, Christine Tessier, George Levesque, Carmen Michaud and Gordon Iaconetti, the Girbauds, Nina Wills, Claude Gagnon, Vicky Apparly, Linda Morisset, Marcelle Danan, Lyse Spenard, Ariane Carle, Maryse Roye, Sandra Angelozzi, Marie Saint Pierre, and many others.

Parachute drew rave reviews through the decade from Canadians and Americans. Don Johnson, detective fashion-plate star of television's *Miami Vice*, wore Parachute's hot weather look in trendy pastels.

The career of Canadian designer Jean Claude Poitras, which began when he worked for Eaton's as a buyer and boutique director, took off in the late seventies when he designed collections under the BOF label for Beverini of Montreal. Poitras launched his own label in 1983, and licensed his women's ready-to-wear through Importations Franck. Later he produced luscious, trendy, and big-scaled shearling coats for Sawyer Canada and International Trademarks Apparel, furs for Amsel and Amsel, and uniforms for a number of corporations. Poitras Design, begun in 1987, was an attempt to have total control over production. Three years later Poitras Design teamed with the highly respected Irving Samuel.

Irving Samuel, known in Canada for over forty years for fine quality and fashionable styling, is a good example of a Canadian company that has kept up with the times. The man behind this singular firm is Samuel Workman whose experience and abilities have helped to create an environment for success.

Other manufacturers, such as Pretty Talk, Shasper Industries, Algo, International Tyfoon, and Miss Style have also lately hired recognized designers. In fact, the clothing industry generally continues to accelerate the trend towards a marriage between designer and manufacturer, as the fashionable Canadian consumer looks harder and longer for an identifiable and prestigious, often Canadian-made, image for her clothing investment. Both manufacturers and designers stand to gain by this liaison.

Although the cities of Montreal, Toronto, and Vancouver have been emphasized here, other Canadian centres from Halifax to Victoria also have emerging fashion personalities. A 1990 report on the apparel industry in Metropolitan Toronto prepared by the Economic Development Division in many ways sums up the problems now faced by the fashion industry across Canada: continuing technological advances, changing global trading patterns, rising production costs, declining retail sales, and free trade are all affecting the way companies market themselves. A growing commitment to develop strong brand name or designer labels is proving an effective strategy against increasing competition, and most Canadian firms are aware of this. "These market-driven firms tend to be more export oriented, and compete on the basis of image and quality as opposed to price. Manufacturers are looking to unique design as one of the key components available to help differentiate their products from that of their domestic and international competitors."[7]

Canadian manufacturers are recognized for producing quality goods and also often have the advantage of experience with flexible short production runs. Other advantages in competition could be developed to include "just-in-time" production agreements, consolidation, or the possibility of manufacturing a certain portion of a firm's products in low-cost centres. But it will be the concerted effort to position and promote an exciting fashion image in the minds of the consumer that will sustain growth for the future. It is in the areas of design development and fashion-consciousness that effective competition counts most. Whatever the future may bring, Canadians will continue to establish their niche in the fabulous and entertaining, always changing, world of fashion.

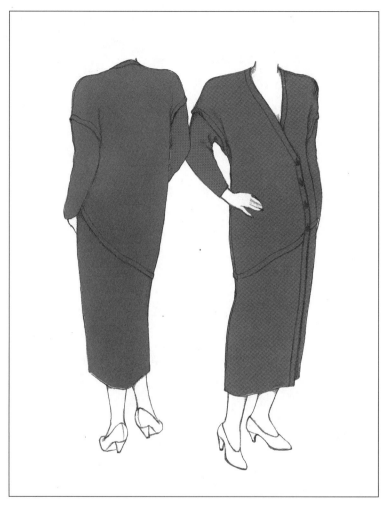

133 CHEMISE

A simple, unlined, asymmetrical chemise in scarlet wool. Padded shoulders and the longer hemline are fashion features. Front V-necked panels overlap, tying on the right underneath and buttoning on the left, leaving a generous slit. The wrapped styling and the self-banded edges are details similar to Sonia Rykiel fashions of the period.

Designer: Debora Kuchmé, Toronto   *The Suddon Collection*

134 SEPARATES

The Japanese look in separates for day: the bold cotton top contrasts fuchsia and teal and adds a touch of yellow ochre in the mandarin collar and stripe on the left sleeve.

The dark, unlined, rib-knit skirt is of twenty percent angora, seventy percent lambswool, and ten percent nylon. The long-line knit has a ribbed waistband encasing a wide elastic band.

Label: [1] *Tokyo, Singapore*
        [2] *Takano*
                                The Suddon Collection

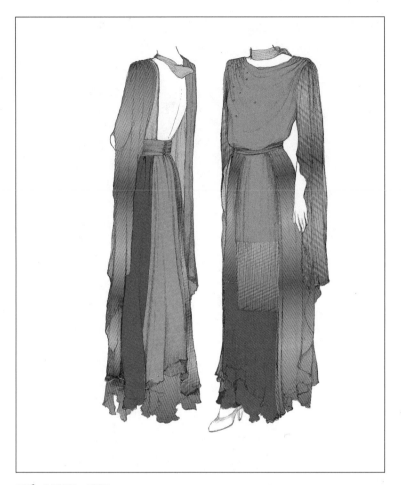

135 DRESS, *1981*

An afternoon or dinner dress in 100 percent polyester georgette. The fluid and sheer georgette is printed with tiny cream and aqua flowers against a dark cherry red ground. The central part of the yoke is in a small geometric print in aqua mainly and matches the elastic shirred waistband. A third printed fabric is pleated on the edges of the yoke at the shoulders. The skirt has six gores. The simple pull-on styling fits all sizes and the fabric is ideal for travel—light, compact, and uncrushable.

Designer: Diane Freis, Vancouver
Label: Made in Hong Kong
Purchased in Vancouver and worn by Caroline Routh   *Private Collection*

136 GOWN, *1982*

A diaphanous gown in multicoloured gradated chiffon. Colours blend from browns through ochres, cream, pink, mauve, and reds. The bodice is draped from shoulders broadened with pads and scattered with pink and clear diamantés. The back is bare above the wide, stiffened chiffon-covered belt. Full-cut layers of skirt are seamed and left to form an irregular hemline.

Designer: Linda Lundström, Toronto   *The Seneca College Collection*

137 PANTS OUTFIT

A two-piece pants outfit in a lightweight printed cotton of fifty percent polyester, fifty percent rayon. Bold black stripes and scattered red floral motifs show a Japanese influence. The black dye bleeds slightly into the white areas giving a "natural indigo" look to the fabric. The pants are full-cut and generously gathered both centre front and centre back but taper to a narrow ankle, reminiscent of Issey Miyake's voluminous pants of 1983. The simple popover top with long raglan sleeves is identical front and back.

Designer: Wayne Clark, Toronto
Label: Wayne Clark for Aline Marelle　　　*The Suddon Collection*

138 GIANT SHIRT

An elongated, white, 100 percent cotton shirt printed with a characteristically erratic postmodern print in neofifties colours: aqua, salmon, yellow, mauve, and black. The shapes of the motifs are also derived from fifties modern design. The hemline is cut away like a man's nineteenth century coat, leaving tails that are vented and buttoned centre back. Worn with black, figure-clinging stirrup pants.

Label: SPIRIT, Weekend Wear, Made in Thailand　　　*The Suddon Collection*

139 AEROBICS SUIT, *1984*

A one-piece aerobics suit in turquoise and black knit of ninety percent cotton and ten percent Lycra spandex. The absorbant stretchy fabric has a comfortable fit to the body. The scooped neckline and high-cut legs are functional and fashionable.

Labels: Phantom, Made in Canada   *Private Collection*

140 SUIT (jacket and skirt)

A soft, unlined, two-piece suit in viscose and acetate. The knee-length skirt is heathered gunmetal grey. The front is nearly covered by a second panel draped from a cluster of pleats to the waistband near the button on left hip. Zipper closes at centre-back seam above a vent.

The jacket fabric is a brocade of small cream polka dots against the heathered gunmetal grey. It is shoulder-padded and faced with self-fabric through the upper area. Buckled tabs at each hip give a curving, fitted silhouette and dark topstitching accents the structure. Worn with moss suede Pino Carina shoes.

Label: Lipton's
Worn by Diane Meaghan   *Private Collection*

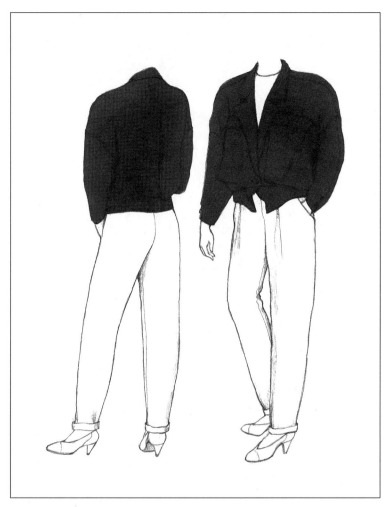

141 JACKET

A soft, lined jacket in black viscose gabardine. The bold geometry of the lines is timely, and the rounded, less aggressive shoulder shows the newer moulded silhouette.

Designer: Jean Claude Poitras, Montreal   *Private Collection*

142 DRESS

An afternoon or dinner dress in lightweight, soft turquoise-green suede. Entirely lined in a light green acetate and cotton fabric, the dress has padded shoulders and a bared lower back with closures of buttons and centre-back zipper. Generous hip pockets and bias seaming emphasize the diagonal line and triangular shapes of postmodern design.

Label: Danier

Worn by Diane Meaghan   *Private Collection*

143 DINNER/EVENING DRESS

A one-piece strapless dress in black and royal blue wool crepe. The black, lined skirt is suspended from the blue satin lining of the bodice. It curves over the thighs with front darts and gores in the back. The bustier bodice shows a satin lapel and double-breasted styling with diamanté buttons. High-heeled black suede shoes with satin ribbons are by Geoffrey Beene.

Designer: Wayne Clark, Toronto
Label: Wayne Clark, Your Choice
Worn by Diane Meagban   *Private Collection*

144 LAPARKA, *about 1986*

A double-layered coat system in off-white wool duffle topped by a lightweight textured outer shell, in scarlet 100 percent nylon. The long wool parka is blanket-stitched together, zips up centre front and has coordinating red "no tears fur" on hood and as hidden storm cuffs. The inner coat also has an Inuit design appliquéd in red wool on the back. The outer coat, with centre-front zip and its own hood, can be worn as a year-round raincoat. It is windproof, machine washable, and rolls up into its own hidden compartment for carrying. The combination of the two coats is perfectly designed for cold Canadian winters.

Designer: Linda Lundström, Toronto   *The Seneca College Collection*

145 SWEATER, *1988*

A traditional Cowichan sweater from the Coast Salish knitters of British Columbia. It is knit of thick, soft, single-ply wool yarn in three natural colours: off-white, pale taupe, and dark brown. The heavy, rain-resistant cardigan zips up centre front, has no side seaming, and has two front slot-pockets edged in dark brown. Cowichan sweaters have been widely available in Canada since the 1930s and internationally popular since the 1970s.

Purchased in Nanaimo and worn by Liz Robinson   *Private Collection*

146 SUMMER OUTFIT

A coordinated set in a mint green rayon sheer and a slubbed mint green rayon plus flax fabric combined with a natural coloured linenlike fabric (seventy-one percent rayon and twenty-nine percent flax). The natural shorts are cut somewhat full with two soft front pleats from the elasticized waist and two generous slot pockets. Trim in mint couching and piping, as well as printed appliquéd medallions, match the long-sleeved sheer blouse with linenlike cuffs and neckline binding. The jacket in mint sheer and mint slubbed has a natural coloured shawl collar, cuffs, and waistband, as well as natural piping and embroidered circular motifs.

Label: Lipton's   *Private Collection*

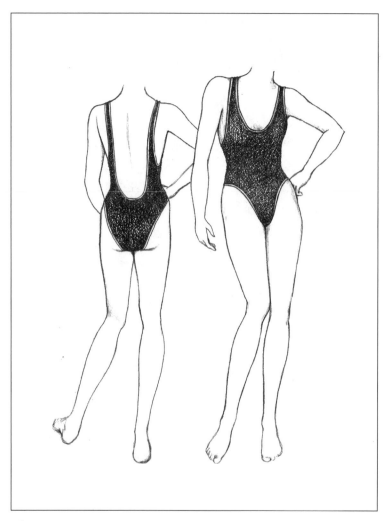

147 SWIMSUIT

A black-and-pink maillot in nylon and spandex. The unlined, silky black suit has a fairly heavy puckered texture, and a comfortable amount of stretch. The edges are bound in bright pink. The leg openings are cut very high in the eighties style to give the illusion of a longer leg.

Label: Christina, fait au/made in Canada, 86% nylon, 14% spandex, Instructions au verso/care on reverse, P/S   *Private Collection*

148 CYCLING SHORTS AND SWEATSHIRT

A sporting outfit for cycling or other activity. The stretchy black pants in eighty percent nylon and twenty percent spandex are made in Canada with a Scott Tinley logo in bright pink. The waist is elasticized and also has a drawstring. The derrière is padded with a soft and lofty fabric for cycling comfort. Leg hems are elasticized, too. The giant sweatshirt shows the postmodern logo design for the 1987 Festival of Canadian Fashion held in Toronto.

Private Collection

◆ N O T E S ◆

The 1900s

1. Full-page advertisement for W.A. Murray and Company, *Toronto City Directory* (1901).

2. O'Brien's labels proudly displayed, "By Royal Warrant to H.R.H. Prince of Wales, By Appointment of Her Excellency the Countess of Aberdeen," and "By Gracious permission of Lady Minto." Examples of this firm's work are in the costume collection of the Royal Ontario Museum. A red wool golf jacket from just before the turn of the century is in the collection of the McCord Museum, Montreal.

3. William Stephenson, *The Store That Timothy Built* (Toronto/Montreal: McClelland and Stewart, 1969), p. 33.

4. Henry Morgan and Company (Morgan's) used the label "The Colonial House" in their fashionable clothing from the 1890s to the 1920s.

5. Advertisement for A.E. Rea and Company, *Toronto the Prosperous* (Toronto: Mail and Empire, 1906).

6. Alan Suddon, "Shirt-waist Must Go!" *Costume Society of Ontario Newsletter*, vol. 12, no. 1 (May 1982), p.10. Suddon states: "the *Toronto Saturday Night* for April 4th, 1903 printed this interesting account of a Dressmaker's Convention fighting a losing battle against progress."

7. Stephenson, *The Store That Timothy Built*, p. 49.

8. *Catalogue 46: Spring/Summer 1901* (Toronto: T. Eaton Co., 1901), p. 5.

9. *Catalogue No. 12: Spring and Summer 1917* (London, Ont.: Smallman and Ingram, 1917), inside front cover.

10. *Northway Garments: Fall Styles 1913* [catalogue] (St. Marys, Ont.: White and May Co., 1913), insert.

11. *Northway Garments*, p. 7.

12. *Northway Garments*, insert.

13. *Catalogue 46: Spring/Summer* (T. Eaton Co., 1901), pp. 10-11.

14. *Catalogue 46: Spring/Summer* (T. Eaton Co., 1901), p. 63.

15. *Everything You've Always Wanted to Know About* (Quebec: Creations Daisyfresh, 1986), p. 3.

16. *M. Davidson Co. Limited: Manufacturing Furriers* [catalogue] (Ottawa: M. Davidson, 1911), p. 5.

17. Eileen Collard, *Decade of Change: Circa 1909–1919* (Burlington, Ont.: E. Collard, 1981), p. 71.

18. Alan Suddon, "Cycles of Fashion: Ladies' Costume," *Costume Society of Ontario Newsletter*, vol. 11, no. 1 (January 1981), p. 8.

19. Suddon, "Cycles of Fashion: Ladies' Costume," p. 8. From a pamphlet "published anonymously, possibly in Canada, and though undated, was almost certainly issued somewhere in the middle of the nineties."

20. Patricia Campbell Warner, "Public and Private: Men's Influence on American Women's Dress for Sport and Physical Education" in *Dress 1988*, vol. 14 (Costume Society of America, 1988), pp. 48-55.

21. *La Mode Dernier Cri* [pamphlet] (Quebec: Dominion Corset Co., n.d.).

The 1910s

1. Eileen Collard, *Decade of Change, Circa 1909–1919* (Burlington, Ont.: E. Collard, 1981), p. 15.

2. Collard, *Decade of Change*, p. 33.

3. Collard, *Decade of Change*, p. 9.

4. Collard, *Decade of Change*, p. 10.

5. Advertisement for the Right House, Hamilton, *Hamilton Herald*, 21 March 1919.

6. *Beaver Brand Knit Goods* [catalogue no. 3] (Stratford, Ont.: R.M. Ballantyne, 1913), introduction.

7. Collard, *Decade of Change*, p. 31.

8. Advertisement for Mrs. M.L. Lynch, *Vancouver World*, 25 March 1916. Public Archives of British Columbia.

9. Collard, *Decade of Change*, p. 40.

10. Collard, *Decade of Change*, p. 29.

11. Advertisement for David Spencer Ltd., *Vancouver Daily Province*, 3 March 1916.

12. *Catalogue No. 20: Spring and Summer 1917* (Toronto: Murray-Kay Ltd., 1917), p. 16.

13. Advertisement for T. Eaton Co., a Toronto newspaper, 14 August 1917.

14. Collard, *Decade of Change*, p. 65.

15. Collard, *Decade of Change*, p. 17.

16. *Goodwin's* [catalogue no. 4] (Montreal: Goodwin's, Fall/Winter 1911–12), p. 55.

17. Collard, *Decade of Change*, p. 19.

18. G. de T. Glazebrook, Katharine B. Brett, and Judith McErvel, *A Shopper's View of Canada's Past* (Toronto: University of Toronto Press, 1969), p. 222.

The 1920s

1. Eileen Collard, *Women's Dress in the 1920s* (Burlington, Ont.: E. Collard, 1981), p. 7.

2. Collard, *Women's Dress in the 1920s*, p. 12.

3. Bevis Hillier, *The Style of the Century, 1900–1980* (New York: E.P. Dutton, 1983), p. 75.

4. "Here and There in the Store, Just from Paris," *Eaton's News Weekly, Autumn Fashions Number*, 27 September 1924, p. 8.

5. Collard, *Women's Dress in the 1920s*, p. 29.

6. Collard, *Women's Dress in the 1920s*, p. 23.

7. *Eaton's News Weekly*, 26 September 1925, p. 5.

8. Collard, *Women's Dress in the 1920s*, p. 41.

9. G. de T. Glazebrook, Katharine B. Brett, and Judith McErvel, *A Shopper's View of Canada's Past* (Toronto: University of Toronto Press, 1969), p. 257.

10. *Mayfair*, May 1957, p. 36. This issue features a look back to 1927, the year *Mayfair* began publication.

11. Don McDonagh, *Dance Fever* (New York: Random House, 1979), p. 44.

12. Collard, *Women's Dress in the 1920s*, p. 13.

The 1930s

1. Veronica Strong-Boag, *The New Day Recalled, Lives of Girls and Women in English Canada, 1919–1939* (Markham, Ont.: Penguin Books Canada, 1988), pp. 41–80.

2. Benjamin D. Singer, "The Period of Social Insecurity," *Advertising and Society* (Don Mills, Ont.: Addison-Wesley Publishers, 1986), p. 36.

3. Strong-Boag, *The New Day Recalled*, p. 57.

4. Yvette Charpentier, "Emancipation," *Les Midinettes* (Montreal: ILGWU, 1962), pp. 79–81.

5. Elsa Schiaparelli, *Shocking Life* (New York: E.P. Dutton, 1954).

6. Betty Guernsey, *Gaby, The Life and Times of Gaby Bernier, Couturière Extraordinaire* (Toronto: Marincourt Press, 1982), pp. 114–16.

7. *Mayfair*, June 1933, p. 78.

8. Eileen Collard, *The Cut and Construction of Women's Dress in the 1930s* (Burlington, Ont.: E. Collard, 1983), p. 18.

9. Strong-Boag, *The New Day Recalled*, p. 118.

10. Collard, *The Cut and Construction of Women's Dress in the 1930s*, p. 32.

11. Robert La Vine, *In a Glamorous Fashion, The Fabulous Years of Hollywood Costume Design* (New York: Scribner, 1980).

12. *Style, 90 Years of Fashion 1888–1978*, Vol. 90, no. 9 (Toronto: Maclean Hunter, 1978), p. 21.

13. T. Eaton's *Fashion Show* [brochure], National Motor Show of Canada, 1936.

14. Peter C. Newman, *The Empire of the Bay* (Markham, Ont.: Viking, 1989), pp. 60-62.

15. *Goodwin's* [catalogue no. 4] (Montreal: Goodwin's, Fall/Winter, 1911–12).

16. *Mayfair*, August 1933, p. 44.

17. *Mayfair*, January 1930, p. 14.

18. David McDonald, *For the Record: Canada's Greatest Women Athletes* (Toronto: John Wiley and Sons, 1981), p. 43.

The 1940s

1. Consumer Branch, The Wartime Prices and Trade Board, *Miracles of Make-Do: A Revision of Re-make Wrinkles* (Ottawa, n.d.).

2. David McDonald, *For the Record: Canada's Greatest Women Athletes* (Toronto: John Wiley and Sons, 1981), p. 72.

3. Evelyn Kelly, "Teens in a New Mood," *Chatelaine*, September 1947, p. 56.

4. Mary Peate, *Girl in a Sloppy Joe Sweater* (Montreal and Toronto: Optimum Publishing International, 1989), p. 67.

5. Peate, *Girl in a Sloppy Joe Sweater*, p. 125.

6. Alan Suddon, "Vets Vote on Fashion," *Costume Society of Ontario Newsletter*, vol. 6, no. 2 (May 1976), p. 2.

7. Betty Guernsey, *Gaby, The Life and Times of Gaby Bernier, Couturière Extraordinaire* (Toronto: Marincourt Press, 1982) p. 101.

8. *Ottawa Citizen*, 22 August 1947.

9. *Montreal Gazette*, July 1947.

10. *Montreal Gazette*, 18 May 1947.

11. *Toronto Star*, 11 September 1947.

12. *Financial Post*, 13 September 1947.

13. *Ottawa Citizen*, 30 September 1947.

14. *Globe and Mail*, 4 May 1948.

The 1950s

1. "Spend Your Money on Quality in 1951," *Mayfair*, January 1951, p. 37.

2. James Lemon, *Toronto Since 1918: An Illustrated History* (Toronto: James Lorimer and Ottawa: National Museum of Man, 1985), pp. 134–6.

3. Maternity fashion advertisement, *Vogue* (New York: August 1950), p. 29.

4. Advertisement for Holt Renfrew, *Mayfair*, February 1951, p. 39.

5. "New York Designers Have New Interest in Canadian Women," *Mayfair*, February 1951, p. 98

6. "Canadian Affairs, Fashion: Mission to New York," *Newsweek* 20 December 1954, p. 47.

7. Betty Guernsey, *Gaby, The Life and Times of Gaby Bernier, Couturière Extraordinaire* (Toronto: Marincourt Press, 1982) pp. 100 and 166.

8. *Frenchshire Style Book* (Montreal, P.Q.: Frenchshire, n.d.), p. 6.

9. Advertisement for Creed's, *Globe and Mail*, 12 September 1951, p. 10.

10. Advertisement for Morgan's, *Mayfair*, February 1951, p. 26.

11. Arlene C. Cooper, "Casual But Not That Casual: Some Fashions of the 1950s," *Dress* (Costume Society of America, 1985), p. 47.

12. Cooper, "Casual But Not That Casual," p. 47.

13. Lisa Birnbach, ed., *The Official Preppy Handbook* (New York: Workman Publishing, 1980), p. 148.

14. "Vogue's Eye View of the Chemise Emergency," *Vogue* (New York: June 1958), p. 71.

15. Bevis Hillier, *The Style of the Century, 1900–1980* (New York: E.P. Dutton, 1983), p. 151.

16. *Style, 90 Years of Fashion, 1888–1978,* vol. 90, no. 9 (Toronto: Maclean Hunter, 1978), p. 50.

The 1960s

1. Barbara Bernard, *Fashion in the 60s* (London: Academy Editions, 1978).

2. *Mary Quant's London*, catalogue of the exhibition held at the London Museum, Kensington Palace, 29 November 1973–30 June 1974.

3. Polly Devlin, "Paris, Twiggy Haute Couture," *Vogue* (New York: March 1967), p. 65.

4. "The He-and-She Trend, Equality of the Sexes," *Mayfair*, October 1957, p. 68.

5. "I Have Been Here Before," theatre program for a production at the Royal Alexandra Theatre in 1938.

6. Marjorie Harris, "The Susie Thing," *Maclean's*, 19 November 1966, p. 12.

7. Joyce Carter, "Canadian Emphasis on the Luxurious," *Globe and Mail*, 23 September 1966.

8. Georgina Cannon, "Fashion," *Toronto Life*, April 1967, p. 32.

9. Margaret Hilton, "Flexibility and Speed Open U.S. Market to Apparel Men," *Financial Post*, 30 January 1971, p. 12.

10. Joyce Carter, "Spectators Rival Elegance of Fashions by Italians," *Globe and Mail*, 14 October 1965.

11. Don McDonagh, *Dance Fever* (New York: Random House, 1979), p. 93.

12. Stasia Evasuk, "Oh, That Exotic Look!" *Toronto Telegram*, 23 November 1966.

13. Edward Lucie-Smith, *Late Modern, The Visual Arts Since 1945* (New York: Praeger, 1976), p. 164.

14. C. Vernon, "Ecology and Dress, Then and Now," *Costume Journal, A Publication of the Costume Society of Ontario*, vol. 21, no. 2 (1991).

15. Joyce Carter, "Paper Wedding Gowns Created by 4 Designers to Test Demand," *Globe and Mail*, March 1968.

16. Helen Meyer, "Wrap Yourself in a Legend," *The Canadian*, 4 May 1968, p. 10.

17. Bevis Hillier, *Art Deco* (London: Studio Vista, 1968).

The 1970s

1. Robert F. Hartley, *Marketing Mistakes* (Columbus, Ohio: Copyright Grid, 1976), p. 123.

2. Eveleen Dollery, "Hot Pants," *Chatelaine*, June 1971, p. 33.

3. Lynn Ball, "Fur Sales Are Booming, More People with Money," *Ottawa Citizen*, 12 April 1976.

4. Joan Sutton, *Clothing and Culture: Contemporary Concepts* (Toronto: McClelland and Stewart, 1975), p. 30.

5. John T. Molloy, *The Woman's Dress for Success Book* (Chicago: Follet Publishing Co., 1977).

6. Mildred Istona, "Dressing for Success: Why Can't a Woman be More Like a Woman?" *Chatelaine*, April 1978, p. 2.

7. Sybil Young, "Moonlight Becomes You," *Canadian Magazine*, 20 July 1974, pp. 16–17.

8. "First Look at Fall," *Style*, April 1976, p. 18.

9. "Canada: Fashioned before the Fact," *Style*, April 1978, p. 20.

10. Joan Kron "The Theories of the Leisure-Class Peasant Look," *New York*, 6 September 1976, p. 40.

11. "The Blouson," *Style*, January 1978, p. 20.

12. Cheryl Hawkes, "The Hand-Knit Sensation," *Toronto Life Fashion*, Winter 1980, p. 58.

13. David Livingstone, "The Dare to Wear," *Toronto Life Fashion*, Fall 1980, pp. 50–51, 84–87.

The 1980s

1. Richard Horn, *Memphis: Objects, Furniture and Pattern* (Philadelphia: Running Press, 1985).

2. David Livingstone, "Modern Dress, Are We Too Buried in the 1960s to Greet the Year 2000?" *Rotunda*, vol. 24, no. 3 (Winter 1991), p. 13.

3. Jay Cocks, "Into the Soul of Fabric," *Time*, 1 August 1983, p. 66.

4. Harold Koda, "Rei Kawakubo and the Aesthetic of Poverty," *Dress* (Costume Society of America, 1985), p. 5.

5. Maggie Paley, "Va-va-va-voom, Return of the Breast," *Elle*, December 1986.

6. *En Ville Montreal, 1991-92* (Montreal: En Ville Publications, 1991).

7. *Metropolitan Toronto*, a paper of the Economic Development Division, May 1990, p. 23.

◆ B I B L I O G R A P H Y ◆

Albrecht, Donald. *Designing Dreams, Modern Architecture in the Movies.* New York: Harper & Row and the Museum of Modern Art, 1986.

Bailey, Margaret J. *Those Glorious Glamour Years.* Secaucus, N.J.: Citadel Press, 1982.

Battersby, Martin. *Art Deco Fashion.* London: St. Martin's Press, 1974.

Birnbach, Lisa. *The Official Preppy Handbook.* New York: Workman Publishing, 1980.

Blum, Stella, ed. *Everyday Fashions of the Twenties.* New York: Dover Publications, 1981.

Brett, K.B. *Women's Costume in Ontario, 1867–1907.* Toronto: Royal Ontario Museum/University of Toronto, 1966.

Charles-Roux, Edmonde. *Chanel and Her World.* New York: Vendome Press, 1981.

Cochrane, Jean; Hoffman, Abby; and Kincaid, Pat. *Women in Canadian Sports.* Toronto: Fitzhenry & Whiteside, 1977.

Collard, Eileen. *Decade of Change: Circa 1909–1919.* Burlington, Ont.: E. Collard, 1981.

———. *Women's Dress in the 1920s.* Burlington, Ont.: E. Collard, 1981.

———. *The Cut and Construction of Women's Dress in the 1930s.* Burlington, Ont.: E. Collard, 1983.

De Bondt, John. *Canada on Wheels.* Ottawa: Oberon Press, 1970.

de la Haye, Amy. *Fashion Source Book.* London: Quarto Publishing, 1988.

de Marly, Diana. *The History of Haute Couture, 1850–1950.* New York: Holmes and Meier, 1980.

Dorner, Jane. *Fashion in the Forties and Fifties.* Surrey, England: Ian Allen, 1975.

Duff, Clarence J. *Toronto, Then and Now.* Toronto: Fitzhenry & Whiteside, 1984.

Glazebrook, G. de T.; Brett, Katharine B.; and McErvel, Judith. *A Shopper's View of Canada's Past.* Toronto: University of Toronto Press, 1969.

Gray, James H. *The Roar of the Twenties.* Toronto: Macmillan of Canada, 1975.

Guernsey, Betty. *Gaby, The Life and Times of Gaby Bernier, Courturière Extraordinaire.* Toronto: Marincourt Press, 1982.

Hartnell, Norman. *Silver and Gold.* London: Evans Brothers, 1955.

Hillier, Bevis. *The Style of the Century, 1900–1980.* New York: E.P. Dutton, 1983.

Horn, Richard. *Memphis: Objects, Furniture and Patterns.* Philadelphia: Running Press, 1985.

Humphries, Mary. *Fabric Handbook 1—Glossary*. Don Mills, Ont.: M. Humphries, 1991.

———. *Fabric Handbook 2—Reference*. Don Mills, Ont.: M. Humphries, 1991.

La Vine, Robert W. *In a Glamorous Fashion*. New York: Scribner, 1980.

Lefolii, Ken. *The Canadian Look, A Century of Sights and Styles*. Toronto: McClelland and Stewart, 1965.

Lemon, James. *Toronto Since 1918: An Illustrated History*. Toronto: James Lorimer and Co., and Ottawa: The National Museum of Man, 1985.

Lindsay, John C. *Turn Out the Stars Before Leaving*. Erin, Ontario: Boston Mills Press, 1983.

MacKay, Donald. *The Square Mile, Merchant Princes of Montreal*. Vancouver: Douglas and McIntyre, 1987.

Maeder, Edwards, ed. *Hollywood and History, Costume Design in Film*. London: Thames and Hudson, 1987.

McDonagh, Don. *Dance Fever*. New York: Random House, 1979.

McDonald, David. *For the Record: Canada's Greatest Women Athletes*. Toronto: John Wiley and Sons, 1981.

Newman, Peter C. *Empire of the Bay*. Markham, Ont.: Viking, 1989.

Nicol, Eric. *Vancouver*. Toronto: Doubleday Canada, 1970.

Packer, William. *Fashion Drawing in Vogue*. New York: Coward-McCann, 1983.

Peate, Mary. *Girl in a Red River Coat*. Toronto: Clarke Irwin and Co., 1970.

———. *Girl in a Sloppy Joe Sweater*. Montreal and Toronto: Optimum Publishing International, 1989.

Pierce, Patricia. *Canada: The Missing Years: The Lost Images of Our Heritage 1895–1924*. Don Mills, Ont.: Stoddart, 1985.

Radice, Barbara. *Memphis: Research, Experiences, Results, Failures and Successes of New Design*. New York: Rizzoli, 1984.

Scagnetti, Jack. *The Intimate Life of Rudolph Valentino*. New York: Jonathan David Publishers, 1975.

Schiaparelli, Elsa. *Shocking Life*. New York: E.P. Dutton, 1954.

Scott, Shirley A. *Canada Knits, Craft and Comfort in a Northern Land*. Toronto: McGraw-Hill Ryerson, 1990.

Singer, Benjamin D. *Advertising and Society*. Don Mills, Ont.: Addison-Wesley, 1986.

Steele, Valerie. *Paris Fashion, A Cultural History*. New York: Oxford University Press, 1988.

Stephenson, W. *The House that Timothy Built*. Toronto: McClelland and Stewart, 1969.

Stevenson, Pauline. *Edwardian Fashion*. Surrey, England: Ian Allan, 1980.

Strong-Boag, Veronica. *The New Day Recalled: Lives of Girls and Women in English Canada 1919–1939*. Markham, Ont.: Penguin Books, Canada, 1988.

Sutton, Joan. *Clothing and Culture: Contemporary Concepts*. Toronto: McClelland and Stewart, 1975.

Toronto the Prosperous. Toronto: Mail & Empire, 1906.

Wise, S.F., and Fisher, D. *Canada's Sporting Heroes*. Don Mills, Ont.: General Publishing, 1974.

The 1900s

a Front cover of *Novi-Modi* [catalogue], (Toronto, Spring 1905). The Suddon Collection.

b Illustration from *Catalogue 46: Spring/Summer 1901* (Toronto: T. Eaton Co., 1901). Courtesy of the Eaton Collection at The Archives of Ontario.

c Advertisement of W.A. Murray and Co. in the *Toronto City Directory 1901*.

d Photograph courtesy of the Textile Department, Royal Ontario Museum, Toronto.

e Illustration from *Style* [catalogue] (Toronto: Morton-Browne Co., 1906). The Suddon Collection.

f Advertisement of the Bon-Ton Co., in *Canadian Pictorial* (Montreal, 1910).

g Illustration from *Northway Garments Fall Styles 1913* [catalogue] (St. Mary's, Ont.: White and May Co., 1913).

h Illustration from *Novi-Modi* [catalogue] (Toronto, Spring 1905). The Suddon Collection.

i Illustration from the *T. Eaton Catalogue Fall/Winter* 1901 (Toronto: T. Eaton Co., 1901). Courtesy of the Eaton Collection at The Archives of Ontario.

j Illustration from *Style* [catalogue] (Toronto: Morton-Browne Co., 1906). The Suddon Collection.

k Illustration from the *T. Eaton Catalogue, Fall/Winter 1906* (Toronto: T. Eaton Co., 1906). Courtesy of the Eaton Collection at The Archives of Ontario.

l Illustration from *Spring Style Portfolio* [brochure] (London, Ont.: J. and D. Ross, n.d.). The Suddon Collection.

m Song sheet cover, "Here's to the Sailor Lassie," 1909. The Suddon Collection.

n Advertisement for the Robert Simpson Company, 25 March 1907. The Suddon Collection.

The 1910s

a Illustration from *Goodwin's* [catalogue no. 4] (Montreal, Fall/Winter 1911–12). The Suddon Collection.

b Illustration from E. Collard, *Decade of Change, Circa 1909–1919*.

c Illustration from *M. Davidson Co.* [catalogue] (Ottawa, n.d.). The Suddon Collection.

d Advertisement for the Dominion Corset Co., Quebec. Reprinted with the permission of Canadelle Inc. The Suddon Collection.

e Illustration from *Novi-Modi* [catalogue] (Toronto, Fall/Winter 1911–12). The Suddon Collection.

f *Murray-Kay Catalogue No. 20, Spring/Summer, 1917*. The Suddon Collection.

g Flyer advertisement for Fairweather's, Toronto, n.d.

h *Beaver Brand Knit Goods* [catalogue no. 3] (Stratford, Ontario, n.d.). The Suddon Collection.

The 1920s

a Illustration from the *Eaton's Catalogue Spring and Summer 1923*, p. 34. Courtesy of the T. Eaton Co. at The Archives of Ontario.

b Illustration from *Pullan Garments* [catalogue] (Toronto, Autumn/Winter 1926–27), p. 8. The Suddon Collection.

c *Eaton's News Weekly*, 13 September 1924. Reprinted by permission of the T. Eaton Co. The Suddon Collection.

d *Mayfair*, May 1927. Reprinted by permission of Maclean Hunter Co. Ltd. The Suddon Collection.

e *Eaton's News Weekly*, 13 September 1924, p. 4 and 26 September 1925, p. 5. Reprinted by permission of the T. Eaton Co. The Suddon Collection.

f *Eaton's News Weekly*, 13 September 1924, p. 11. Reprinted by permission of T. Eaton Co. The Suddon Collection.

g *Eaton's News Weekly*, 27 September 1924, pp. 9 and 13. Reprinted by permission of the T. Eaton Co. The Suddon Collection.

h *Eaton's News Weekly*, 26 June 1926, p. 13. Courtesy of the T. Eaton Co. at The Archives of Ontario.

The 1930s

a Illustration by Marcel Vertes for Schiaparelli's Shocking perfume.

b Newspaper advertisement for Simpson's, 1932. Reprinted by permission of the Hudson's Bay Co. The Suddon Collection.

c Pattern page from *The Chatelaine*, December 1931. Reprinted by permission of Maclean Hunter Co. Ltd.

d Front cover of *Mayfair* (January 1934). Reprinted by permission of Maclean Hunter Co. Ltd. The Suddon Collection.

e Illustration of a brassiere, about 1930. Courtesy of Canadelle Inc.

f Fashion illustration. The Suddon Collection.

g Pattern illustrations from *Women's World*, April 1934, p. 28.

h Pattern illustrations from the *Pictorial Review*, December 1930, p. 70.

i Front cover of *Joseph and Milton Ltd.* [brochure] (Toronto, about 1937). The Suddon Collection.

The 1940s

a Cover of *Miracles of Make-Do: A Revision of Re-make Wrinkles* [booklet] (Ottawa: Wartime Prices and Trade Board, n.d.), also p. 26. The Suddon Collection.

b Advertisement for silk hosiery at W.J. Griffith, June 1940. The Suddon Collection.

c *Miracles of Make-Do*, p. 28.

d Unknown

e Photograph courtesy of Barbara Ann Scott.

f Advertisement for Eaton's in a concert program for Massey Hall (Toronto, 24 October 1947). Reprinted by permission of the T. Eaton Co. The Suddon Collection.

The 1950s

a *Your Fall Wardrobe from Frenchshire* [booklet] (Hamilton, Ont.: French Dress Shop, n.d.) p. 5. The Suddon Collection.

b Illustration from an Eaton's staff training booklet. Reprinted by permission of the T. Eaton Co. The Suddon Collection.

c Ashley-Crippen photograph of a collection of evening gowns by Cornelia in the 1950s, courtesy of Cornelia.

d *Career Girls' Wardrobe Guide* (Toronto, 1958), p. 21. Courtesy of the Wool Bureau of Canada. The Suddon Collection.

e *Career Girls' Wardrobe Guide*, p. 15.

f Illustration by Jean Miller from the *Career Girls' Wardrobe Guide*, p. 24.

g Cover of the program, *Eaton's Fall Fashion Presentation, 1957* (Toronto, Eaton Auditorium, commentary Dora Matthews). Reprinted by permission of the T. Eaton Co. The Suddon Collection.

The 1960s

a Unknown

b Unknown

c Author's illustration of two Susie Kosovic designs of 1966.

d Photograph of 1966 EEDEE winner, courtesy of David E. Rea.

e Cover of the program for *Eaton's Spring Fashion Presentation 1962*. Reprinted by permission of the T. Eaton Co. The Suddon Collection.

f Fashion illustration courtesy of Jean Pierce and Seneca College.

g Illustration by Theo Dimson, reprinted by permission of Liptons International Ltd. The Suddon Collection.

The 1970s

a Illustration of a Tom d'Auria design, about 1974, courtesy of the Mary Stephenson Collection, Seneca College.

b Illustration of a Nicola Pelly design, about 1975, reprinted by permission of Bagatelle.

c Graphic design by Theo Dimson, 1970s, courtesy Liptons International Ltd.

d Photograph of designs by Claire Haddad about 1975, courtesy of Claire Haddad.

e Photograph of a design by Lilly Dee about 1973, courtesy of Lilly Dee.

The 1980s

a Fashion illustration, 1984, courtesy of Fatima Melito.

b Cover design for *Fashion Blooms, 1988*, courtesy of The Fashion Cares Group of Toronto.

c Photograph for the 1990 collection, courtesy of Zapata.

d Photograph by Karen Levy of a design from the 1990 collection, courtesy of Elvira Vali.

e Photograph for a design from the 1992 collection, courtesy of Comrags.

f Photograph from the LaParka collection, courtesy of Linda Lundström.

g Photograph courtesy of Jean Claude Poitras.

h Photograph courtesy of Irving Samuel.

◆ I N D E X ◆